KidSavvy™ Westchester

A parents' guide of information & inspiration

Betsy Cadel and Laura E. Wilker

With
Jane Fogelson, Alisa Herschaft and Pam Marzano

SUBURBAN GODDESS PRESS, INC., HARTSDALE, NY

Cover design and illustration by Greg Paprocki (www.gregpaprocki.com)

Book design by Connie McCraw

Library of Congress Control Number: 2006929457
ISBN: 978-0-9727477-1-4

Publisher's Note
Neither Suburban Goddess Press, Inc. nor the authors have any interest, financial, personal or otherwise, in the locations and services listed in this book. No fees were paid or services rendered in exchange for inclusion in these pages. While every effort was made to ensure that information regarding phone numbers, hours, admission fees and prices was complete and accurate at the time of publication, it is always best to call ahead to verify. Any slights of people, places or organizations are unintentional. We recommend that readers discuss all health-related issues with their medical practitioner before acting.

Acknowledgements

It would be an out-and-out lie to say that this book would have been possible without the assistance, input and dogged research provided by three very special Suburban Goddesses: Jane Fogelson, Alisa Herschaft and Pam Marzano. These ladies tirelessly tracked down information, made phone calls and were wizards on the Internet. We thank you so much.

To Connie McCraw, who did far more than just make the book look "pretty." You kept us on our toes, redefined "quick turnaround," and your design skills are unparalleled. We're delighted with the result.

To Leyla Aker, our amazing editor, fact-checker and advisor. We were so thrilled to work with you again and hope it is only the second of many more projects.

To Greg Paprocki, our illustrator extraordinaire, who made us wish people would judge our book by its cover.

To everyone who e-mailed us encouraging words and wonderful ideas, this book is better because of you.

The biggest "thank you" goes to all of our boys: Andrew, Sam, Ben, Andy and Simon. Thank you for realizing that KidSavvy is more than a hobby. We hope we've made you proud.

Lastly, to our extended families—and in loving memory of Laura's mom and dad and Betsy's father, who are no longer with us—for helping us become the moms we are today. You were great role models and inspirations, and you were KidSavvy long before it was stylish.

Table of Contents

The More Things Change...

The first edition of **KidSavvy Westchester**™ *was "conceived" of when, thanks to a slowing economy, we became full-time stay-at-home moms.* Since we weren't spending our days working in Manhattan anymore (and we were no longer shell-shocked mothers of newborns), we were eager to take advantage of family-friendly Westchester. We went to the local bookstore to pick up a resource guide, but, to our surprise, none existed. Impossible! There were literally dozens of books written for city parents, but none for all those of us who had made the move north to the 'burbs.

After we got over the initial surprise, we got busy. Drawing on Betsy's background as an advertising copywriter and Laura's years of experience in public relations, we formed Suburban Goddess Press, Inc. We researched activities and classes, scoured local websites and free monthly publications, and quizzed our network of contacts, friends and playgroups. Nearly a year—and tons of research—later, we self-published the first edition of *KidSavvy Westchester* in June 2003. To our delight, the book was well-received by long-time residents and newcomers alike, as well as by businesses and realtors. Our sons, too young at the time to truly understand what was going on, were just excited that their pictures were in a real book! It was so gratifying to get e-mails from parents thanking us for making their lives just a little bit easier, since that, in a nutshell, was the whole idea.

Since that time a lot of things have changed. Laura had another son, Ben, in June 2004. She also went back to work and is now doing PR at a major global accounting and consulting firm. The two of us went from being friends and co-authors to being neighbors too, when Laura and her family bought the house across the street from Betsy's. When we were writing the first edition, Sam and Simon were just toddlers. Now, several years later, we've been through preschool hunts, "separation and socialization," and summer camps, not to mention several more caregivers. In the fall, our "big boys" will start second and first grade respectively, and Ben—now a toddler himself—will start preschool.

Not surprisingly, this edition of *KidSavvy* reflects these changes in our lives. There were topics we hadn't covered in the first edition that we knew parents would appreciate—such as how to select a preschool, ways to donate and sell the things your kids have out-grown, specific restaurant recommendations—and so we've added them in new chapters and sections. This time around we wanted to make certain that parents with children of all ages—not just infants and toddlers—knew that this guide would be helpful in countless ways, so we expanded the classes, activities, and, of course, the shopping sections. We also added some amazing day-trip and weekend getaway ideas, as well as a chapter on summer camps.

One thing that hasn't changed is our desire to make *KidSavvy Westchester* the most comprehensive and reliable parents' guide around. It's still the one-and-only insider's listing of classes, indoor playspaces, parks, museums, services, invaluable websites and more. The entries are still followed by detailed descriptions, including locations, phone numbers, age-appropriateness and spe-cial "What to Know Before You Go" sections, with tips you won't find anywhere else. Once again we've done the homework for you, and we've included dozens of "Savvy Suggestions," "Savvy Savings" and "Savvy Superlatives" throughout the book that give you advice, ideas and cost-saving tips.

We're like any parents: *KidSavvy Westchester*—our first "baby"—provided us with tremendous joy, a fair amount of anxiety and a valuable learning curve. Even though we're now slightly more sea-soned moms, we still want what all suburban parents really want (besides a good night's sleep): useful information at our fingertips.

Thank you for all the feedback and input that went into this edition of *KidSavvy Westchester*. We hope you find it even better than the first one and that you continue to be part of the *KidSavvy* family. We truly appreciate all of your support and encouragement. And remember, we're always looking for your insights and advice, so please e-mail us at **suburbangoddess@kidsavvy.net** or go to **www.kidsavvy.net**.

Enjoy!

Chapter 1

Great Expectations & Beyond

Clothing, Furniture & Baby Stuff

Help with Breast-Feeding

Baby Nurses & Doulas

Getting Rid of the Baby Weight

Mommy & Me Classes

We know that when you're expecting, parents, friends and even complete strangers are full of "helpful" advice. Why should we be any exception? And so our best advice is: get the support you need, whether it comes in the form of meeting other moms to bond with, babysitters to give you a little time off or classes that can help you with the needs of a newborn. As Hillary says, "it takes a village," so take full advantage of yours.

The second piece of advice we have is that even though there's a baby in there, there's also your inner suburban goddess. Pamper her. The good news is that doing so is now easier than ever. With stores offering everything from incredibly stylish clothes to the very latest in maternity spa treatments, we're willing to bet that—swollen feet aside—this might just be the best nine months of your life!

Savvy Suggestion

Before or after your baby is born, call formula, diaper and baby food companies to get on their mailing lists for coupons.

Savvy Suggestion

Great Places to Meet Other New Moms

* The women's rooms at Nordstrom and Neiman Marcus at The Westchester. (Also great for breastfeeding.)
* A Mommy & Me program, or other classes for newborns.
* Your neighborhood—get outside with that carriage and take a walk!
* Your local playground. Even if their children are too small to play, mothers congregate there anyway.
* Starbucks—if you get an empathic smile, start a conversation!
* Any store that carries baby stuff is a great place to compare notes and share sleep deprivation stories.

CLOTHING, FURNITURE & BABY STUFF

If you're pregnant, the only thing growing faster than your waist-line is the number of stores, services and classes that are popping up all over Westchester specifically aimed at you and other mommies-to-be. We've listed below some standout stores for getting yourself, your child and the nursery looking their best.

Clothing

BabyStyle
125 Westchester Ave., White Plains
(914) 948-9511
www.babystyle.com

Another catalog comes to life with this new addition to The Westchester Mall. This store features super stylish clothes for moms both pre- and post-baby, as well as for kids. They also carry unique toys, hip accessories and lots of other things to make your baby's nursery a totally "cool crib." Try to plan your excursions on Wednesdays mornings to coincide with the in-store Storytime at 11 am; kids will be entertained and maybe you can really get some shopping done!

Hours: Monday-Saturday 10 am-9 pm, Sunday 11 am-6 pm

Destination Maternity
The Source (Fortunoff's building)
5 Maple Ave., White Plains
(914) 948-1279
www.destinationmaternity.com, www.edamamespa.com

The new Destination Maternity superstores provide moms-to-be with fashion offerings from three different collections: exclusive "A Pea in the Pod," contemporary "Mimi Maternity," and value-priced "Motherhood Maternity." The stores also offer products to pamper the pregnant woman and classes to enlighten the mind and condition the body. One of our favorite touches is the complimentary water bottles, orange juice and saltines. They also take care of daddies-to-be by providing them with comfy leather seats and a big screen TV to watch while waiting. And there's a self-contained toddler play area too. But the pampering doesn't stop there. Destination Maternity's in-house spa, Edamame, features luxury treatments catering exclusively to expectant women, including facials to counter the effects of hormonal changes and therapeutic massages to relieve lower back and hip discomfort. All treatments are given by certified massage therapists and estheticians. Luxurious robes, soothing teas and the tranquil sound of a gentle waterfall complete the experience.

Hours: Monday-Saturday 10 am-9 pm, Sunday 11 am-6 pm

Furniture

While both of the megastores (Babies 'R' Us and Buy Buy Baby) listed below in the "Baby Stuff" section can't be beat when it comes to selection, Westchester has several specialty shops that you may also want to check out, whether you're looking for a crib or a big kid's bed. Following are some of our favorites for children's furniture. There are a lot of options out there, and you should feel free to do what works best for you; Laura has managed to raise her two kids without a changing table by putting a pad on a bureau and often using the floor.

Savvy Shopping

Feeling very, very pregnant and want to indulge in some "retail therapy"? You can find great, stylish and inexpensive maternity clothes at places like Target, Old Navy and even www.gap.com.

Bellini Baby and Teen Designer Furniture
495 Central Park Ave., Scarsdale
(914) 472-7336
www.bellini.com

This is a company that believes in quality over quantity. Every crib converts to either a junior or twin-sized bed and they are the only store that carries a tall changing table that can transform into drawers with bookshelves, for when your child is out of diapers. The store features many hand-painted, personalized options for accenting your child's room and they also carry a few lines of bedding, including their own exclusive styles. They have an in-home delivery and assembly service starting at $95.

Hours: Monday-Saturday 10 am-6 pm (Thursday until 7 pm), Sunday 11 pm-5 pm

Crib & Teen City Expo
183 South Central Park Ave., Hartsdale
(914) 686-3331
159 Rte. 4 West, Paramus, NJ
(201) 843-1505
www.cribteencity.com

This store strikes a comfortable balance between the high-end boutiques and the baby megastores. Their slogan is, "We take your baby from cradle to college," so it's no surprise that you'll find a wide range of furniture to select from. For the "big kids" they have a superb assortment of twin beds, bunk beds, loft/desk combinations and more.

Hours: Monday and Wednesday 10 am-9 pm, Tuesday and Thursday-Saturday 10 am-6 pm, Sunday 11 am-5 pm

Kid's Supply Co.
14 Railroad Ave., Greenwich, CT
(203) 422-2100
1343 Madison Ave., New York, NY
(212) 426-1200
www.kidssupply.com

If you're looking for both style and substance, this is a store you won't want to miss. They do have quite a few items in stock, but their real specialty is custom-made furniture for children; their items have been featured in many children's and design magazines. They do not make cribs but do carry several readymade lines. They create custom bedding as well.

Greenwich Hours: Monday-Friday 9:30 am-5:30 pm, Saturday 10 am-5 pm

NYC Hours: Monday-Friday 10 am-6 pm, Saturday 10 am-5 pm, Sunday 12 pm-4 pm

Millers
335 Mamaroneck Ave., Mamaroneck
(914) 698-5070
www.millerstoys.com

In addition to toys, Millers also has a small but sweet selection of baby furniture. Though only a few cribs and pieces of furniture are on display, you can look through catalogs to find the perfect items to order for your nursery. They specialize in several European brands but can get you the most popular American ones as well. The staff is helpful and experienced, and if you're coming with another child in tow, she'll most likely be mesmerized by the train display, giving you a chance to get your shopping done. They will stay open late for you on Thursdays if you schedule an appointment.

Hours: Monday-Saturday 9 am-6 pm. Later hours offered on Thursdays by appointment. Extended hours around the winter holidays.

Savvy Shopping

Aside from sonograms, putting together a layette is one of the most exciting times of your pregnancy. You definitely need to check out the usual suspects like Baby Gap, Children's Place, Target, Gymboree, and local baby supply and department stores. Denny's Children's Wear is also worth a look. The trained staff can help you choose your entire layette, and they also have clothes that your "cool kids" will love as they get older. And, when your kids are ready for sleepaway camp, Denny's will organize everything from clothes to labels, trunks and duffle bags.

Denny's Children's Wear
925 Central Park Ave. (Midway Shopping Center)
Scarsdale
(914) 722-6077

Hours: Monday, Tuesday, Friday and Saturday 10 am-6 pm; Wednesday and Thursday 10 am-9 pm; Sunday 11 am-5 pm

Pottery Barn Kids

125 Westchester Ave. (The Westchester), White Plains
(914) 949-4947
www.potterybarnkids.com

If you've ever looked through their catalog you know what to expect: cute, fun furniture and accessories that are often small-scale versions of their grown-up lines. They don't carry everything in the store but you will save on shipping charges for those items they do stock. You can feel free to allow your child to play with the display items, and the sales help is just that—helpful.

Hours: Monday-Saturday 10 am-9 pm, Sunday 11 am-6 pm

Baby Stuff

When it comes to giving you the most choices for products, bigger is certainly better. Following are two baby megastores and a specialty store every Westchester parent should know about.

Babies 'R' Us

2700 Central Park Ave., Yonkers
(914) 722-4500
www.babiesrus.com

Part of the Toys 'R' Us/Kids 'R' Us family, this spacious, multilevel store has it all. They cater to children ages 0-2, with baby gear, clothing, furniture, toys, supplies, strollers, bedding, books and more. At times, finding sales help can be challenging, and some of the salespeople could be more familiar with the products. However, this store does have the largest selection of merchandise

Savvy Safety

As of 2005 New York State law requires that all car passengers under age 7 sit in an appropriate child restraint system. The same law previously applied only to kids under age 4, so for most 4-to 6-year-olds this means a booster seat is now mandatory. Getting caught without one will result in a fine of $25-$100. Some experts recommend using a booster until the child reaches eighty pounds or is large enough for a seat belt to fit properly across the shoulder and over the upper thigh.

and it's a great place to go if you know exactly what you're looking for. There's also an in-house portrait studio.

Hours: Monday-Saturday 9:30 am-9:30 pm, Sunday 11 am-7 pm

Buy Buy Baby
1019 Central Park Ave, Scarsdale
(914) 725-9220
www.buybuybaby.com

This store has everything for children ages 0-4. You will find a staggering array of baby gear, clothing, furniture, toys, supplies, strollers, bedding, books and more. The staff is readily available to help you and they're generally very knowledgeable about the products carried. There's also a very convenient self-scanning system that makes purchasing a breeze. This is the perfect place for when you only want to make one stop.

Hours: Monday-Saturday 9:30 am-9:30 pm, Sunday 11 am-7 pm

The Right Start
5 Maple Ave. (Inside Destination Maternity), White Plains
(914) 686-5880
www.therightstart.com

Fans of the catalog can now check out in person these unique and useful products for newborns, babies and toddlers. They have a good selection of strollers and car seats as well as tons of adorable gift items.

Hours: Monday-Saturday 10 am-9 pm, Sunday 11 am-6 pm

HELP WITH BREAST-FEEDING

Feeding a newborn is supposed to be the most natural thing in the world. However, it's fairly common to have difficulty with breast-feeding. Betsy found that each nurse in the maternity ward had her own specific advice on how to do it, which left her a bit confused. And, Laura had vastly different experiences breast-feeding Sam and Ben, so if you have difficulty the first time, it doesn't mean you shouldn't try again.

If you're having problems or just want reassurance that your breast-feeding is going well, some one-on-one attention by a trained, specialized professional might be in order. Breast-feeding consultants work in hospitals, pediatric offices, and private practices, and they also make home visits. They can help you with issues regarding nipple or breast pain, latching-on difficulties, flat or inverted nipples, low milk supply, premature babies, twins and triplets, pumping and storing breastmilk, and more.

Contact the **International Board of Certified Lactation Consultants,** at www.ilca.org, for many useful resources and to locate a consultant near you.

The Breastchester, Inc.
(845) 227-8636 or (888) 225-7512
www.breastchester.com

After your baby is born, your self-image may be in need of some special attention. Think sexy lingerie and cool, comfy clothes have to be put away while you're breast-feeding? Think again. The Breastchester specializes in high-end and designer nursing clothing and bras, and also offers pumps, breast pads, nursing covers, nursing pillows, hands-free accessories, novelty items for baby and more, including many things you won't find in stores. Even better, in-home consultants will bring the clothing items to you for you to try on and have properly fitted in the comfort of your own home. Consultants will also teach you about the various nursing products and can perform pumping demonstrations.

Savvy Suggestion

The Perfectly Packed Diaper Bag

* A spacious changing pad
* Diapers (one more than you think you'll actually need)
* Burp cloths
* Baby wipes
* Rash ointment
* Hand sanitizing gel
* Change of baby clothes
* Receiving blanket
* Nursing pads or extra bottle/nipple/formula
* Bottled water
* Extra pacifier
* Plastic bags in a couple of sizes
* A clean shirt and a snack for you

We liked packing a "mini" bag inside the diaper bag with just the bare essentials for quick stops, to avoid the crushing weight of carrying the entire arsenal at all times.

BABY NURSES & DOULAS

Anyone who has had a baby will tell you that the first few weeks are a blur of sleepless nights followed by, well, exhausting days. This is the time when most people can use a little extra support, not to mention a chance to catch a few zzzz's while your baby is being cared for.

Baby Nurses

Baby nurses live in for a week or two, but some families desire the extra help for far longer. A baby nurse is there to assist you with new-baby care twenty-four hours a day. She will bottle-feed the baby or bring the baby to you to breast-feed. She will assist with bathing, changing diapers, doing laundry and anything else you need to help get you settled with your newborn. Most important-ly, she will help you get some rest, whether it's daytime naps or letting you get back to bed while she rocks the baby back to sleep after a middle-of-the-night feeding. Baby nurses generally cost $120–150 per day, and you provide room and board. While she will be available to you 24/7 during her stay, if you plan on keeping her longer than two weeks you will need to arrange for one or more days off.

The best way to find a baby nurse is through a referral from a friend. There are also many agencies that place baby nurses; if you think you're interested in hiring one through an agency, be sure to register in advance. Generally, they can't guarantee you a specific person since she may be working on another job if you give birth early. Although it runs contrary to every maternal instinct you have, you may end up hiring a baby nurse "sight unseen." When Betsy hired her baby nurse she was able to speak with another mother who had hired the same woman. Beyond that she had to trust that the agency she was dealing with was as good as everyone said it was. She was reassured by the agency's promise that if she wasn't comfortable with the nurse for any reason they would find a replacement right away. As it turned out, her nurse was wonder-ful and Betsy has recommended her highly to other moms. There are some baby nurses that work independently, in which case you may be able to meet them in advance and "reserve" them for your due date.

Doulas

In addition to pregnancy and labor support, doula services provide postpartum support for moms and babies up to four months. Services can include infant care, sibling care, overnight care, cook-ing meals, running errands, doing light housekeeping and taking you to doctor's visits. There is usually a required minimum number of hours, and this care isn't cheap, averaging about $25 an hour. But if you don't have family nearby—or if you just want a professional to help you stay sane—doulas can certainly be a worthwhile investment (and may be covered by your insurance). Generally, your contract includes a block of hours (the minimum is usually twenty), and you can use these any way you want to. One thing to keep in mind is that you will probably have more than one doula working for you, though most agencies try to keep the "rotation" to a minimum.

To locate a doula, contact **Doulas of North America at (888) 788-DONA or www.dona.org**. Or contact one of the following local doula agencies.

Northeast Doulas
(845) 208-3246
www.northeastdoulas.com
Contact: Barbara Ryan or Debbie Aglietti
Cost: $30.00/hour

MothersCare Doula Services
(203) 931-1850
www.motherscaredoula.com
Contact: Susan Keeney or Sheila Marley
Cost: $28.00/hour daytime, overnight $24.00/hour

GETTING RID OF THE BABY WEIGHT

No sooner are they born than we start expecting to spring back into our pre-baby shape. Well, as the experts say, nine months up, nine months down. Of course we all have those friends we love to hate who fit back into their skinny jeans two weeks after their baby was born, but for most of us it takes a little bit of time, patience and work. Many gyms do provide child care and there are

Savvy Suggestion

If you have a winter baby and outdoor walks aren't in your immediate future, take a few laps around a mall or megastore. You're bound to get some exercise along with the opportunity to pick up a few essentials.

even some options for you and your baby to get a little fresh air while you exercise.

Stroller Mamas

(914) 589-6862

www.strollermamas.com

Meet at Juliane's Park in Pelham (6th St. & 3rd Ave.) for forty-five minutes of brisk stroller pushing followed by fifteen minutes of strength training led by certified personal trainer (and mom) Colleen O'Connor. O'Connor will also bring the class to you (for a minimum of three adults)—either outdoor sessions or indoor exercise/playgroup sessions—using either resistance bands or your children as weights!

Fee: $10

Stroller Strides

(914) 977-3038

www.strollerstrides.com

This fitness program was created specifically for new parents who bring their children in strollers. The hour-long, challenging workout utilizes power walking with stops for strength training using resistance tubing, the environment and body weight while also weaving in fun children's songs and activities to keep the young ones happy and content. All Stroller Strides instructors are nationally certified and have special training in pre- and postnatal fitness. In addition, Stroller Strides offers playgroups and other support group activities for mothers with young children to help them socialize and share their parenting experiences.

Fee: $15 per class, or a 10-pack can be bought for $115. They also offer a monthly membership for $65, which requires a one-time registration fee of $75 and comes with a choice of T-shirt or baby hat and resistance bands.

Locations: Following are the class locations at the time we went to press. However, more are being added all the time, so check the website to see if there is a program near you.

Briarcliff Manor (except in the winter), at Law Memorial Park, 1025 Pleasantville Rd. Park, in the back of the Atria lot

Hours: Mondays and Thursdays, 9:30 am

What to Know Before You Go: In bad weather, classes will be held at The White Plains location below.

Kensico Dam Plaza at Kensico Dam Park in Valhalla

Hours: Tuesdays and Saturdays, 9:30 am

What to Know Before You Go: There is free, ample parking at the park and a snack bar should you need to do some carb-loading before or after your workout. Meet at 9:15 in the parking area.

White Plains (during the winter and inclement weather), at The Westchester, 125 Westchester Ave.

Hours: Mondays and Thursdays, 9:30 am

What to Know Before You Go: For the White Plains location, park in the West Garage and take the J Elevator bank to Retail Level 3 (Near Crate & Barrel and The Disney Store). The 10-pack purchase includes free parking until noon on Stroller Strides days and enrollment in the Simon Mall Kidgits program.

Savvy Suggestions

For New Parents

* Join a group: connecting with other new parents is really important.
* Keep your diaper bag packed. Refill it when you get home, so it's ready to go next time.
* Don't be a superparent—learn to ask for help.
* Enjoy yourself—go to a museum or someplace fun (the baby won't mind).
* Wear a snuggly or sling around the house so you can get things done and keep the baby warm, happy and quiet.
* And above all, remember: it's a marathon, not a sprint. So always look at the big picture; one less-than-perfect feeding or skipped nap isn't the end of the world.

MOMMY & ME CLASSES

For many parents, adjusting to the new "bundle of joy" is a process that extends far beyond sleep deprivation and trying to find a single piece of clothing that doesn't have some sort of baby-induced stain on it. Signing up for a Mommy & Me program (which can include daddies and caregivers, too) can be a great way to connect with other moms, share your experiences and get advice from a child development specialist. Most programs consist of playtime for moms and kids together, followed by a discussion led by a facilitator while the kids are watched by baby-sitters. Classes

are usually grouped by children's ages, so the issues you are dealing with will be similar to the other parents' concerns.

Mommy & Me programs for older children are often aimed at laying
the groundwork for parent/child separation. This may mean children
are in one room doing arts & crafts or having a snack while moms are
in a room across the hall—close enough if separation anxiety sets in,
regardless of whether it's your child's or your own!

In addition to the classes listed below, check with your local
religious institutions and community centers as they often offer
these types of programs. Lastly, be sure to check out Chapter 2 for
support group listings. Betsy and Laura actually solidified their
friendship through a mother's group and are huge advocates of
forming a support network, especially when your children are young.

Mount Kisco
The Parent Center
15 S. Bedford Rd.
(914) 378-5007

A nonprofit cooperative, the center offers playgroups for children
from newborn to 4 years. Children participate in a variety of activities, including arts & crafts. A special group is offered for first-
time parents with children under 9 months.

White Plains
Mommy & Me at White Plains Hospital Center
Davis Ave. at East Post Rd.
(914) 681-2515
www.wphospital.org

Exercises designed for mom and new baby (from 6 weeks to crawling).

Parent's Place
3 Carhart Ave.
(914) 948-5187

Parent's Place strives to increase a parent's knowledge and confidence
in a supportive environment while allowing infants and preschoolers to play and explore in a stimulating and fun setting. The skilled
staff is made up of social workers and early childhood educators. This
is a drop-in facility, meaning no registration is necessary; you may come
as often or infrequently as you like.

Hours: Mondays, Thursdays and Saturdays 10 am-12 pm (age 5 and
under), Tuesdays 10 am-12 pm (ages 2 and under by 9/1), Tuesdays
1:15 pm-2:45 pm (ages 9 months and under)

CONNECTICUT

Just Wee Two

Three locations:
464 Round Hill Rd. (First Church of Round Hill), Greenwich
113 Pemberwick Rd. (William Yantorno Community Center), Greenwich
31 Cascade Rd. (North Stamford Congregational Church), Stamford
(800) 404-2204
www.justweetwo.com

Programs for children ages 14 months to 3 years, taught by early childhood teachers. Children are encouraged to explore, discover and interact through activities such as music, arts & crafts, playtime and stories. There are partial separation, preschool readiness and total separation programs.

ROCKLAND COUNTY

Rockland Parent-Child Center

137 First Ave., Nyack
(845) 358-2702
www.rocklandparentchild.org

Free support groups for parents of infants (ages 12 months and younger) and toddlers (ages 1-3 years). Sessions include a discussion led by a social worker or facilitator. One evening a week there is also a support group for single parents.

Savvy Suggestion

Put the "om" in mom. Taking yoga classes can keep your body limber, flexible and strong, which can not only make for an easier delivery but also help with all the bending, stretching and lifting you'll be doing with your new bundle of joy. Yoga also offers a quiet atmosphere in which to think, focus and relax (which, once your baby is born, may be a rare thing). In Chapter 4 we list a lot of yoga facilities, most of which offer both pre- and postnatal classes as well as ones you can take your kids to.

Being Well-Connected

Community Centers

Support Groups & Newcomers Clubs

Local Publications

Local & National Websites

School District Websites

Hotlines

We're big advocates of finding the support you need, particularly in those first months of your child's life, when your life has undergone a seismic shift. In this chapter we provide some valuable sources for help and information, ranging from the "old-fashioned" (community centers) to the Internet-age (parenting websites).

COMMUNITY CENTERS

Community centers, such as Ys and JCCs, are great places to start when you're looking to connect with other parents. They're also great places to find parenting workshops, programs for toddlers and children (including nursery school, child care and school holiday programs) and classes for your child and for you, including Mommy & Me, Gymnastics, Play, Music, Arts & Crafts, Dance, Martial Arts, Swimming and Foreign Language classes. Some of these facilities have playgrounds, children's theaters or pools where you can go for free swim. Many also have fitness centers, so you can exercise while your child enjoys one of the dozens of activities offered. Another advantage to these all-in-one facilities is that you will find community-centered programs or support groups where you can meet other families and take part in many adult programs.

At some community centers, membership entitles you to a discount for classes and workshops; at others, membership is required. **To find a community center, these websites are most helpful: www.ymca.net, www.ywca.org and www.jcca.org.** Below are the local listings.

Mount Kisco

Boys & Girls Club of Northern Westchester
351 Main St.
(914) 666-8069
www.boysandgirlsclubnw.org

Mount Vernon

The YMCA of Mount Vernon
20 S. Second Ave.
(914) 668-4041
www.mtvymca.org

YM-YWHA of Southern Westchester
30 Oakley Ave.
(914) 664-0500

New Rochelle

New Rochelle YMCA
50 Weyman Ave.
(914) 632-1818
www.nrymca.org

Pleasantville

Richard G. Rosenthal JCC of Northern Westchester
600 Bear Ridge Rd.
(914) 741-0333
www.rosenthaly.org

Port Chester

Port Chester/Rye Brook Family Center
400 Westchester Ave.
(914) 939-7800

Rye

Rye YMCA
21 Locust Ave.
(914) 967-6363
www.ryeymca.org

Scarsdale

JCC of Mid-Westchester
999 Wilmot Rd.
(914) 472-3300
www.jccmidwestchester.org

Tarrytown

Family YMCA at Tarrytown
62 Main St.
(914) 631-4807
www.ymcatarrytown.org

JCC on the Hudson
371 S. Broadway
(914) 366-7898
www.jcconthehudson.org

White Plains

YWCA of White Plains and Central Westchester (North Street Y)
515 North St.
(914) 949-6227
www.ywcawhiteplains.com

YMCA of Central & Northern Westchester
250 Mamaroneck Ave.
(914) 949-8030
www.ymca-cnw.org

Yonkers

YMCA of Yonkers
17 Riverdale Ave.
(914) 963-0183

YWCA of Yonkers
87 S. Broadway
(914) 963-2752
www.ywcayonkers.org

CONNECTICUT

Greenwich Family YMCA
50 E. Putnam Ave., Greenwich
(203) 869-1630
www.gwymca.org

MANHATTAN AND THE BRONX

92nd Street Y
1395 Lexington Ave., Manhattan
(212) 415-5500
www.92ndsty.org

Riverdale YM-YWHA
5625 Arlington Ave., Bronx
(718) 548-8200
www.RiverdaleY.org

ROCKLAND COUNTY
Rockland County YMCA
35 S. Broadway, Nyack
(845) 358-0245
www.rocklandymca.org

JCC-Y of Rockland
900 Rte. 45, Ste. 15, New City
(845) 362-4400
www.jccyofrockland.org

SUPPORT GROUPS & NEWCOMERS CLUBS

When you first get home with that bundle of joy, it can be a very daunting experience—particularly if it's your first. Because this can also be a very isolating time, the best thing you can do is reach out to other moms.

Many community centers and hospitals sponsor groups, including general support and discussion groups for new moms. Some focus on a specific topic, such as breastfeeding, child safety, CPR, baby care or adapting to parenthood, and some address a specific group, such as mothers of multiples. **For more information, check out www.newcomersclub.com and www.westchestergov.com (under Family Services), or call the Westchester Self-Help Clearinghouse, which maintains a comprehensive database of parenting support groups, at (914) 949-7699.** We've listed many of Westchester's support groups and newcomers clubs below.

Support Groups

Adoptive Parents Committee
Connecticut/Hudson chapter: (914) 997-7859
hudsonapc@yahoo.com
www.adoptiveparents.org

Chappaqua Preschool Parenting Association
(Only Not Lonely Kids and Playgroups)
(914) 238-0809

Katonah Village Library New Mothers' Group
(914) 232-3508

Latina Mothers' Network
Northern Westchester Hospital
(914) 666-1111
www.nwhc.net

Mom's Club of Rye Brook
(914) 937-6626

Mothers & More
Lower Westchester chapter:
chapterleader@momsofwestchester.com
www.momsofwestchester.com

The Mother's Connection
(914) 737-8976

Mothers of Multiples
Larchmont chapter: Sophie Dassesse-Cowles (914) 833-5011
Westchester/Putnam chapter: (914) 273-3913, twinmom9997@aol.com
(both are affiliated with the National Organization of Mothers of Twins Clubs)
www.nomotc.org

MOPS (Mothers of Preschoolers)
Bedford Hills: (914) 666-5384

New Moms Support Group
(914) 666-1370

New Mommies' Network
(212) 665-7956
www.newmommies.com

New Mothers Talking
Hudson Valley Hospital Center
(914) 736-0218
www.hvhc.org/wellness.html

Parents Without Partners
(914) 779-0265
www.pwpchapter21.com

The Place for Single Parents
Jewish Community Center of Mid-Westchester
(914) 472-3300, ext. 412
www.jccmidwestchester.org

Rockland Parent-Child Center
(845) 358-2702

Second Shift
(212) 492-4013
www.secondshift.org

Single Parent Support Group
White Plains chapter: (914) 761-3584
Nyack chapter: (845) 358-2702

Twins Plus Club
(914) 736-9633

Newcomers Clubs

Chappaqua Parents Preschool Association
(For residents of the New Castle community)
(914) 320-CPPA
hlwny@hotmail.com

Larchmont Newcomers Club
(For residents of Larchmont, Mamaroneck and New Rochelle)
(914) 973-LNC1

Pleasantville Parents Preschool Association
rapley@mindspring.com

Newcomers Club of Pound Ridge
(914) 764-5172
cshepre@aol.com

Purchase Newcomers Club
(For residents of Purchase, West Harrison and Harrison)
newcomers1@hotmail.com

Rye Newcomers Club
(For residents of Rye, Rye Brook and Port Chester)
ryenewcomers@yahoo.com

Scarsdale/Hartsdale Newcomers Club
(For residents of Scarsdale, Hartsdale and Edgemont)
vgfam@aol.com

Somers Newcomers Club
(For residents of Somers)
sncpresident@yahoo.com

LOCAL PUBLICATIONS

There are several local publications that cover Westchester and will provide you with topical information and monthly calendars of events and family-friendly activities. Some are geared towards children and families, and some towards adults.

* **Parent Guide**–Free, found in supermarkets, community centers, libraries and schools
* **Westchester County Times**–Free, found in newspaper dispensers around the county
* **Westchester Family Magazine**–Free, found in supermarkets, schools, libraries and some kids' stores
* **Westchester Parent Magazine**–Free, found in supermarkets, schools, libraries and some kids' stores
* **Westchester Magazine**–Found in some area stores, or by subscription (for information, call (800) 254-2213 or visit www.westchestermagazine.com)
* **Westchester Wag**–Free, found in area stores

LOCAL & NATIONAL WEBSITES

What did we do before the Internet? If you're looking for information–on anything from planning a day trip to finding local events to seeking child-related developmental or medical information–the Internet is the place to start. The sites below provide advice and resources, organized online communities and an abundance of shopping opportunities.

Local Sites

* www.americantowns.com–Information and events in Westchester, listed by town
* nyc.babyzone.com–New York City information, plus articles and resources for pregnancy through parenthood
* www.daytrips.org–Hudson Valley daytrips
* www.essentialmom.com – Listings of Westchester events, classes and resources
* www.greatschools.net/modperl/bycounty/?stateselect=ny&county=Westchester–An online guide to schools K-12, with information about school districts, local resources and more
* www.hudsonriver.com–Historic River Towns of Westchester website; lists attractions and historical sites
* www.hudsonvalley.org–Historic Hudson Valley website; information on mansions, parks, etc.

* www.kidsevents.com – Listings for events, classes, party resources and summer camps in Westchester and Fairfield.
* www.lhric.org/schools/index.html–Lists schools and districts with hyperlinks to their websites
* www.parenthoodweb.com–A national website with local listings
* www.parentsknow.com–Articles, resources and local calendar information
* www.townlink.com/community_web/–Community pages, Westchester and New York State links
* www.westchester1.com–local directories and listings
* www.westchestergov.com–Westchester County government website; lists news, information and events
* www.westchesterny.com–Westchester County Office of Tourism; provides listings and local events

National Child-Related Websites

There are lots of pregnancy, baby- and child-related websites to choose from. They offer articles, advice, information, resources, online communities and shopping. Some of the most popular and comprehensive websites of this type are:

* www.babycenter.com
* www.busyparentsonline.com
* www.thebabycorner.com
* www.iparenting.com
* www.parentcenter.com
* www.parentsoup.com

And this one deserves special mention: **www.fathersworld.com** is chock-full of information, resources, support and education for fathers and their families.

And, if you're looking for health-related advice, try these sites:
* www.aap.org–American Academy of Pediatrics website
* www.kidshealth.org–Medical information geared toward children
* www.zerotothree.org–Website focused on infant/toddler development, with content provided by doctors
* www.kidsgrowth.com–Website developed by pediatricians,with advice and articles by topic
* www.postpartumny.org–Postpartum Resource Center of New York website, with healthcare referrals, educational materials and support
* www.womenshealthnetwork.org–National Women's Health Network website, with information, articles and resources by topic

SCHOOL DISTRICT WEBSITES

Once your children enter the public school system, these district websites are a great way to say in the loop regarding PTA meetings, school budget information, as well as upcoming events.

Bedford: www.bedford.k12.ny.us

Blind Brook: www.blindbrook.org

Brewster: www.brewsterschools.org

Briarcliff Manor: www.briarcliffschools.org

Bronxville: www.bronxville.k12.ny.us

Chappaqua: www.chappaqua.k12.ny.us

Croton-Harmon: www.croton-harmonschools.org

Dobbs Ferry: www.dfsd.org

Eastchester: www.eastchester.k12.ny.us

Edgemont: www.edgemont.org

Elmsford: www.elmsfordschools.k12.ny.us

Greenburgh: www.greenburgh.k12.ny.us

Hastings-on-Hudson: www.hastings.k12.ny.us

Irvington: www.irvingtonschools.org

Katonah-Lewisboro: www.klschools.org

Mahopac: www.mahopac.k12.ny.us

Mamaroneck: www.mamkschools.org

Mount Pleasant: www.mtplcsd.org

Mount Vernon: www.mtvernoncsd.org

New Rochelle: www.nred.org

Ossining: www.ossiningufsd.org

Pelham: www.pelhamschools.org

Pleasantville: www.pleasantvilleschools.com

Pocantico Hills: www.pocanticohills.org

Port Chester: www.portchesterschools.org

Rye: www.ryecityschools.lhric.org

Rye Neck: www.ryeneck.k12.ny.us

Scarsdale: www.scarsdaleschools.k12.ny.us

Somers: www.somers.k12.ny.us

Tarrytown: www.tufsd.org

Tuckahoe: www.tuckahoeschools.org

Valhalla: www.valhalla.k12.ny.us

White Plains: www.wpcsd.k12.ny.us

Yonkers: www.yonkerspublicschools.org

Yorktown: www.yorktown.org

HOTLINES

We've listed some hotlines in case you want to speak to a real, live person; the organizations below will provide you with information and help on a variety of topics. Hopefully you'll never need any of these numbers, but you should have them at the ready just in case.

* Poison Control Center: (800) 222-1222
* Public Health Hotline/Westchester County Dept. of Health: (914) 813-5000
* Domestic Violence Hotline: (800) 942-6906
* My Sister's Place: (800) 298-SAFE (7233) (a safe shelter)
* National Child Abuse Hotline: (800) 422-4453
* Toy Safety Hotline: (800) 851-9955

Savvy Suggestion

ICE (stands for In Case of Emergency) ensures that emergency services workers can contact a loved one should it be necessary. Enter contact information for your spouse, friend or neighbor into your cell phone under the heading ICE. If you have more than one person you'd like them to call use ICE2, ICE3,etc.

Chapter 3

Desperately Seeking Mary Poppins

Day Care Centers

Nannies

Au Pairs

Babysitters

Background Checks & Nanny Cams

Employment Tax Services

Of course you love your kids more than anything, but at some point it's necessary for you and your spouse to take a break. Maybe it's time for you to head back to work. Or maybe you just want to drink a Venti Soy Half Caf Macchiato in peace. No matter the reason, whether you're looking for someone to watch your child for four hours a week or for forty, it's time to talk about child care.

As we pointed out in the first edition of *KidSavvy Westchester*, the prospect of hiring a caregiver can be anxiety-provoking, to say the least. There are decisions to be made. There are interviews to be conducted. There's separation anxiety—perhaps the baby's, definitely yours—to overcome. And then there's the leap of faith you must take when leaving your child in someone else's care. We have gained even more experience in hiring and working with caregivers since the first edition of this guide was published, and although we're no experts we're happy to share with you what we've learned.

They're Out There—Be Patient

Don't panic. It's a big decision, and it can seem a little daunting, but there really is someone or someplace great out there that will fit (most of) your needs. Don't settle for a situation that won't work for you.

At the Same Time, Be Realistic

As with any decision, you will have to make trade-offs. Laura adored her first nanny even though she didn't have a driver's license, which limited the options for Sam's and Ben's extracurricular activities to what could be reached by walking or by taking the train or bus. That was a trade-off that Laura and her family were more than willing to make for almost seven years of great child care. Before you start looking for someone in earnest, think about what compromises you would be willing to make and what would be a deal-breaker for you.

Write Up a Wish List

Take a few minutes to sit down and really figure out what your needs are. Do you need child care for just a few hours a few times a week so you can make it to the gym or run errands that are decidedly more difficult with a child in tow? Do you want someone who will help out with housework? Cook? Do laundry? If you're looking for full-time help, do you want her to live in or live out? Is cost a big issue?

Writing down a wish list will help considerably in your search. And try to be honest with yourself—you may love cooking, but after a really full day (and possibly a commute home) it might be nice to have dinner ready and waiting. And also try to think ahead—if you have an infant, you're probably not concerned about toilet training yet, but someday you will be. The rules or attitudes of the child care provider are important to know about ahead of time.

Narrowing Down Your Search

Once you've written your wish list, it should become more clear what type of situation will suit you best. In this chapter we cover four main areas of child care: day care, nannies, au pairs and baby-sitters. (Baby nurses and doulas are covered in Chapter 1.)

We feel that no matter which child care option you choose, nothing beats word-of-mouth recommendations when it comes to finding a good person or place. So once you have an idea of what you're looking for, the first thing to do is ask your friends and neighbors. After you've done that, take a look at the suggestions below to help you find the right situation for you and your family.

DAY CARE CENTERS

Day care centers offer group care, and as a result are probably the most affordable route to take (about $900–1,200 per month) if you're going to need your child looked after for many hours. Unfortunately, there are long waiting lists for many Westchester facilities, some as long as a year!

Location is certainly a primary consideration, as you'll probably want the center to be near your home or work for easier drop-off and pick-up. You'll also want to make sure that they have coverage for enough hours. Most day care centers that Laura looked at for Sam closed by 7 pm; she and her husband both work in New York City, and they weren't sure they'd be able to make it by closing time every night. In New York State, the teacher-to-child ratio is mandated, but some centers may exceed the State standards, so it's worthwhile to ask.

❓ Some Other Things to Consider ❓

* ✳ Are the caregivers or teachers engaged and energetic? Are they caring and attentive, especially when children need help or attention?
* ✳ Does it feel safe? What are the rules for protecting your child?
* ✳ What are the facilities like? Is it clean? Do they have a good variety of toys, books and playthings? Is it bright and cheerful?
* ✳ How do they handle issues like separation anxiety, discipline and toilet training? What are their policies or rules?
* ✳ How do they handle emergencies? (If neither parent is working close by, you'll need to identify another contact person, just in case.)
* ✳ Most importantly, do the children look happy? Are they having fun?

Visit several centers, so you can gain some perspective and form a basis of comparison. Go when the kids are there, so you can see the center in action. Try to ask the same questions at each place you visit. And take your time—get a feel for the place. Usually the head of the center will give you a tour, discuss policies and rules, spend some time with you and answer your questions. If you want to talk further with the caregivers or teachers, hang around or come back when they aren't in session so they can give you their undivided attention. Ask all your questions, and trust your instincts. You'll know in your gut when you've found the right place.

As you begin your search, check out the following resources.

Child Care Aware
(800) 424-2246
www.childcareaware.org

A nonprofit initiative that provides information and resources on child care.

Child Care Council of Westchester
470 Mamaroneck Ave., Suite 302, White Plains
(914) 761-3456
www.childcarewestchester.org

A private, nonprofit organization that provides tons of resources and information on child care, as well as referrals in Westchester.

Daycareproviders.com
www.daycareproviders.com

Nationwide online child care directory (providers pay a fee for listing), plus information and links.

Medline Plus
www.nlm.nih.gov/medlineplus/childdaycare.html

Articles, research and information on child care. This website is run by the National Library of Medicine and the National Institutes of Health.

Savvy Suggestion

For information on New York State licensing standards, click on **www.daycare.com/newyork**

NANNIES

Nannies generally work full-time and are either live-in or live-out. There's a wide range of salaries on the market, but you should expect to pay $350–700 per week. As we said before, the first place to start when looking for a nanny is to let everyone know you're looking. Also, ask your friends' nannies if they know anyone looking for a job—there's often a strong placement network among nannies. Once you've exhausted those two avenues, there are others to be explored.

Nanny Agencies

The theory here is that you will save time by having access to a prescreened group of women who are matched with prospective employers according to their specific needs. Use your wish list to tell the agency what these needs are (including nationality— some agencies even specialize in placing women from a particular country), and make sure you're clear about what you're looking for in terms of days and hours per week, salary, duties and so on.

You can work with multiple agencies at the same time, but some agencies require you to pay a registration fee prior to receiving information about candidates. Most agencies have done prelimi- nary background checks (criminal record, driving violations) that they will provide to you along with the basic application the can- didates filled out. They usually have also done an initial reference check to see what kind of experience a former employer has had. In return for this "safety net" you can generally expect to pay a fee equal to one or two months of the nanny's salary or 10–15% of the annual salary.

Agencies will usually give you three to five candidates at a time to consider. The logic is that since they're sending you high-quality applicants that suit your needs, you won't have to interview lots and lots of people.

When you work with an agency, they might play an active role in salary negotiation, or that might be left up to you to work out with the prospective employee. Usually the agency will give you an idea of what pay range the candidate is looking for, or at least what she was making before.

Once you've picked someone, agencies generally give you a trial period of about a week to see if your new nanny is going to work out before requiring you to pay the commission. If you're still not sure at the end of the week, ask for a few extra days—the agency will probably agree. However, you are still responsible for paying the nanny the predetermined salary during this trial period.

Once you pay the agency commission, you'll have another one- or two-month trial period. If the candidate leaves or is fired within this period, most agencies agree to find you someone else for no additional charge. Certainly these services market themselves via their good reputation, but bear in mind that once they have your commission they may not be quite as motivated as they were the first time around. (That said, one agency that Laura worked with said they would provide a prorated refund if they were unable to find a replacement.)

Both of us have found nannies by going through agencies. The first time Laura looked for a nanny she worked with three agencies and felt the candidates to be of all-around higher quality than the others she met; the woman she ended up hiring stayed for almost seven years. On the other hand, Betsy's first nanny, who was found through an agency, lasted only seven weeks and a replacement was never found (read: Betsy was out several thousand dollars). After using agencies, we've both also found nannies by other means. You can find someone terrific either way; there's no right or wrong answer since obviously everyone's experience is different.

Classified Ads

If you ever start to doubt that the right person is out there, take a look at the classified listings in some of our recommended publications and sites. There are literally dozens of women looking for positions and it only takes one to be your Mary Poppins.

Both of us have placed ads in *The Irish Echo* and we each received more than 130 calls. Let your answering machine field the calls, or give your cell phone number only and record a specific message asking candidates to leave their names, phone numbers and any other piece of pertinent information you may be looking for. (For instance, "The job is live-out, Monday through Friday, from 7 am to 7 pm. If you are not able to work those hours, please do not leave a message.") Many applicants will be weeded out by this process: Did they follow your instructions? Were they pleasant? Call the ones you are interested in back and conduct a phone interview. (Remember to change your answering machine message back afterward!)

A better option is to reply to an ad. For Laura's recent search she responded to ads on craigslist.org that seemed to meet her current criteria, which included someone who could drive. Refer to your "wish list" to decide what your primary needs are. Perhaps you are looking for a candidate who has previous experience with twins, or is CPR certified, or has a flexible schedule. Or, best of all, her current employer placed the ad on her behalf to help her secure a good position. Generally this means they had an extremely positive experience and are giving up their nanny due to a change of circumstance (they're moving, the children are older, etc.). But, again, caveat emptor: one woman we know discovered that the candidate had placed the ad herself, posing as a previous employer.

Savvy Suggestion

If you have a fax or separate dedicated phone line, attach your answering machine to it during your search and shut off the volume. Candidates can call any time (day or night) and this way you can listen to messages when your schedule allows.

Another popular way of finding someone is to put up fliers at supermarkets, community centers, libraries, preschools and other places that nannies may frequent. Often you can find fliers hung by people looking for positions (again, some may be posted by current or previous employers).

Interview How-To

Conduct the initial interview by phone. Use this as an opportunity to let your instincts guide you. Is the person pleasant? Accommodating? Does she seem responsible? Is there any language barrier that may be a problem? Find out where she's worked and for how long, the age of the children she took care of, whether or not she has children herself and how old they are. If she is not from this country you should find out if she is going to need to return home anytime in the near future (say, within a year). You can start to form an overall impression about a candidate and decide whether or not you want to move to the next step and meet her in person. Make sure that she understands the parameters of the position and is able and willing to fulfill them. If there is any hesitation, consider that a red flag.

For candidates that interest you, get references. It can be helpful to check them prior to the actual interview. This is your chance to do the deep digging about someone else's experience. You'd expect the references the candidate provides to give glowing reviews, but you never know what you'll find out. And you can ask former employers some pointed questions and compare them to answers you receive from the candidate, like: What were her responsibilities? What was her typical day like? How did your children interact with her? What did she do with them that you really liked? What did she do (or not do) that you would have changed? Did she do a thorough job or did you need to remind her to follow through on responsibilities? How often did she call in sick? Why did she leave? If you had to do it all over again, what would you look for that's different from this person? How were conflicts resolved? The more specific your questions are, the more helpful their answers will be. You can use some of the information in your interview with your prospective nanny. For instance, "Wendy said that you occasionally prepared meals for the family. Is that something that you would do here?"

Still interested? Arrange to interview the candidate in person. If she's taking public transportation, it's customary to compensate her for the round-trip fare. Unless you are trying to replace a nanny currently in your house, conduct the interview in your home so you can pick up some useful insights and see how the candidate interacts with your child (or children). When Betsy asked one of her applicants if she had any questions after the interview the woman asked if her son had any allergies and when Betsy was planning on starting the potty training process. These and other thoughtful questions were geared towards being able to better take care of Simon. Not surprisingly, she got the job. When Laura met her first nanny at the train station, the woman immediately put on her seatbelt, which none of the other candidates had done. At the house, she offered to change Sam's diaper, and did it lovingly and playfully (and washed her hands before and after). That meant a lot.

Another good idea: make copies of your wish list, title it "Job Description," and give it to prospective candidates so they have a clear, written understanding of what you're looking for. It not only saves time during the interviewing process but can also be used for reference once you've hired someone.

Betsy found it very helpful to have a basic information sheet for each candidate to fill out. Name, address, cell and home number, and anything else you may want to have on record. You'll also want to ask the candidate some of the same questions you asked her references. Some other things you might want to know: How would she comfort a crying baby? How flexible is her schedule? (If she has small children, it may be less so.) How would she handle a tantrum? What are her attitudes on discipline? What types of activities would she do with your children? Think in advance about what answers to these questions would be okay with you. And again, let your gut be your guide.

If you get a good feeling for someone, ask her to come for a day as a trial (you'll need to pay her for this). You can do the laundry, make phone calls and catch up on household chores while you observe her in action. And remember: good caregivers are pure gold. When you find someone terrific you'll want to hold onto her until your kid goes to college.

Following are some publications and websites where you can place an ad for a nanny (or look for posted ads).

Craig's List
http://newyork.craigslist.org/wch/kid

You can post and respond to ads on this website for free.

Irish Echo
14 East 47th St., New York
(212) 686-1266
www.irishecho.com

Ads run on Wednesdays; you must submit your ad by the previous Friday at 2 pm. The costs are $30 for three lines, $10 for each additional line (30 characters/spaces per line).

Irish Voice
875 Avenue of the Americas, Suite 2100, New York
(212) 684-3366
www.irishvoice.com

Ads run on Wednesdays; you must submit your ad by the previous Tuesday at 1 pm. Twenty-five words cost $38.50 for one week or $70 for two weeks.

Nanny Locators
(800) 706-7747
www.nannylocators.com

A sixty-day subscription costs $129 and allows you to place ads as well as respond to ads placed by prospective nannies.

New Mommies Network
www.newmommies.com

Go to the "Nanny Share" link at the bottom of the home page; you'll find employers looking to place nannies either full- or part-time as well as posts placed by nannies themselves. There is no charge for this service site.

The agencies listed below are ones we used and liked or ones our friends recommended.

Domestically Yours
535 Fifth Ave., New York
(212) 986-1900

Frances Stuart Agency
1220 Lexington Ave., New York
(212) 439-9222

Larchmont Employment Agency
4 Gilder St. (at Larchmont Ave.), Suite 1, Larchmont
(914) 834-1611
www.thelarchmontagency.com

The Nanny Authority
26 Ferry Street, Newark, NJ
(973) 466-2669
www.nannyauthority.com

To search for a nanny agency (and also to order a background check or use the nanny tax calculator) try this website:
www.nannynetwork.com

AU PAIRS

"Au pair," literally translated from French, means "on par"—as in, this person is not an employee but a temporary member of your family. These young (generally eighteen- to twenty-six-year-old) foreign women are usually in college or have just completed their studies. They come from all over the world to take part in a one- to two-year "cultural exchange program" with a host family in the United States. They should be included in family meals, activities and outings or trips. In return for free room and board, they help out with your child care needs, but not necessarily with things like housework, cooking or laundry (except as it relates to the kids).

By law, au pairs are not allowed to care for infants less than three months old. If they wish to be placed with a family who has a child under two years old, they must have completed 200 documented hours of child care, but they are still not child care professionals and may have limited experience. Nevertheless, they can form wonderful relationships with your children, and your children will have the opportunity to learn about other countries and cultures (and maybe even a second language!). Au pairs are generally paid $140–250 per week, making this a relatively inexpensive option.

As Simon got older Betsy decided to look for an au pair. She had always been rather hesitant about the idea, since she wouldn't be able to meet the person in advance and would have to rely too heavily on the recommendations the agencies would provide. However, a friend told her about a website, **www.greataupair.com**, that works in essentially the same way a dating service does: prospective employers and prospective au pairs register themselves on the site and are each able to specify certain criteria that they're looking for. (For example, a family might be looking for an au pair from a specific country, with a valid driver's license; an au pair might be looking for a host family near a specific city.) Betsy was able to find an au pair who matched her needs and her au pair was able to find a situation that suited her placement wishes as well. Although in the end you'll most likely need the help of one of the handful of government-approved agencies to bring an au pair to the country, the process is relatively seamless.

Betsy's best advice when it comes to hiring an au pair is to communicate as much as possible with her. Speak on the phone, e-mail, send photos and start to integrate that person into your family before she arrives. Let her know, in writing, exactly what her duties will be, give her a general idea of her schedule, and try to iron out all the little things that can be awkward to address after someone has already moved in (for instance, how you feel about overnight guests, any restrictions on use of the family car, and what activities are off-limits for your child).

For Betsy, having someone who could help out with running errands, pitch in with shuttling Simon from activity to activity and offer her tremendous scheduling flexibility was exactly what was needed. She admits that being someone's "host mother" is a far different situation from being someone's employer, but she has really enjoyed the change and forged great bonds with her au pairs.

Before you decide that this option is the one for you, here are a few important facts to consider.

There are significant up-front costs. Most au pair agencies get around $6,000 to cover visa costs, training and commissions. Also, you must pay up to $500 towards the au pair's post-secondary education, as she is required to take six class credits while in the U.S.

Hours are strictly regulated. You cannot require an au pair to work more than ten hours a day and forty-five hours a week. They are required to have one full weekend off each month and a day-and-a-half off every week. However, unlike other caregivers, their schedules are generally far more flexible, which is ideal if yours fluctuates frequently.

Their duties are limited to child-related responsibilities. She is not required to do heavy housework or chores, like cooking for the entire family. However, some au pairs enjoy cooking or sewing or have other skills that they may want to share with their host families. Because au pairs must have international driver's licenses, they can also take care of bringing your children to school or to classes.

Congratulations, you just had a 19-year-old girl! Often families who take on au pairs feel like they've adopted a teenager. These girls are interested in the same things all girls their age are—shopping, socializing and, well, boys. You have not imported a nun, so make sure you have the nerves to deal with her social life.

An au pair's stay is limited. Until recently, they were only permitted to stay in the country for twelve months (plus four extra weeks at the end to travel if they wished), but the laws have changed. Now au pairs are allowed in some circumstances to stay for another year. Even so, all good things must come to an end: there will be some difficult good-byes, and the "changing of the guard" as the new au pair arrives can be tough for your family and especially for your children.

To find an accredited au pair agency contact: Department of State at (202) 401-9810 or http://exchanges.state.gov.

Savvy Suggestion

Sign your au pair or nanny up for a "Visa Buxx™" card. It's a debit card that you fill up with a specific amount of money, and the daily transaction records are e-mailed to you. It makes things a lot easier if you need her to run out and grab a gallon of milk. Go to www.visabuxx.com to get started.

BABYSITTERS

As much as you've been enjoying staying home with your newborn, maybe you're looking for a little freedom in your week, just a few hours to shop, work out or grab a "grown-up" lunch with a girlfriend. Maybe you want to start "dating" your hubby again, whether it's a night out once a month or every Saturday night. It's time to find a baby-sitter. And we guarantee you, you'll be glad you did. Just remember, the steadier the gig, the easier it is to line up a super sitter.

Of course, the best place to find a babysitter is through a referral from a friend or neighbor, but you'll find that even your closest friends may clam up when it comes to revealing the name of their

Savvy Suggestion

Avoid a last-minute rush before you go out by having on hand a pre-typed information list for your babysitter as well as a list of emergency numbers by every phone. Leave a "fill in the blank" line where you can write in the phone number of your destination.

precious Saturday Night Sitter. They may be willing, however, to see if their sitter has a friend who's available. Also check with high-school-age kids and senior citizens in your neighborhood. And keep your eyes and ears open. A friend of ours was grocery shopping and—desperate for an evening out with his wife—asked the clerk if she babysat. When she arrived later that night, his wife saw the multiple piercing and Technicolor hair and was understandably panicked. But the sitter got along great with the kids, lived right down the street and had her own car; she became their steady sitter two afternoons a week and every Saturday night. So you just never know.

If you want less regular babysitting (e.g., every other Saturday night), you might want to hook up with a friend or neighbor to share a sitter; if you ensure her a regular gig, it'll be a more stable arrangement for all of you. There are also services that provide sitters. Although they won't necessarily guarantee that the person you love will be yours every Saturday evening, they are a great source for experienced help. And in case your favorite sitter is in demand, you might want to line up several once-in-a-while sitters so that you have a comfortable "stable" of sitters to select from. You should expect to pay a babysitter $9-12 an hour.

In addition to the clerks at the supermarket, you might want to try the following resources to find a babysitter.

Hartsdale Fire Station
300 W. Hartsdale Ave., Hartsdale
(914) 949-2325

Sponsors an annual "Babysitters Course" comprised of twenty hours of specialized training in how to care for children and handle emergency situations. The fire station provides a list of course graduates as a public service.

Chappaqua Library
195 S. Greeley Ave., Chappaqua
(914) 238-4779

This library course trains sitters ages ten and up. Visit the library to see the list of babysitting graduates.

The Service
(914) 834-7050

Serves lower Westchester only. Sitters get $10–12 an hour (depending on how many children you have and their ages). There is a four-hour minimum plus a $5 transportation fee. An agency fee of $12 covers twenty hours of sitting.

Larchmont Employment Agency
4 Gilder St. (at Larchmont Ave.), Suite 1, Larchmont
(914) 834-1611
www.thelarchmontagency.com

Sitters get $12–15 an hour, depending on experience level. The agency fee is 30% on top of that (i.e., $3.60–$4.50 an hour).

There are also many less formal ways to find a sitter. Many local high schools, synagogues and churches have job boards and can be a great source for babysitters. In addition, you can post an ad on MonsterTRAK, a website for college students. You can target local campuses, including Manhattanville, Mercy, Sarah Lawrence and SUNY Purchase, and run your ad for two weeks for $25 per school. **Contact this site at (800) 999-8725 or www.monstertrak.com.**

Savvy Safety

Learn CPR at home with "Family & Friends CPR Anytime," developed by the American Heart Association. It doesn't provide certification in CPR, but it's a great short course or refresher for parents, grandparents and babysitters. Each $30 kit contains a 22-minute DVD, an American Heart Associate CPR booklet and an inflatable CPR mini-mannequin.

Learn more at **www.cpranytime.org**

If you find sitters you like through one of these avenues, you'll want to make sure they are well prepared for the job—particularly if they're young. For a babysitting course that covers caring for and supervising children, preventing accidents and what to do in an emergency, contact the resources listed above or the Red Cross.

American Red Cross
Westchester County Chapter
106 N. Broadway, White Plains
(914) 946-6500
www.westchestercounty.redcross.org

Greenwich, CT Chapter
99 Indian Field Rd., Greenwich
(203) 869-8444
www.greenwich.ctredcross.org

Babysitter's Training is offered frequently. This eight-hour course is designed for ages 11–15 and includes numerous hands-on learning experiences. Participants receive a Babysitter's Guide, a checklist and a Red Cross Certificate.

BACKGROUND CHECKS & NANNY CAMS

If you've picked a child care provider but still want a little extra comfort, there are many services that can provide it. You may want to order a background check, particularly if your nanny didn't come through an agency (which will usually do them for you). In addition, if you're so inclined, you can buy or rent a "nanny cam," which will allow you to videotape activities in your home. Another option is remote video monitoring, which allows you to keep an eye on your home from anywhere at any time via a high-speed, always-on internet connection like DSL or cable modem. One suggestion: if you hire more than one nanny in your child's life, or plan on monitoring for an extended period of time, in many cases you can buy a system for the same cost as renting it.

Care Check
1056 Fifth Ave., New York
(212) 360-6640

Offers video surveillance sales (approximately $999) and remote video monitoring (approximately $2,100). Rentals are also available ($250 for two days or $350 for three days), and you can apply the cost of the rental to a future sale.

icaml
www.icaml.com
(914) 741-1991

Offers remote video monitoring ($2,300–2,600, and ongoing service is $1 per day). Provides free in-home estimates.

Knowyournanny.com
300 Grand River Blvd., Dover Township, NJ
(888) MYBABY-1 (692-2291)
www.knowyournanny.biz

Provides background checks, including a state criminal check, a driver's license check and a credit check ($129). Offers video surveillance sales ($199–369) as well as rentals ($99.95 for ten days). Also offers remote video monitoring (approximately $800).

Nanny Check
55 State St., Hackensack, NJ
(800) 788-3937
www.nannycheck.com

Provides a variety of packages for pre-employment screening and background checks ($49–300+). Also offers video surveillance sales ($300–700) and rentals (approximately $100 per week).

EMPLOYMENT TAX SERVICES

You can certainly file household employer taxes on your own, but those of you who don't like filling out forms each quarter may want to find some help. See the following resources.

GTM Associates
7 Halfmoon Executive Park Dr., Clifton Park, NY
(888) 4EASYPAY or (518) 373-4111
www.gtmassociates.com

Household tax and payroll services.

Household Employment Taxes Online
www.householdemploymenttaxes.com

An on-line service for household payroll and taxes, plus free resources for do-it-yourselfers.

Nannytax
51 E. 42nd St., Suite 601, New York
(888) NANNYTAX or (212) 867-1776
www.nannytax.com

Full-service tax preparation for employers of domestic help.

Chapter 4

Class Acts

Arts & Crafts

Cooking

Dance

Drama

Enrichment & Tutoring

Foreign Language

Gymnastics & Play

Martial Arts

Music

Rock Climbing

Special Needs

Sports

Swimming

Yoga

Before your child is old enough to attend school, a class is a fun way to provide some structure to her day and will give you something entertaining to do as well. As your child grows older, classes can teach her a wide range of skills and expose her to new activities and experiences.

When your child is quite young, you'll probably be enrolling more for *you*—Laura signed up Sam in Gymboree at six weeks to get out of the house and meet other parents. Classes provide a setting in which your child can learn to socialize and engage with other children and in which you can meet other parents and make friends. We both came out of classes with long-lasting friendships for our kids and ourselves.

When enrolling younger children, be forewarned: the minute you sign up for a class that works perfectly for Junior's routine and plunk down a check, his nap time is guaranteed to change. Maybe it's just Murphy's Law, but it's true. Anyway, it's best not to second-guess when you think his nap time will be; most often the programs are flexible enough to let you switch from one time or day to another. Other considerations in selecting a class include location, class size and program structure and philosophy. Also, since the success of the class is largely dependent on the specific teacher, ask around for recommendations. If you find teachers you like, stick with them.

As your child grows you'll want to match your choices to her disposition—if she's a regular Mexican jumping bean, a gymnastics class might be a better choice than a sit-still arts & crafts program. Bear in mind that for most kids these classes are opportunities to try out new things: your child might jump from ice-skating to ballet to karate to pottery. He might find his passion, or a great hobby or two, but with rare exceptions most of us are not dealing with prodigies, so there's no need to stick with one thing exclusively. At the end of the day, these classes should be teaching your children one thing: how to have fun.

There's no shortage of classes in the Westchester area (even retail stores have started getting into the act), so once you've decided on what kind you want it's really a matter of finding one that works for your child's schedule. Also, we cannot stress enough that you should check with your local community center (see Chapter 2) when you're looking—most offer a wide variety of classes for kids. **One final note: most places that offer classes also host birthday parties, so if your son loves his weekly music class, he may be thrilled to share it with his friends for his birthday.**

ARTS & CRAFTS

Ever since Martha Stewart let us know that there is, indeed, a right and a wrong way to glue rubber stars onto a piece of wood, classes that specialize in arts & crafts projects have multiplied exponentially. Of course, this may also have something to do with the fact that when it comes to paint, clay and glue, "better your place than mine" is usually a parent's sentiment. Either way, here are places where your children can create to their hearts' content. You'll have new objets d'art to proudly display around your home, and you won't have to pick sparkles out of the carpet for the next two years.

Chappaqua

New Castle Art Center
939 Hardscrabble Rd.
(914) 238-3606
www.newcastle-ny.org/artcenter.html

Classes in art, woodworking and ceramics for ages 2-13.

Cortlandt Manor

Croton-Cortlandt Center for the Arts
293b Furnace Dock Rd.
(914) 739-4320
http://nystatearts.org/orgs/

A variety of classes for ages 3-17 (some require a caregiver), including "Clay Creations," "Young at Art" and "Authors and Illustrators." Workshops include "Marvelous Mobiles" and "Make Your Own Musical Instrument."

Dobbs Ferry

Art In Us
127 Main St.
(914) 591-5377
www.artinusonline.com

Multimedia classes for age 2 and up (some require a caregiver). For the younger set it's mostly arts & crafts, while the classes for children age 6 and up focus more on drawing and painting. In the past they've also offered storytimes, and jewelry and yoga classes.

Pottery-on-Hudson
145 Palisade St., Studio 2-S
(914) 478-2762
www.potteryonhudson.com

Pottery classes for ages 6-18 in which children learn different handbuilding methods, experience wheel throwing and become familiar with studio equipment and tools. "Parent-Child Clay Workshops" for younger children (ages 4-10) are available on select Sundays.

Eastchester

Monet's Child
20 John Albanese Pl.
(914) 337-6202
www.monetschild.com

Students ages 3-8 explore a variety of mixed media (including oil pastels, tempera and watercolors) and are introduced to the works and techniques of famous artists.

Golden's Bridge

Children's Center of Golden's Bridge

5 Anderson Ln.
(914) 232-6813
www.childrenscenterofgb.com

A variety of multimedia arts classes for children ages 10 months to 10 years, including Fine Arts Master Class (ages 3-5 and 5 and up), After Arts (age 5 and up), and ArtSmart (ages 3-5), which combines art, music and movement. Parents and caregivers can relax with a cup of coffee in "Mom's Café." Walk-ins are welcome, but reservations are suggested.

Jefferson Valley

Gymboree Play & Music

3631 Hill Blvd. & Rte. 6
(866) 477-3700
www.gymboree.com

This national chain offers age- and developmentally-appropriate art classes for ages 6 months to 5 years. Classes include painting, sculpting and designing, as well as singing, dressing up and other imaginative activities.

Katonah

Katonah Art Center & Gallery

77 Bedford Rd.
(914) 232-4843
www.katonahartcenter.com

This center has classes for ages 2-18 (some require a caregiver). "Little Rembrandts" (ages 2-3) includes many materials and techniques. In "Petite Picassos" (ages 4-5) children create an arts & crafts masterpiece each week. Classes for older children include mixed media, sculpting with clay, drawing and painting, and cartooning.

Larchmont

Children's Creative Corner

7 Addison St.
(914) 833-2880

A variety of classes for ages 5-14, including painting, drawing and ceramics.

Paint Your Art Out
2005 Palmer Ave.
(914) 833-2321
www.paintyourartout.com

Classes offered for ages 6 and up include drawing, painting, glass fusing and mosaics.

Pelham

Pelham Art Center
155 Fifth Ave.
(914) 738-2525

A variety of classes for ages 9 months and up, including Adult & Tot workshops, crafts, ceramics, dance and drama. There are also workshops for children in various media, coordinated with gallery openings.

Port Chester

Clay Art Center of Westchester
40 Beech St.
(914) 937-2047
www.clayartcenter.org

Ceramics classes for age 8 and up.

Rye

Rye Arts Center
51 Milton Rd.
(914) 967-0700
www.ryeartscenter.org

They offer more than twenty different classes for children age 2 and up, including clay, drawing, painting, sculpture, cartooning, photography, musical theater and more.

Rye Brook

Little Rembrandt
116 S. Ridge St. (Rye Ridge Shopping Center)
(914) 939-1400
www.littlerembrandt.info

This facility offers a variety of classes for children ages 18 months to 12 years. "Mommy & Me" classes are geared towards school readiness, concentrating on fine motor skills, attention span and language development through art. They also offer preschool mixed media and drawing classes.

Scarsdale

Gymboree Play & Music
450 Central Park Ave.
(866) 477-3700
www.gymboree.com

See the listing under Jefferson Valley for more information.

Smart Art at The Scholastic Store
450 Central Park Ave. (Scarsdale Park Mall)
(914) 725-7201
www.scholastic.com/aboutscholastic/stores/store-scarsdale.htm

"Smart Art" is available for boys and girls ages 4-5. Each week the store offers a different theme from their company-owned "Klutz" line of books, including Pop Beads, Hand Art, Tiaras and more.

Young At Art Workshop
1088 Central Park Ave.
(914) 723-9229
www.youngatartworkshop.com

Painting, collage, puppet and construction classes for ages 2-10. For the younger set, there is "Mommy & Me"; for children ages 3-10, classes are two-hour drop-offs. All classes include two art projects, creative movement, a story and snack.

CONNECTICUT

Greenwich Art Society
299 Greenwich Ave., Greenwich
(203) 629-1533
www.greenwichartsociety.org

This nonprofit visual arts education organization offers several multimedia classes, including "Art Workshop for Juniors" (ages 7-10) and "Paint-A-Masterpiece" (ages 6-8 and 9-15).

Gymboree Play & Music
31 Mill Place Rd., Danbury
(866) 477-3700
www.gymboree.com

See the listing under Jefferson Valley for more information.

PUTNAM COUNTY

Garrison Arts Center
23 Garrison's Landing, Garrison
(845) 424-3960
www.garrisonartcenter.org

A variety of classes for ages 5-12, including pottery, painting, drawing, mixed media and sculpture. They also offer workshops and school vacation camps.

ROCKLAND COUNTY

Rockland Center for The Arts
27 S. Greenbush Rd., West Nyack
(845) 358-0877
www.rocklandartcenter.org

A variety of classes for ages 3-18, including mixed media, ceramics, painting and drawing. There are also parent/child workshops where you can learn to make things like mosaics, snow globes and wrapping paper.

Savvy Savings

Instead of always going to the brand name stores, hit the discounters like dollar stores, and the large warehouse clubs for huge savings on things like toys, arts & crafts materials and wrapping paper.

COOKING

Cooking combines two things that children really enjoy: getting messy and eating yummy foods of their own creation. It also teaches important skills like measuring, following directions and patience, not to mention the sense of pride they share when presenting their final masterpiece. In addition to providing the groundwork for a wonderful family activity at home, cooking classes can teach children to appreciate how much effort actually goes into cooking dinner every night! Some of these classes take place at a facility, others can be set up at your home as a weekly playgroup activity.

Kids 'r' Cookin'
(914) 937-2012
bandy@kidsrcookin.com

Geared towards teaching your kids a love of cooking and baking, these ten-week sessions take place at your home or other location. You can choose group, private or customized classes for you and your children to enjoy together, and you can even arrange to have classes take place during a playgroup. The best part is, they'll bring all the utensils, food and ingredients you need. Children will receive a chef hat, apron and laminated recipe card so they can recreate their culinary masterpieces again and again. Classes for younger children (ages 3-5) must be attended with a parent or caregiver, classes for preschoolers (ages 4-5) with or without.

Hartsdale

Chef Central
45 S. Central Ave.
(914) 328-1376
www.chefcentral.com

They offer classes several times a week for children ages 3-5 and 6-8. (By the way, they offer lots of great hands-on classes and tastings for adults too). Advance registration is required.

Mamaroneck

Medium Rare
114 Boston Post Rd. (at It's My Party)
(914) 777-7273
www.mediumrarellc.com

These aren't classes in decorating pre-made treats but rather hands-on interactive cooking classes where kids will create cakes, pretzels, pancakes, pasta and candy from scratch. Kids' classes are recommended for children ages 4 and older. Medium Rare also offers classes for grown-ups that teach you how to make meals from simple family dinners to impressive dinner parties.

DANCE

Few of us can resist the opportunity to see our daughters in frilly pink tutus at least once. And for those of us with sons, this is the perfect way to impart some semblance of rhythm and coordination to them so that they can be the coolest ones on the dance floor when they get older. With irresistible cuteness and coolness on offer, it is not surprising that there are tons of dance classes in Westchester. The style of dance varies—some facilities focus exclusively on ballet, while others offer a wide range of classes, including less traditional forms like hip-hop, Broadway, Irish step and acrobatic.

Bedford Hills

The Pulse Performing Arts Studio
196 Rte. 117 (Bypass Rd.)
(914) 241-0200
www.performthepulse.com

The Pulse Performing Arts Studio brings the vibe of the city to Westchester County, with programs ranging from creative movement classes for preschoolers to performance ensembles for the most serious teenage future stars. Dance styles include tap, ballet, jazz, Duncan, hip-hop, modern and theater.

Chappaqua

Ballet des Enfants
18 S. Greeley Ave.
(914) 238-6733
www.balletdesenfants.net

"Fairytale Ballet" is a traditional, ballet-based creative movement program with a unique twist: the first half of the class is spent on terms and movements followed by a story; the second half of the class is spent in costume, "dancing out" that story using props. For little ones, Ballet des Enfants offers a Mommy & Me class (age 2) and an independent class (ages 2 1/2-3 1/2) called "Just Me," followed by "Leaps & Bounds" (ages 3-4). "Classical Kids" (ages 5-6) is a pre-ballet program.

Dance Emotions
75 S. Greeley Ave.
(914) 238-8974
www.danceemotions.com

This facility is in its twenty-fifth year of operation. Their style is child-friendly but structured, and even the youngest student will learn some "real" dance moves. There's "Pre-Dance" (ages 2 1/2-5), "Ballet/Tap" (ages 4-5), "Kinderkids" (ages 5-6) and "Ballet/Theatrical Jazz/Tap Combo" (age 7 and up). From there, children can take hour-long classes or "intensives" in ballet, tap, jazz, hip-hop and lyrical. They also have pointe classes for advanced dancers. There is a year-end show at the Horace Greeley School Theater as well as an annual "Nutcracker" performance.

Steffi Nossen School of Dance
191 S. Greeley Ave. (St. Mary the Virgin Church)
(914) 328-1900
www.steffinossen.org

This school offers a wide range of classes for all ages and levels. Two-year-olds (with a parent or caregiver) can enjoy "Mommy & Me" (or Daddy & Me) or "Classical Story Ballet," where they'll learn classical ballet movement and vocabulary by dancing to stories using props and costumes. These classes are also offered independently for 3-, 4-, and 5-year-olds; preschool classes are also offered in creative movement and modern. For slightly older children, there is hip-hop, jazz and, of course, ballet.

Cortlandt Manor

Dance Magic
2050 E. Main St.
(914) 736-1110

A smaller, "boutique" studio that believes in the magic of dance. "Move & Groove" (age 3) features tumbling, obstacle courses, instruments and props, ballet, jazz and creative movement. "Ballerinas to Be" (age 4) is a combination of tumbling, jazz, ballet, and instruments and props. "Tumble Jazz" (ages 5-6) focuses on building skill and coordination while teaching the basics of dance. All classes are limited to eight children. Classes go through 12th grade, and older students have the opportunity to join the "Dance Team," which performs at the Westchester County Center every other year and also travels to and performs at places like Disney World.

Eastchester

Hendry School of Irish Dance
98 Stewart Ave. (St. Luke's Church)
(914) 961-5640

Competitive and non-competitive Irish Step dance classes offered for ages 5 and up.

Studio B. Dance Center
375 White Plains Rd.
(914) 793-2799

This facility offers pre-ballet/creative movement (ages 2-3), ballet/tap (ages 4-5), and ballet, tap and jazz classes (age 6 and up). There are also modern dance, with instrumental and percussive music, (age 5 and up) and hip-hop (age 8 and up) classes. The Company programs (age 6 and up) are for those children who are serious about studying dance (the classes are two hours long) and wish to participate in community service performances. All students are invited to show off their talents at the annual spring recital.

Golden's Bridge

Children's Center of Golden's Bridge
5 Anderson Ln.
(914) 232-6813
www.childrenscenterofgb.com

Dance classes including Pre-Ballet (ages 3-5) and Ballet 1 (age 6 and up). Parents and caregivers can relax with a cup of coffee in "Mom's Café." Walk-ins are welcome, but reservations are suggested.

Harrison

Magical Movements
33 Halstead Ave.
(914) 381-6185
www.magicalmovements.net

A wide variety of dance classes for age 2 and up, including "Mommy/Daddy & Me" (ages 2-3), "Just Me" (ages 2-3), "Dance Beginnings: Creative Movement & Ballet" (ages 3-4), "Ballet" (ages 4-12), "Tap & Ballet" (ages 4-12), "Jazz/Hip-Hop" (ages 5-10) and "Tap & Jazz" (ages 8-12). For preteens, teens and adults, they also offer ballet technique & pointe, tap, jazz, hip-hop, hip-hop aerobics and belly dancing.

New York Dance
222 Harrison Ave.
(914) 835-5252
www.newyorkdance.com

This professional performance company offers courses with a focus on correct technique and training while developing the student's individual strengths in a warm and nurturing environment. Classes for ages 3 and up include ballet, pointe, jazz, tap, hip-hop, modern, creative movement, and Mommy & Me. For those who want to take their talents a bit further, there are opportunities with several performing companies around the metropolitan area at junior, teen and senior levels.

Hastings-on-Hudson

Broadway Training Center
10 Washington Ave.
(914) 478-5825
www.broadwaytraining.com

Preschool programs (ages 3-4 and 4-5) include pre-ballet, creative dance and fairytale theatre (for budding actors and actresses). For older children (age 5 and up), there are classes in ballet, jazz, modern dance, tap, hip-hop, acting, improv, singing and musical theater. Junior Ensemble (ages 6-13) and Senior Ensemble (ages 12-18) meet at least two days a week and build up to live perform-ances of Broadway shows at a local theater.

Kids Co-Motion
7 Farragut Ave. (St. Matthew's Lutheran Church)
(914) 476-8368
www.kidsco-motion.com

This facility provides a learning atmosphere, beginning with classes in motion, music, tumbling and song for very young children (with caregivers). "Mommy & Me" classes include "Tots" (ages 12-21 months) and "Toddlers" (ages 22-40 months). They also offer "Creative Movement" (ages 3-5) and "Beginning Modern Dance" (ages 6-9).

On Hudson Fitness & Dance Studio
558 Warburton Ave. (V.F.W. Bldg.)
(914) 478-0508
www.onhudsonfitness.com

They have variety of classes, including "Tumblin' 2s" (ages 18 months–2 years), "Creative Ballet" (age 3), pre-ballet and pre-ballet/tap (ages 4-5), ballet (including pointe), tap, jazz/hip-hop (age 6 and up) and modern (8 and up). Ballroom workshops are offered throughout the year for parents with their children, and fitness classes are on offer for teens and adults.

Hawthorne

Rose's School of Dance
338 Elwood Ave.
(914) 769-7077
www.rosesschoolofdance.com

In business for more than forty years, this dance studio offers chil-dren 3 years and up (ages 3-4, 5-7, 8-10, 11-12) courses in classical ballet, pointe and jazz with live piano accompaniment. They also have acrobatics (age 5 and up), competition teams (age 8 and up), private vocal instruction, and classes for teens and adults. Students can take part in an annual recital.

Katonah

Arts Caravan
Bedford Rd., Rte. 117
(914) 666-3917 or (914) 772-7348

A creative program for preschoolers (age 3 and up) in tap, jazz, ballet or theater. They also offer "Musical Theater Workshop" (ages 4-17), salsa and ballroom dance classes for teenagers and adults.

Siobhan Moore School of Irish Dance
117 Valley Rd. (St. Mary's Church)
(914) 232-4081
This school offers classes in all levels of Irish Step dancing.

Larchmont

A Dance Studio
2094 Boston Post Rd.
(914) 834-2432
www.adancestudio.com

This studio offers "Preschool Beginner Classes" (ages 3-5), a combination of creative movement and some tap. As children get older and more confident, they can opt for ballet or a tap/jazz combo class (ages 5-9), and hip-hop classes (age 8 and up).

Ballet des Enfants
1290 Boston Post Rd. (Ferndale Shopping Center)
(914) 834-5443
www.balletdesenfants.net
See the listing under Chappaqua for more information.

Lorna London School of Ballet
1810 Palmer Ave.
(914) 833-1267
www.lornalondonballet.com

It's "pure ballet" at this school, owned and operated by Lorna London herself for over sixty years, with classes now being taught by her daughter, Constance, also a professional ballerina. They offer beginner, intermediate and advanced classes for all ages: their students range in age from 3 to 73! For children, there are pre-ballet (ages 3-4) and ballet (ages 5-15) classes, and each class is divided by age and ability.

Mamaroneck

Dance Cavise
273 Halstead Ave.
(914) 381-5222
www.dancecavise.com

This facility offers classes in "Creative Movement" (ages 3-4); pre-ballet, tap or jazz (age 5); and ballet, tap, or jazz (age 6 and up). As kids get older they can also take other types of lessons like hip-hop, modern and pointe (for advanced dancers).

Steffi Nossen School of Dance
546 E. Boston Post Rd. (United Methodist Church)
(914) 328-1900
www.steffinossen.org

See the listing under Chappaqua for more information.

Mount Kisco

Monique's
145 Kisco Ave.
(914) 244-0435

This facility offers age-specific programs to coordinate with children's varied abilities. "Baby Dream Jam" is an interactive musical and movement "jam session" for moms and their babies (ages 6-24 months). In "The Dream Jam Book Club" (ages 2-4), books come alive through the use of sets, props, music, movement and art activities; each child receives a new book each week. There are also hip-hop dance classes for ages 4-11.

The Dance Connection of Mount Kisco
35 Main St.
(914) 244-4224

This facility offers classes in "Creative Movement" (ages 3-4), "Kindergarten Ballet, Jazz & Tap" (ages 5-6), "First/Second Grade Ballet" (ages 7-8) and "Jazz & Broadway Tap" (ages 7-8).

New Rochelle

Lynn Academy of Irish Dance
36 Division St. (Irish Benevolent Society)
(914) 420-9742
www.lynnacademy.com

This facility offers Irish Step dance classes in all levels for ages 5 and up.

Rooftop Rhythms Dance Studio
10 S. Division St., #7
(914) 576-6027
www.rooftoprhythms.com

This newly expanded studio offers a variety of classes for ages 3-18, including tap/ballet (ages 3-4, 5-6 and 7-9), jazz/ballet (ages 7-9), hip-hop (age 6 and up, grouped by age) and boys-only hip-hop (ages 8-13). The year culminates with a recital at the White Plains Performing Arts Center.

Ossining
Logrea Dance Academy
2 Dale Ave.
(914) 941-2939
www.logreadance.com

This academy teaches a wide variety of ballet classes, including "Pre-Ballet" (ages 3-4, children must be out of diapers), "Elementary 1" (ages 4-5), "Elementary 2" (ages 5-6), "Ballet 1" (ages 6-8) and "Ballet 2" (ages 7-9). For kids age 7 and up, they teach other dance styles, including tap, jazz and modern.

Peekskill
Siobhan Moore School of Irish Step Dancing
341 Railroad Ave. (Kelly's on the Green)
(914) 232-4081

See the listing under Katonah for more information.

Pelham
Ballet Arts/The Performing Arts Center of Southern Westchester
504 Fifth Ave.
(914) 738-8300
www.ballet-arts.net

Ballet Arts provides classes for ages 2 through adult for every skill level in ballet (with piano accompaniment), creative movement, tumbling, jazz, hip-hop, yoga, Pilates, Irish Step, ballroom and modern/improvisation. A babysitting service is available on-site for adult classes.

Beverly Dance Studio
139 Wolfs Ln.
(914) 738-5277

This studio offers "Shake, Rattle & Roll," a unique class for ages 0-5 (with a caregiver) that incorporates music and movement. For ages 3 to 6, there is a "Dance Basics" class that incorporates ballet and tap and includes a performance at the end. They also offer ballet, tap, jazz and hip-hop classes, divided by level and age.

Lynn Academy of Irish Dance
1415 Pelhamdale Ave. (Christ Church of the Pelhams)
(914) 420-9742
www.lynnacademy.com

See the listing under New Rochelle for more information.

Pleasantville

Academy of Dance Arts
17-19 Marble Ave.
(914) 741-5678
www.academyofdancearts.info

The classes for little ones include "Baby Steps" (ages 12-24 months), "Tiny Toes" (ages 2-3) and "Creative Movement" (ages 3-5), as well as pre-ballet for preschoolers. For age 6 and up, they offer classes in ballet, jazz, tap, theatre dance, hip-hop, acrobatic, lyrical (ballet/modern) and creative movement.

Steffi Nossen School of Dance
600 Bear Ridge Rd. (The Richard G. Rosenthal JCC)
(914) 328-1900
www.steffinossen.org
See the listing under Chappaqua for more information.

Woods School of Irish Dancing
Corner of Saratoga & Garrigan Aves. (Our Lady of Pompeii Church)
(845) 735-4283
www.wsoid.com

Irish Step dancing classes for students ages 5-15 begin with the basics in reel and jig time. Competitive and non-competitive classes are available.

Port Chester

Westchester Dance Academy
181 Westchester Ave.
(914) 690-1501
www.wdacademy.com

The have a variety of classes for young children, including Mommy & Me (ages 18 months-2 years), "Creative Movement" (ages 2 1/2-3), "Ballet/Tap Combo" (ages 3-4 and 5-6) and "Ballet/Jazz Combo" (ages 3-4 and 5-6). For older kids, there is ballet (ages 5-7), jazz (age 6-7), acrobatics and tumbling (ages 6-7), boys' jazz (ages 6-8), lyrical (age 9) and hip-hop (age 11 and up). This center also has advanced programs for children of increasing age and experience.

Rye

The Ballet Class
51 Milton Rd. (The Rye Arts Center)
(914) 967-0912
www.theballetclass.com

This studio offers "Pre-Ballet" (ages 5-6), "Ballet I" (ages 6-8), "Ballet II" (ages 7-9), "Ballet III" (age 8 and up, two classes a week mandatory), as well as more advanced classes that require prior experience and an audition. There is a recital at the end of the year.

Scarsdale

Central Park Dance
450 Central Park Ave.
(914) 723-2940
www.centralparkdance.com

Celebrating twenty-five years in business, they offer over a hundred classes in more than ten different styles of dance, plus classes in acting, aerobics (including "Japanese Aerobics"), fitness, Pilates, and voice. There is a preschool program, "Tot & I" (ages 2 1/2-3), and then classes for ages 3-4, 4-5 and 5-6. Children age 6 and up can choose from classes in ballet, jazz, hip-hop, funk, theater jazz, tap and more.

Scarsdale Ballet Studio
696R White Plains Rd. (Vernon Hills Shopping Center)
(914) 725-8754
www.scarsdaleballetstudio.com

"Creative Ballet" (ages 3-5) is a creative movement class that focuses on rhythm and coordination as children are introduced to the joy of dance. For older kids, "Pre-Ballet" (age 6) and "Elementary Level I" (age 7) focus on classical ballet training and technique. Levels progress from there based on age and ability. They also offer jazz dance classes for ages 8 to adults.

Steffi Nossen School of Dance
Popham Rd. at Autenrieth Rd. (Scarsdale Community Baptist Church)
(914) 328-1900
www.steffinossen.org

See the listing under Chappaqua for more information.

Sleepy Hollow

Sleepy Hollow Performing Arts Center
38 Beekman Ave.
(914) 333-0663
www.outsiderart.com/shpac/

A variety of styles for a variety of ages, including pre-ballet/tap (ages 2-3 and 4-5), "Creative Movement" (ages 3-5), ballet (ages 4-7), hip-hop (ages 6-9), boys-only beginning breakdance/hip-hop (ages 7-12), hip-hop/jazz (ages 5-7, 6-8 and 7-9) and beginning breakdance (ages 6-10).

Tappan Zee Dance Group
362 N. Broadway
(914) 631-6692
www.tzdg.org

For the little ones, there is "Creative Movement" (ages 3-4). For older kids, there's "Dance Prep," a pre-ballet class (ages 5-6).

Tarrytown

Dance by Audrey St. Vincent
27 S. Washington St. (UMC Arts Center at the United Methodist Church)
(914) 439-4532

With over thirty years of experience, Audrey and her staff will give your child proper technical training and correct body alignment in a fun-filled, nurturing atmosphere. For the younger set, they have a general creative movement class called "Tots in Motion" (ages 3-4). Other classes include classical ballet and pointe, "Little Feet Ballet", pre-jazz, jazz and even salsa.

Lynn Academy of Irish Dance
42 N. Broadway (Reformed Church of the Tarrytowns)
(914) 420-9742
www.lynnacademy.com

See the listing under New Rochelle for more information.

White Plains

City Center Dance
236 E. Post Rd.
(914) 328-1881
www.citycenterdance.com

They offer dance classes for children age 3 and up. Choose from creative movement, ballet, tap, jazz, hip-hop, lyrical, modern, musical theater and a breakdance/pop n' lock class. All students except preschoolers perform in the end-of-the-year student showcase.

O'Rourke Academy of Irish Dance
430 North St. (Trinity Lutheran Church)
(917) 453-0375
www.orourkeirishdancers.com

This traditional Irish dance school offers classes in Irish Step for children age 5 and up. There's a recital at the end of the year.

Steffi Nossen School of Dance
(Two locations)
82 Prospect St. (St. Bartholomew's Church)
216 Central Park Ave. (Westchester Conservatory of Music)
(914)328-1900
www.steffinossen.org

See the listing under Chappaqua for more information.

Yonkers

Christine Murray School of Irish Dance
1455 Nepperhan Ave.
(914) 968-2698

Offers Irish Step dance at all levels for age 5 and up. Their "Dance-Out Group" gives students ages 10-19 an opportunity to perform at local schools, dinner dances and other community events.

Hip Hop Kidz
1 Odell Plaza
(914) 457-0405
www.hiphopkidz.net

Kids ages 4-18 can learn the freshest hip-hop dance moves from top music videos. Classes for younger kids include "Pee Wee Hip Hop Kidz" (ages 4-5), and "Hip Hop Kidz I and II" (ages 6-11). For older children there are opportunities to be part of select dance troupes that perform at venues ranging from TV shows to The Macy's Thanksgiving Day Parade.

Dawn McMahon School of Dance
1455 Nepperhan Ave.
(914) 968-2698

Classes for pre-schoolers through adults in ballet, tap, jazz, hip-hop and modern dance.

Flynn School of Irish Dance
990 McLean Ave. (Aisling Irish Community Center)
(914) 588-9200

This facility welcomes boys and girls age 4 and up for Irish Step dance classes. There is also a location in Riverdale.

Tara Circle
1097 N. Broadway (Alder Manor)
(914) 964-8272
www.taracircle.org

Irish Step dancing classes offered for ages 6-9 and 10-14. Students learn the basic jig, slipjig and reel steps.

Yorktown Heights

Siobhan Moore School of Irish Step Dancing
137 Moseman Rd. (St. Patrick's Church)
(914) 232-4081

See the listing under Katonah for more information.

Westchester Ballet Center
1974 Commerce St.
(914) 245-2940
www.westchesterballetcenter.com

For younger children, they offer "Pre-Ballet" (ages 3-5) and "Ballet" (ages 5-8). For dancers ages 8 to 18, they offer ballet, modern, tap, jazz, pointe, hip-hop, flamenco, Hawaiian dance and Classical Indian dance for all skill levels.

CONNECTICUT

Ballet des Enfants
722 Post Rd., 3rd Fl., Darien
(203) 662-9800
www.balletdesenfants.net

See the listing under Chappaqua for more information.

Ballet des Enfants
2000 West Main St. (Shoprite Plaza), Unit 450
Old Greenwich/Stamford
(203) 973-0144
www.balletdesenfants.net

See the listing under Chappaqua for more information.

PUTNAM COUNTY

The Dance Shop
54 Miller Road Plaza, Mahopac
(845) 628-2312

A variety of classes are taught, including "Mommy & Me" (ages 18 months-2 1/2 years), "Creative Movement" (ages 2 1/2-4) and combo classes (ages 4-5) such as ballet/creative movement, ballet/tap or ballet/jazz. For older kids (age 6 and up), there are classes in ballet, tap, jazz, hip-hop and modern.

DRAMA

We think you'll agree that when it comes to drama, children are naturals. You've seen them perform such heart-wrenching scenes as "The boo-boo so bad I'm going to need my leg amputated" and "If I don't wear this dress today I will actually die." So why not harness some of that natural talent and let them put it to good use? Drama classes teach many important skills, like articulation, memorization and self-confidence. Some drama classes are geared towards a specific end-of-session performance; others change week to week and end with a final "showcase" of your children's talents. Remember, almost all Oscar-winners thank their parents even if they run out of time to thank anyone else on their list!

In addition to the listings by town below, this franchise chain has numerous Westchester locations:

Drama Kids International
Northern Westchester/Putnam County (Briarcliff Manor, Cortlandt Manor, Mount Kisco, Ossining, Pleasantville): (914) 762-2279
Lower Westchester (New Rochelle, Pelham, Rye, White Plains): (914) 712-7484
www.dramakids.com

This program for ages 5-17 has a creative drama curriculum and teaching methods that include speech, verbal dynamics, creative movement, language development, structured improvisation, dialogue development, snippets, scene starters and mini-scripts. There are Parent Day presentations and an end-of-the-year production. Groups include Lower Primary (ages 5-8), Upper Primary (ages 9-12) and a Youth Theater program (ages 13-17).

Bedford Hills
The Pulse Performing Arts Studio
196 Rte. 117 (Bypass Rd.)
(914) 241-0200
www.performthepulse.com

Programs range from creative movement classes for preschoolers to performance ensembles and theater dance for the most serious teenage future stars.

Katonah
Arts Caravan
Bedford Rd., Rte. 117
(914) 666-3917 or (914) 772-7348

A creative program for preschoolers (age 3 and up) in tap, jazz, ballet or theater. They also offer "Musical Theater Workshop" (ages 4-17) and "Story Improvisation" with a performance at the end of the session.

White Plains

Class Act Studios
77 Tarrytown Rd.
(914) 946-3391
www.classactstudios.com

Class Act Studios has decades of experience training children of all ages. They offer "Tiny Tots" workshops, which are designed specifically for the non-reader, with an emphasis on role-playing, creative drama and improvisation. Classes are available for children, teens and even adults.

Star Kidz
468 Rosedale Ave. (Community Unitarian Church)
(914) 921-0006

An afterschool program for children ages 4-16, combining instruction in singing, acting and hip-hop dancing. All classes stress the fun of performing and are taught by professional Broadway performers. Parents are invited to observe the final class.

The Play Group Theater
200 Hamilton Ave., #4B
(914) 946-4433
www.playgroup.org

Children and teens in The Play Group work in an environment of creativity, mutual respect and fun—and in the end the whole family enjoys the product! "Little Theatre" classes include "Pre-Theatre" (ages 3-4) and "Theatre Skills" (ages 5-6). For children ages 7-17 they offer beginning, intermediate and advanced acting classes in addition to musical theatre, improv and dance.

ENRICHMENT & TUTORING

We've all heard that young children have brains like sponges, so how about letting them soak up a little knowledge? If your child has difficulty learning or just needs a little extra help with certain school subjects, a tutor can be a great way to help them "learn to learn." These services provide students with the opportunity to catch up, keep up or get ahead in reading, writing, math, study skills and more. Shhhhh, don't tell them about all the stuff they're learning! They'll just think they're having fun.

Armonk

Tutoring Club
475 Main St.
(914) 273-2353
http://armonkNY.tutoringclub.com

This national chain provides students from kindergarten through 12th grade with individualized programs in reading, writing, math, PSAT/SAT preparation, study skills and more.

Bronxville

Sylvan Learning Center
850 Bronx River Rd.
(914) 237-4396
www.educate.com

After a diagnostic assessment to pinpoint your child's strengths and weaknesses in reading, writing and/or math, they will design a program suited to his or her needs and carry out ongoing assessments to track progress.

Hartsdale

Huntington Learning Center
441 Tarrytown Rd. (Crossroads Shopping Center)
(914) 946-7800
www.huntingtonlearning.com

They diagnose what is keeping your child from doing his or her best, and then create an individualized program that includes instruction in such subjects as reading, writing, mathematics, study skills and/or phonics. For children ages 5-17.

Katonah

Tutoring Club
173 Katonah Ave.
(914) 232-2317
http://katonahNY.tutoringclub.com

See the listing under Armonk for more information.

Mount Kisco

Sylvan Learning Center
41 South Moger Ave.
(914) 241-7020
www.educate.com

See the listing under Bronxville for more information.

Rye

Imagine Tomorrow
44-46 Purchase St.
(914) 921-2024
www.imaginetomorrow.com

They offer classes, Mommy & Me and Preschool & Kindergarten enrichment programs to help children learn keyboard and computer basics, thinking and problem solving, early reading and writing, and listening comprehension as well as Internet and digital communications. Classes are kept small for a stronger teacher-to-student ratio. They also offer summer camp.

SCORE! Education Center
25 Purchase St.
(914) 925-8840
www.escore.com

This national facility helps children of all learning levels, from Pre-K to 12, make academic progress in math, reading, writing and more, in a fun, motivating environment. They also help develop goal-setting skills and increase older children's preparedness for state tests.

Rye Brook

FasTracKids
27 Rye Ridge Plaza
(914) 937-6977
www.fastrackids.com

These enrichment programs are geared towards children ages 3-6. Instruction is provided in twelve subject areas—from astronomy and creativity to mathematics and natural sciences—in two-hour, weekly classes. Classes are built around the FasTrack Learning Station—a combination of computers, LCD projection and an interactive white board.

Scarsdale

Dicker Reading Method
75 Brook St.
(914) 997-0975

No matter what level your child is reading at, even if he or she is diagnosed as learning disabled, dyslexic, or with ADD or ADHD, the Dicker Reading Method pledges immediate reading achievement, increased comprehension and a marked improvement in vocabulary development.

Huntington Learning Center
721 White Plains Rd. (Eastchester Shopping Center)
(914) 722-6100
www.huntingtonlearning.com

See the listing under Hartsdale for more information.

Imagine Tomorrow
158 Summerfield St.
(914) 572-7950
www.imaginetomorrow.com

See the listing under Rye for more information.

SCORE! Education Center
450 Central Park Ave.
(914) 722-6070
www.escore.com

See listing under Rye for more information.

White Plains

Brain Builders Tutoring
280 Dobbs Ferry Rd.
(914) 328-1258

Brain Builders' goal is to make it possible for your child to learn without frustration and heartache. Special education teachers trained in Orton-Gillingham and Lindamood Bell programs teach at this small private practice. They design programs tailored to the student's specific learning needs. Also offered are educational evaluations, consultations, advocacy, and classes for writing, organizational and study skills.

Sylvan Learning Center
180 S. Broadway
(914) 948-4116
www.educate.com

See the listing under Bronxville for more information.

FOREIGN LANGUAGE

It may seem like your child can already say "no" in every conceivable language. But if you want to expand her repertoire, there are many language classes available. Westchester is also a popular area for foreign professionals to relocate in temporarily or to settle in on a more permanent basis. If you're a bilingual family—particularly if you are planning on returning to your original country within a few years—these classes can help your child learn your native language while still attending day school with the neighborhood kids.

Larchmont

Armelle's Language Studio
2 East Ave.
(914) 833-0781
www.home.earthlink.net/~languagestudio

Children age 6 months and older learn French or Spanish through songs, allowing them to assimilate the language while having fun. The classes focus on imitation, comprehension and repetition, and include interactive songs, sing-along games, finger-play and puppets.

Peekaboo Learning Center
4 Chatsworth Ave., Suite #4
(914) 833-9755
www.peekaboolearningcenter.com

Classes in French, Spanish, English, Italian and Chinese for school-age children and adults are given either privately or in a small group (with a maximum of four people) in your home. Children's classes focus on the rhythms and sounds of a foreign language, and on learning basic vocabulary through songs, coloring and games.

Rye

The Little Language League
22 Purdy Ave.
(914) 921-9075
www.languageleague.com

The Little Language League stresses learning in context and adheres to the fundamentals of Montessori philosophy. "Language Together" is an immersion class in French, Spanish, Italian or German for children ages 6 months-3 years (with caregiver). "Language for Kids" (ages 3-10) develops French, Spanish or Italian language skills through art, music and theater. "Shine Theater" (age 3 and up) introduces children to the performing arts through speech, movement and song, and is available in English and French.

Scarsdale

ABC Language Exchange at The Scholastic Store
450 Central Park Ave.
(914) 725-7201
www.scholastic.com

Classes teaching the basics of Mandarin, French or Spanish for children ages 2-9 (separated by age).

Language Link Center
270 Ardsley Rd. (Greenville Community Church)
(914) 779-LANG (-5264)

Instruction in a wide variety of languages, including French, German, Spanish, Latin, Greek, Mandarin, Italian, Russian, Portuguese, Japanese and more. Mommy & Me classes are offered beginning at 12 months, and individual lessons or small group classes are available for children and adults at their site or your location.

Tuckahoe

La Piazza Di Carolina
116 Alta Vista Dr.
(914) 793-2629
www.lapiazzadicarolina.com

An Italian immersion program for ages 6 months through adult. Children learn through stories, games, songs, dance, theater and arts & crafts. Mommy & Me classes include: "I Piu Piccoli" (ages 6-13 months), "I Primi Passi" (ages 14-23 months) and "Pronti a Correre" (ages 2-3). There are also classes for ages 3-5, 5-6, 6-7, 8-10, 11-13, and a "Full Immersion Summer Camp" for 3-5 or 6- to 12-year-olds.

White Plains

Berlitz Language Center
1 N. Broadway
(914) 946-8389
www.berlitz.us

Classes in Spanish, Italian and French for children ages 4-11. Kids learn through play, songs, stories and other activities, and learn the new language the same way they learned their first one—naturally, through conversation. They offer private and group off-site classes as well.

Savvy Suggestion

Osmosis makes award-winning educational products that include brightly illustrated board books, DVDs and activities that focus on English-Spanish and English-Italian instruction. The products are divided into different topics like "Casa—Things Around the House," "Cuerpo—Body Parts" and more. Available at Buy Buy Baby, The Right Start and on-line at www.learningbyosmosis.com.

Connecticut

The Language Exchange
205 E. Putnam Ave., #9 (Mill Pond Shopping Center), Cos Cob
(203) 422-2024 or (888) TLE-LANG
www.foreignlanguageexchange.com

Both facility-based and in-home instruction in eighteen languages for all ages, from six months old to adults. Classes are organized by age and level, depending on the child, and focus on learning through age-appropriate activities.

The Little Language League
59 E. Putnam Ave. (First United Methodist Church), Greenwich
(914) 921-9075
www.languageleague.com

See the listing under Rye for more information.

Berlitz Language Center
350 Bedford St., Suite #408, Stamford
(203) 324-9551
www.berlitz.us

See the listing under White Plains for more information.

GYMNASTICS & PLAY

If your kid loves to tumble, run and jump, check out these classes. But know what you're looking for first; while your child doesn't need to be a budding Olympian, some of these programs are actually pre-gymnastics programs that are geared towards continued training in the sport. "Developmental gymnastics"—essentially, noncompetitive gymnastics—focuses on basic skills, coordination, balance and strength. Some classes are built around an obstacle course format on real gym equipment for younger kids, with increasingly advanced gymnastics for grade school children and competitive gymnastics for older children. Some other programs are really more play classes, but they all involve movement, tumbling and stretching.

Bedford Hills

American Gymnastics
317 Railroad Ave.
(914) 241-1997

Preschool classes include "Mom & Me I" (ages 1-2), "Mom & Me II" (ages 2-3), "Ameri-Cubs" (ages 3-4) and "Ameri-Bears" (ages 4-5). There is a special program just for 5-year-olds. Programs for older kids (ages 6-12) are grouped by age and ability. This facility also offers competitive gymnastics.

Chappaqua

World Cup Gymnastics
170 Hunts Ln.
(914) 238-4967
www.worldcupgymnastics.com

Gymnastics classes for ages 3 months to 18 years, including "Romperee" parent/child classes (ages 3-24 months), preschool classes (age 2-5) focusing on early gymnastics skills, and recreational programs (ages 5-16) to develop beginner through advanced gymnastic skills. There are also competitive teams and exhibition teams (ages 6-18).

Cortlandt Manor

Gymnastics City
2121 Crompond Rd.
(914) 734-1616
www.gymnasticscity.com

Gymnastics classes for ages 18 months to 12 years. "Mom & Tot" (ages 18 months-2 years) and preschool classes (ages 3-5) are based on an obstacle course format. General gymnastics classes for girls (ages 6-9, 10-13 and 14 and up) and boys (ages 6-8 and 9 and up) provide instruction based around the main Olympic events (e.g. floor, vault, bar).

Croton-on-Hudson

Straddles Gymnastics
420 S. Riverside Ave.
(914) 271-2400

They offer "Split Peas" (ages 18 months-3 years), "Tumble Weeds" (ages 3-5), and general classes for ages 5-18, separated by age and ability.

Elmsford

Gymtime
326-328 Saw Mill River Rd. (Multiplex Shopping Center)
(914) 948-1868
www.gymtimeplace.com

Parent/child recreation programs for infants and toddlers include "Hello World," (ages 3-11 months), "First Steps" (ages 9-17 months), "Toddlers" (ages 13-24 months), "Runners" (ages 18-30 months) and "Jumpers" (ages 30-48 months). Classes focus on exercise and movement, and include songs, obstacle courses and parachute play. Gymtime has an unlimited class policy, which means that once you register for the class of your choice you can attend any other classes in your child's age group at no additional charge.

Harrison

International School of Gymnastics (ISG)
151 Crotona Ave.
(914) 835-0010

Gymnastics classes for ages 10 months–14 years. Classes requiring a caregiver include "Tumbling Bunnies" (ages 10-18 months), "Gyminy Crickets" (ages 1-2) and "Chipmunks" (ages 2 -3). For older children there is "Pre-School Girls & Boys" (ages 3-5), as well as age-appropriate classes for ages 5-6, 6-7, 8-12 and 12-14.

Hawthorne

Westchester Gymnastics
5 Skyline Dr.
(914) 592-2324

Preschool classes include "Parent & Tot" (ages 18 months-2 years and 2-3 years), "Beginner Gym" (ages 3-4), and "Advanced Gym" (ages 4-5). They also offer recreational classes (ages 4-18) and a competitive team (ages 6-17).

Jefferson Valley

Gymboree Play & Music
3631 Hill Blvd. & Rte. 6
(866) 477-3700
www.gymboree.com

The Gymboree Learning Program is a series of progressive age- and developmentally-appropriate play and movement classes for children from birth to age 5. In addition to seven levels of traditional Gymboree classes—with play equipment, parachute time, songs and bubble time—there are also "Mommy and Baby Fitness," "Baby Signs," "Yoga Fun," "Fitness Fun" and "Global Kids," a multi-cultural "journey" that explores play, music, dance, customs and activities from around the world.

Mamaroneck

Gym Dandy
546 Boston Post Rd. (Methodist Church)
(914) 422-9123

Full-hour classes for ages 6 months to 3 years, including warm-up exercises, songs, puppets, arts & crafts, and parachute play.

Mohegan Lake

Dynamic Gymnastics
1949 E. Main St.
(914) 528-5437
www.dynamicgymnasticsny.com

This facility offers "Terrific Twos" (ages 18 months-3 years, with caregiver), preschool and kindergarten classes, and recreational gymnastics for ages 5-14, separated by age and ability. They also offer advanced classes and team gymnastics.

Mount Kisco

Jodi's Gym
25 Hubbels Dr.
(914) 244-8811
www.jodisgym.com

"Mommy & Me" classes (ages 9-12 months, 12-17 months, 18-24 months, 25-30 months and 30-35 months) include gym, gym/art combo, gym/music combo and gym/music/art combo. For preschoolers there is "Tumbling Tots" (ages 3-4 and 4-5) and for kindergarteners there's "Kindergym". School-age children (ages 6-12) are grouped by age and ability in "Developmental Gymnastics," "Accelerated Gymnastics" and "Advanced Gymnastics." There is also a Manhattan location.

Ossining

Locomotion
255 N. Highland Ave.
(914) 923-1700
www.locomotion4kids.com

They offer "Gym Stop" (ages 6 months-5 years), "Music Stop" (ages 6 months-5 years) and "Loco Movement", a movement, nutrition and sports skills program for ages 4-7.

Pelham

Gym Dandy
1415 Pelhamdale Ave. (Christ Church of the Pelhams)
(914) 422-9123

See the listing under Mamaroneck for more information.

Spotlight Gymnastics
901 Pelhamdale Ave.
(914) 738-7305
www.spotlightgym.com

"Parents and Tots" (ages 2-3) focuses on introductory gymnastics. Class programs (ages 3-16, grouped by age and ability) develop basic gymnastics skills.

Scarsdale

Gymboree Play & Music
450 Central Park Ave.
(866) 477-3700
www.gymboree.com

See the listing under Jefferson Valley for more information.

Gymtime
1 Heathcote Rd. (Scarsdale Congregational Church)
(914) 948-1868
www.gymtimeplace.com

See the listing under Elmsford for more information.

Little Gym
777 White Plains Rd. (Shoppes at Eastchester)
(914) 722-0072
www.tlgscarsdaleny.com

Infant/toddler classes include "Bugs" (ages 4-10 months), "Birds" (ages 10-18 months), "Beasts" (ages 19 months- 2-years) and "Super Beasts" (ages 2-3). Preschool and kindergarten classes include "Funny Bugs" (ages 3-4), "Giggle Worms" (ages 4-5) and "Good Friends" (ages 5-6). Grade-school gymnastics (ages 6-12) include "Flips" (beginners), "Twisters" (intermediate) and "Aerials" (advanced). For developing sports skills, they offer "Mini Jacks" (ages 3-4) and "Cracker Jacks" (ages 4-6). There is cheerleading, karate and dance for 6-12 year olds.

Savvy Suggestion

Hitting the gym is not for just parents anymore. Children in Motion is a forty-five-minute exercise program in an assisted circuit. It's designed for kids ages 7-14 to be fun and challenging. The workout includes cardio exercise and safe hydraulic resistance equipment that allows for all strength levels. A cue alerts your child to change stations every thirty seconds. They also offer yoga.

Children in Motion
125 Marbledale Rd., Tuckahoe
(914) 337-0837
www.childreninmotion.net
Hours: Monday-Friday 3 pm-7 pm, Saturday and Sunday 9 am-6 pm

Tumble Bugs
826 Scarsdale Ave.
(914) 713-1113
www.tumblebugsny.com

Gymnastics and pre-gymnastics classes for ages 9 months-6 years. For the younger set, there are "Baby Bugs" (12-18 months) and "Snuggle Bugs" (18-24 months), both requiring caregiver participation. "Tumble Bugs" (ages 2-6, 2-year-olds requiring a caregiver) are movement education classes grouped by age and are focused on developing confidence, physical ability and coordination.

White Plains

New York Sports Club for Kids
4 City Center
(914) 428-2020
www.mysportsclubs.com

They offer many recreational athletic programs, including: "Mini Gymi's" (ages 6-36 months), a parent/tot class; "Gymtastics" (ages 1-15), a basic gymnastics skills class; "Cardio Kids" (ages 3-6), an age-appropriate sports skills development class; "Dancexperience" (ages 3-15); "Cheertastics" (ages 5-15); "Kickboxing Kids" (ages 6-12) and "Kidspin Theatre" (ages 7-15).

Yonkers

Gym Cats Gymnastics Center
1 Odell Plaza
(914) 965-7676
www.gymcats.net

"Tiny Cats" is divided into three age-appropriate, co-ed categories that focus on basic movement education: "Mom & Me" (age 2), and classes for ages 3 and 4. "Little Cat" classes (ages 5-6 1/2) for boys and girls focus on beginner level skills. "Big Cat" classes (6 and up) for boys and girls concentrate on skills and routines. There are also "Super Cat" girls' and boys' classes (age 7 and up), by invitation only, and cheerleading and acrobatics for ages 12 and up.

CONNECTICUT

Gymboree Play & Music
31 Mill Place Rd., Danbury
(866) 477-3700
www.gymboree.com

See listing under Jefferson Valley for more information.

Tumble Bugs
6 Riverside Ave. (behind St. Catherine's Church), Greenwich
(203) 637-3303
www.tumblebugsny.com

See the listing under Scarsdale for more information.

Putnam County

Gym Magic Gymnastics
Brewster Business Park, Rte. 22, Brewster
(845) 278-2076

Preschool classes include "Parent & Tot" (ages 18 months-2 years and 3-4), and "Advanced Gym" (ages 4-5). They also offer recreational classes (ages 4-18) and a competitive team (ages 6-17).

Odyssey Gymnastics
288 Rte. 6, Mahopac
(845) 621-4924

Classes include "Parent & Tot" (ages 2-3) and "Pre-School" (ages 3-5). They also offer recreational classes (age 6 and up) and a competitive team (ages 6-17).

Rockland County

New York Sports Club for Kids
1000 Palisades Center Dr. (The Palisades Center Mall), West Nyack
(845) 358-1818
www.mysportsclubs.com

See the listing under White Plains for more information.

MARTIAL ARTS

Martial arts courses teach physical techniques, but they also cultivate mental attributes such as focus, attention, respect and discipline—hopefully teaching kids to use their heads before using their hands. You can enroll your child in most programs when she is as young as 3, sometimes even younger. You may even find yourself donning a *gi* as well.

Ardsley

Chai Karate Do
4 American Legion Dr.
(914) 674-4893
www.chaikaratedo.com

"Little Dragons" (ages 5 and under) is a basic introduction to karate. Classes are then divided by age and skill.

Bedford Hills

Black Dragon's Martial Arts and Fitness Center

717A Bedford Rd.
(914) 244-8888
www.blackdragon2K.com

For the little ones, this center offers "Little Dragons" (age 3 and up). They also have "Junior Martial Arts" (ages 7-14) and "Family Classes".

Traditional Karate America

178 Harris Rd.
(914) 241-0222
www.tkadojo.com

This is a traditional Japanese facility teaching Shotokan style karate. They offer "Little Dragons" (ages 5-7) and "Junior Basic" (ages 8-13), as well as a "Family Class".

Eastchester

Black Belt Tae Kwon Do Center

360 White Plains Rd.
(914) 779-8000
www.blackbelttaekwondo.net

This facility offers "Tiny Little Dragons" (ages 3-4), "Little Dragons" (ages 4-6) and a Children's Class (ages 6-12), as well as classes for teens and adults. Students are certified as they move through the ranks. This is a traditional school, but the emphasis is on a fun environment in which to learn the proper technique and mindset while building coordination and focus.

Harrison

Bruce Chung's Tae Kwon Do

250 Halstead Ave.
(914) 835-0665
www.brucechung.com

Classes for children ages 3-12, teenagers and adults (divided by age). They also offer "Gym-Mini Kick-it," a Mommy & Me program for ages 12-24 months, 16-28 months and 24-36 months.

Hastings-on-Hudson

New York Goju Karate

558 Warburton Ave.
(914) 478-0508
www.onhudsonfitness.com

They teach karate classes for all ages and abilities. For young children, they have "Tiny Tigers" (ages 3-4 and 4-5).

Larchmont
Hiawatha's Martial Arts & Fitness
6 Depot Way West
(914) 834-1971

The classes for kids at this academy include "Ninjas" (ages 4-5), "Dragons" (ages 6-11) and "Lions" (ages 8-12).

Mount Kisco
Black Belt Tae Kwon Do Center
507 E. Main St.
(914) 241-9400
www.blackbelttaekwondo.net

See the listing under Eastchester for more information.

Kang Tae Kwon Do & Hapkido
77 Kensico Dr. (The Saw Mill Club)
(914) 241-0797
www.kangmartialarts.com

Classes for kids age 4 and up. (Classes for adults are available too.)

Ossining
Black Belt Tae Kwon Do Center
246 S. Highland Ave. (Arcadian Shopping Center)
(914) 923-9600
www.blackbelttaokwondo.net

See the listing under Eastchester for more information.

Pleasantville
Black Belt Tae Kwon Do Center
25 Broadway
(914) 769-5600
www.blackbelttaekwondo.net

See the listing under Eastchester for more information.

Scarsdale
Jujitsu Concepts
79 Montgomery Ave.
(914) 723-7818
www.safeandfit.com

Jujitsu, kick-boxing and self-defense classes for age 4 and up.

Kang Tae Kwon Do & Hapkido
455 Central Ave. (Scarsdale Plaza Mall)
(914) 723-0777
www.kangmartialarts.com

See the listing under Mount Kisco for more information.

The Little Gym
777 White Plains Rd.
(914) 722-0072
www.tlgscarsdaleny.com

The offer introductory level karate for children 4-6 years old.

Westchester Judo Club
1495 Weaver St.
(914) 723-8006
www.westchesterjudo.com

Judo classes for kids age 4 and up, as well as for adults.

Thornwood

Bushido School of Karate
1008 Broadway (Thornwood Town Center)
(914) 741-1177
www.bushidokarate.com

For younger students, this school offers "Little Eagles" (ages 30-48 months). For older children, there are karate classes (ages 4-6 and 7 and up) divided by age, weight and experience.

White Plains

Grand Master Byung Min Kim Tae Kwon Do
60 S. Broadway (Westchester Pavilion Mall)
(914) 428-0085
www.ilovetaekwondo.net

The Grand Master offers Tae Kwon Do classes for young children (ages 3-5), older kids and adults, divided by ability.

Toshindo Karate & Fitness Center
196 Maple Ave.
(914) 285-9001
www.toshindokarate.com

For younger children, this facility offers "Tiny Tigers" (ages 3-5) and "Little Dragons" (5-10), separated by age and rank. For older students they offer "Juniors" (10-18) and "Adult Karate" (16 and up). Advanced Black and Brown Belts can participate in "Kobudo" (weapons) instruction.

Yonkers

Tiger Schulmann's Karate
2500-10 Central Park Ave. (in the Best Buy Shopping Center)
(914) 779-4900
www.tsk.com

The "Karate Cubs" preschool program stresses "advancement and growth based on each child's individual pace." Classes are taught by child care professionals trained to provide motivational instruction. Intermediate and advanced classes are also available as skill increases.

CONNECTICUT

Tiger Schulmann's Karate
(Two locations)
15 Backus Ave. (Danbury Square Mall), Danbury, (203) 790-5425
2333 Summer St., Stamford, (203) 969-0352
www.tsk.com

See the listing under Yonkers for more information.

Kang Tae Kwon Do & Hapkido
263 Sound Beach Ave., Old Greenwich
(203) 637-7867
www.kangmartialarts.com

See the listing under Mount Kisco for more information.

PUTNAM COUNTY

Bushido School of Karate
1511 Rte. 22 (Lakeview Shopping Center), Brewster
(845) 279-8500
www.bushidokarate.com

See listing under Thornwood for more information.

MUSIC

There's no question that children love music and moving around. Perhaps that's why there are so many places that offer music classes here in Westchester. The classes tend to fall within four general styles: Music & Movement, Kindermusik, Dalcroze Eurhythmics and the Suzuki Method.

In the first three types of classes, children and their parents or caregivers explore rhythm and tonal patterns, musical styles and simple musical instruments. Kids and parents not only listen to and sing or play along with the musical selections but also have a chance to get down and boogie. Some classes use old favorites, some use original music. Some teachers play the guitar, piano or autoharp as children sing along, while others use an accompanist. A number of classes are grouped by age to include developmentally appropriate activities, while others are mixed-age classes (clearly better for parents wanting to enroll two children of different ages in the same class). And some classes provide you with a CD and other materials to use at home.

The fourth type of class uses the Suzuki Method, a more formal style of teaching in which children use scaled-down instruments like pianos, guitars or violins. This method combines listening, proper technique, repetition, reinforcement and active parent involvement. If you feel you have a budding Beethoven on your hands, this may be the right choice for you.

Some programs believe children will benefit most from a highly structured environment. They may expect children to remain seated at certain times and encourage children and parents or caregivers to follow a specific routine. Other programs believe children will benefit just by being in the room and are less focused on getting twelve toddlers to bang their drums "just so." To find out which style works best for you, check out a few different classes prior to signing up. Almost every program allows a free preview class if you make a reservation in advance.

Remember, these classes are designed for young children. You may find the songs or the teacher painfully corny, but the true test of a great teacher is how the child responds. Also keep in mind that the more into it you are, the more into it your child will be, so just (rock and) roll with it, baby.

In addition to the listings by town, below, the following three music classes are offered at numerous Westchester locations.

Music Together
www.musictogether.com

Mixed-age music and movement classes for children from birth to 4 years old, with their parents or caregivers. Classes are forty-five minutes long and the program includes two CDs, a songbook and a parent education guide. This is a franchise with many locations, including Armonk, Bedford Village, Briarcliff, Chappaqua, Croton Falls, Croton-on-Hudson, Dobbs Ferry, Katonah, Larchmont, Mamaroneck, Mount Kisco, Pelham, Pound Ridge, Rye, Scarsdale, South Salem, Tuckahoe, White Plains, Yonkers and Yortown Heights, so consult the website to get more information on the class located closest to you.

Musical Munchkins
(914) 771-7000
www.musicalmunchkins.com

In this music and movement program, classes are divided by age as follows: "Babies" (ages 6-13 months), "One's" (ages 13-24 months), "Two's" (24-35 months), "Three's" and "Four's" (ages 35 months and up), and "Friends & Family" (ages 1-4, in the summer only). Classes are forty-five minutes long and usually include familiar songs that you and your children will recognize. (All classes require a parent or caregiver to attend.) There are locations in Bronxville, Dobbs Ferry, Larchmont, Mount Kisco/Bedford Hills, New Rochelle, Pawling, Pleasantville, Rye, Scarsdale and White Plains. They also offer residents-only classes in Armonk, Pelham and Somers.

Musicville
(914) 378-5040
www.musicville.org

Another franchise with multiple Westchester locations, including Armonk, Bedford Hills, Chappaqua, Mount Kisco and Rye Brook. Classes include "Baby Butterflies" (birth-6 months), "Tootin' Tigers" (6 months-3 years) and "Jammin' Giraffes" (ages 3-5).

Bedford

Amadeus Conservatory
382 Cantitoe St. (St. Mathews Church)
(914) 234-7280
www.amadeusconservatory.com

Classes are limited to seven children and feature real instruments such as violins, recorders, drums and more. There is an accompanist in addition to the teacher, and parent or caregiver participation is essential.

Chappaqua

Amadeus Conservatory
201 King St.
(914) 238-0388
www.amadeusconservatory.com

See the listing under Bedford for more information.

Eastchester

Crestwood Music
453 White Plains Rd.
(914) 961-3497
www.crestwoodmusic.com

This facility focuses strictly on private lessons on all instruments for all ages and levels. Free trial lesson available.

Elmsford

Musictime
326-328 Saw Mill River Rd. (Multiplex Shopping Center)
(914) 948-1868
www.gymtimeplace.com

This music and movement program is for children ages 9 months to 4 years. Classes are multi-aged and limited to ten children. Gymtime has an unlimited class policy, which means that once you register for the class of your choice you can attend any other classes in your child's age group at no additional charge. The program cost also includes a book, CD and tape.

Golden's Bridge
Children's Center of Golden's Bridge
5 Anderson Ln.
(914) 232-6813
www.childrenscenterofgb.com

Music and movement classes for children ages 10 months to 10 years, including "BabyTime!" (ages 10-23 months), "Feeling Groovy" (ages 3 and up) and "ArtSmart" (ages 3-5), which combines art with music and movement. Parents or caregivers can relax with a cup of coffee in "Mom's Café." Walk-ins are welcome, but reservations are suggested.

Jefferson Valley
Gymboree Play & Music
3631 Hill Blvd. & Rte. 6
(866) 477-3700
www.gymboree.com

Age- and developmentally-appropriate music and movement classes for children ages 6 months to 5 years. The enrollment fee includes CDs and a songbook.

Larchmont
Larchmont Music Academy
2089 Boston Post Rd.
(914) 833-8941
www.larchmontmusicacademy.com

The Kindermusik program is available for children from birth to 6 years. The classes are divided by age into "Village" (ages 0-18 months), "Our Time" (ages 18 months-3 years), "Imagine That" (ages 3 1/2-4 1/2) and "Young Child" (ages 4 1/2-6). Classes are forty-five minutes long for younger children and an hour for older ones. Home materials are also distributed.

Music for Aardvarks
157 Larchmont Ave.
(914) 834-3383
www.aardvarksrocks.com

Created in 1997 by rock musician-turned-father-of-three David Weinstone. His sophisticated songs feature themes universal to all children, in a range of musical styles. Add in instrument jams, free-form dance breaks and an element of spontaneous silliness and you have a music class that really rocks! Classes are mixed ages from 6 months through pre-school.

Mamaroneck

The Music Academy
895 Mamaroneck Ave.
(914) 777-5488

They provide private, semi-private and group lessons for ages 4 and up (and adults) on all instruments and all levels.

Mount Kisco

Jodi's Gym
25 Hubbels Dr.
(914) 244-8811
www.jodisgym.com

These music classes are held in a gym setting. There are a wide variety of classes, separated by age, and all have live music. "Mommy & Me Music & Movement" is for children from 9 months to walking age. "Mommy & Me Gym & Music Combo," an hour-and-fifteen-minute class with a story and snack dividing the music portion from the gym time, is separated into sections for children ages 12-17 months, 18-24 months, 25-35 months, and 3-4 years.

New Rochelle

Joy of Music
1270 North Ave.
(914) 654-8753

Programs are available for children 9 months and older. Classes are broken up by age into "Your Baby Needs Music" (ages 9 months-2 years and 2-3 1/2), "Preschool Music Program" (ages 3 1/2-5 1/2), "Fun with Pianos" (ages 5 1/2-8) and "Fun with Guitar" (ages 5 1/2-8). They also offer private instruction in flute, guitar, piano and voice as well as classes for special needs children.

Pelham

Joy of Music
1023 Esplanade Ave.
(914) 654-8753

See the listing under New Rochelle for more information.

Rye

Amadeus Conservatory
260 Stuyvesant Ave. (Wainwright House)
(914) 967-0987
www.amadeusconservatory.com

See the listing under Bedford for more information.

Rye Arts Center
51 Milton Rd.
(914) 967-0700
www.ryeartscenter.org

In "Fun with Melody & Rhythm" (ages 4-5), children are introduced to the basics of music and rhythm using a Suzuki-based method. Children in this class must have group experience and know the alphabet. In "Rise, Sing & Act" (age 6 and up) children sing and act out Broadway, pop and children's songs. Suzuki classes are offered for guitar and violin. Private lessons are also available.

Scarsdale

Belle School of Music
1088 Central Park Ave.
(914) 961-5511
www.belleschool.com

This is a more "serious" Kindermusik program for children age 2 years and older. Here every child has his or her own piano to learn on as well as other rhythm instruments. Class size ranges from four to eight children. They use an exclusive patented "magnet system" to teach children to read music; it makes learning fun and enjoyable. Each session has classes that meet once a week for four months. Books and supplies are included.

Gymboree Play & Music
450 Central Park Ave.
(866) 477-3700
www.gymboree.com

See the listing under Jefferson Valley for more information.

Hoff-Barthelson Music School
25 School Ln.
(914) 723-1169
www.hbms.org

This is a more structured setting where children enjoy singing and movement while learning to follow directions and take turns. Classes for children ages birth to 5 years utilize the Dalcroze Eurhythmics technique and include "Love and Lullabies" (0-4 months), "Learning in the Lap" (4-12 months) and "Guppies" (12-18 months). Early Musicianship Classes for 3-, 4- and 5-year-old children (without grown-ups) include movement, music games, listening, singing and improvising with rhythm instruments. There are group recorder classes for young children as well as Suzuki programs for violin, viola, cello and piano for children ages 4-6 years. Lastly, there is a certified preschool center for 3- and 4-year-olds offering two- or three-hour classes, depending on the age group.

"Little Maestros" at The Scholastic Store
450 Central Park Ave.
(914) 725-7201
www.scholastic.com

"Little Maestros" is a live music program for children ages 3 months to 3 years (with a caregiver). You and your child will experience music from Bach to rock while gaining letter and number recognition (and more) through puppet shows, parachutes and songs.

White Plains

Belle School of Music
283 Tarrytown Rd.
(914) 287-0066
www.belleschool.com

See the listing under Scarsdale for more information.

Music Conservatory of Westchester
216 Central Ave.
(914) 761-3900
www.musicconservatory.org

In addition to Music Together classes, the Music Conservatory of Westchester offers its own classes, group lessons and individual instruction. For younger kids, classes include "Introduction to Music" (age 3 and up); "Introduction to Instruments" (ages 5-6); Suzuki classes for violin, piano and cello (age 4 and up); and group lessons for violin, piano, recorder and guitar (ages 5-8).

Yonkers

Belle School of Music
1537 Central Park Ave.
(914) 961-5511
www.belleschool.com

See the listing under Scarsdale for more information.

MANHATTAN

Jazz at Lincoln Center's WeBop!
Broadway at 60th (Time Warner Center)
(212) 258-9999
www.jalc.org/jazzED/subs/webop.html

An early-childhood music education program in which children (ages 8 months-5 years) and their parents or caregivers sing, move and play with the soulful rhythms and great melodies of jazz. The classes are forty-five minutes long and are divided into "Hipsters" (ages 8-23 months old), "Stompers" (ages 2-3), "Gumbo Group" (ages 3-5) and "Syncopators" (ages 4-5).

Savvy Suggestion

Save cardboard rolls from toilet paper and paper towels. You and your child can decorate them with stickers, markers, paint and glued-on objects. Put some beans or rice inside the roll, cover the ends with tin foil and seal them with rubber bands to make a maraca. Or just let your child use the tube as a "horn" by singing and tooting into it as you march around the house.

CONNECTICUT

Gymboree Play & Music
31 Mill Place Rd., Danbury
(866) 477-3700
www.gymboree.com

See the listing under Jefferson Valley for more information.

ROCK CLIMBING

You've heard the expression "my kids were climbing the walls"? Well, now they really can. Rock climbing teaches focus and determination, and it's a great way to build upper-body strength. However, note that these facilities are not "drop in on a rainy Saturday" kinds of places: they give thorough instruction in the required techniques for your children (and you) to enjoy rock climbing safely. Most of them are fairly new and represent a growing interest in an activity that has been enjoyed on the West Coast for years. As moms, we were intrigued by the idea of doing an activity that by all accounts absolutely does not allow for letting your mind wander onto "to do" lists and work problems. Talk about taking the high ground!

New Rochelle

The Rock Club
130 Rhodes St.
(914) 633-ROCK (-7625)
www.ClimbRockClub.com

This new facility at the New Rochelle Racquet Club has classes for children as young as four years old. (There is a 30 lb. minimum weight requirement to properly fit into the harness.) The Rocks section—a separate climbing area that's completely enclosed—is designed specifically for kids. Classes, which teach appropriate climbing and related skills development, are divided by age: "Pee Wees" (ages 4 -5), "Rock Rats" (ages 6-11) and "Teen Rock" (ages 12 and up). Other programs include: birthday parties, scout merit badge opportunities, climbing teams, camps and more.

Valhalla

The Cliffs
1 Commerce Park
(914) 328-ROCK (-7625)
www.thecliffsclimbing.com

Three-week "Learn to Climb" classes (ages 9-16) emphasize safety and teach knot tying, verbal commands, belaying and more. Each class is three hours long. "ClimbTime," two-hour sessions on Saturday and Sunday mornings (ages 6-14), let your kids have non-instructional climbing fun while supervised by the professional staff.

CONNECTICUT

Go Vertical
727 Canal St., Stamford
(203) 358-8767
www.govertical-ct.com

They offer two-day youth certification classes for kids 13 to 17 years old, afterschool programs for kids 8 to 13 years old, and birthday parties for those as young as 9. Passing the certification course is a requirement for anyone who wants to use the climbing walls without supervision by an adult.

SPECIAL NEEDS

Some parents who have children with special needs may find that their kids have difficulty participating in some conventional programs. Certain classes may be overly stimulating, too physically advanced or have some other component that doesn't work for your son or daughter. Fortunately, there are a growing number of programs geared towards special-needs kids so that they can enjoy the same types of activities (like dancing, arts & crafts, or karate), but in a modified environment and with instructors who are trained to help with their specific issues.

Ardsley
Greenburgh Parks & Recreation Department
11 Olympic Ln.
(914) 693-8985, ext. 128
www.greenburghny.com

A variety of recreational classes are offered for the special-needs child age 5 and up, including cooking, horseback riding, swimming and much more. An intake interview is required. Classes are held at several different locations.

Hastings-on-Hudson
New York Goju Karate
558 Warburton Ave.
(914) 478-0508
www.onhudsonfitness.com

The G.R.O.W. martial arts program was developed four years ago by Dr. Jonathan Slater and Shihan James Chillemi specifically for children with special needs. The focus in not on competition or "self-defense" but on improving physical coordination, self-esteem, mental concentration and balance in life.

Scarsdale
Jewish Community Center of Mid-Westchester
999 Wilmot Rd.
(914) 472-3300, ext. 361
www.jccmidwestchester.org

The S.N.A.A.C. Program (Special Needs Academic and Arts Center) provides enrichment programs that are appropriate for children with ADHD, speech and language delays, learning disabilities, Asperger's Syndrome, PDD or various other social and emotional problems. Classes are offered as afterschool programs and on Sundays. Pre-K classes (age 3 and up) are in social skills, art, music, sports and theatre. In addition to these, for the K-6th grader there's also personal training, chess, karate, reading wizards, writer's workshop, Little Einstein and more. "SIBSHOP" (ages 5-15) provides brothers and sisters of children with special needs the opportunity for peer support and education in a group setting. "Sunday/Funday" is a three-hour all-inclusive program (ages 3-16, groups divided by age) featuring sports, social skills, art, computer and music. They also offer birthday parties customized for special-needs children.

Tarrytown
Jewish Community Center on the Hudson
371 S. Broadway
(914) 366-7898
www.jcconthehudson.org

A variety of self-contained and inclusion enrichment programs offered for children with learning or developmental disabilities, including: "Shalom K'Tanim" (ages 3-5); "Shalom Chaverim" (grades K-2); "Pre-Ballet Plus" (ages 3-5); "Karate for Kids" (grades 1-6); "X-Ray Vision Club" (grades 3-6); "SKIP: Special Kids Interesting Places" (grades K-6), which provides full-day outings during school holidays; "Special Children's Program" (ages 6-12 years); and "Almost Home," where children participate in activities like arts & crafts, games, computers and homework help in a warm, safe and stimulating environment. An intake interview is required.

White Plains
Wonder Kids
470 Mamaroneck Ave., Suite #204
(914) 421-8270
www.wonderkidstherapycenter.com

Yoga, music and social skills classes offered for the special-needs child (ages 3-5 and 5-8).

SPORTS

You know what it's like. Your daughter comes home wanting to be Mia Hamm, so you do what any supportive, loving parent would do: you buy every conceivable piece of soccer equipment, register her for classes and sign up as coach for the school league. And then—whammo!—she decides that what she really wants is to play lacrosse. When it comes to your kids and their ever-changing "favorites," these sports facilities are a great option because they provide a range of classes in a variety of sports, giving kids the prerogative to change their minds without driving you out of yours.

Briarcliff Manor
Club Fit for Kids
584 North State Rd.
(914) 762-3444
www.clubfit.com

There are a wide variety of classes for kids, from tumbling to introductions to different sports. Classes include "Just for 3s," an introduction to sports and games, and "Junior Kinder Sports" (age 4) and "Kinder Sports" (age 5), which focus on physical and creative movement. "A Little More Sports" (ages 5-8) includes kick-ball, soccer, floor hockey and more. For older kids they also offer lacrosse, basketball, flag football and baseball.

Jefferson Valley

Club Fit for Kids
600 Bank Rd.
(914) 245-4040
www.clubfit.com

See the listing under Briarcliff Manor for more information.

Montrose

Premier Athletic Club
2127 Albany Post Rd.
(914) 739-7755
www.premierathletic.com

They offer kids' programs that are available to the general public, including swimming, tennis, racquetball, fitness, soccer and basketball. Members' children can also enjoy free programs such as supervised gym, yoga, swimming, ballet and creative movement.

New Rochelle

Golden Touch Soccer
10 Mill Rd. (Holy Trinity Greek Orthodox Church)
(914) 654-9297
www.goldentouchsoccer.net

These are indoor soccer classes, directed by former professional soccer player Winston Buddle. Because indoor soccer is played in a smaller space, children can better learn to control the ball and develop their skills. Classes are for boys and girls ages 4-9, and children are grouped by age and experience. They also offer advanced soccer skills training for select boys and girls ages 15-17, as well as private classes and outdoor classes for ages 7-19.

Purchase

Backyard Sports
735 Anderson Hill Rd. (SUNY Purchase Athletic Facility)
(914) 304-4052
www.byardsports.com

This program currently offers basketball classes but will be expanding soon into soccer and baseball for boys and girls Pre-K to 8th Grade. Classes are taught by professional educators who provide a high level of skill instruction and show kids how to enjoy the fun and the positive lessons of team sports without being overly competitive. Sessions take place in the off-season, so as not to compete with school and town recreational programs.

White Plains

New York Sports Club for Kids
4 City Center
(914) 428-2020
www.mysportsclubs.com

They offer many recreational athletic programs, including "Mini Gymi's" (ages 6-36 months), a parent/tot class; "Gymtastics" (ages 1-15), a basic gymnastics skills class; "Cardio Kids" (ages 3-6), an age-appropriate sports skills development class; "Dancexperience" (ages 3-15); "Cheertastics" (ages 5-15); "Kickboxing Kids" (ages 6-12) and "Kidspin Theatre" (ages 7-15).

Frozen Ropes
55 S. Broadway
(914) 993-6355
www.frozenropes.com

In addition to the indoor batting cages and pitcher's mounds, this national chain for baseball and softball training has classes for kids as young as 3 years. "Born to Play" (ages 3–5) teaches balance, hand-eye and color coordination, hitting, throwing and correct terminology. "Basic Fundamentals" (age 5 and up) is about advancing skills and techniques.

ROCKLAND COUNTY

New York Sports Club for Kids
1000 Palisades Center Dr. (The Palisades Center Mall), West Nyack
(845) 358-1818
www.mysportsclubs.com

See the listing under White Plains for more information.

SWIMMING

Swimming classes for babies? Think of them more as aquatic appreciation classes. These programs teach kids to enjoy being in and around water so that they will be more comfortable when they get old enough to really learn strokes, breathing techniques, diving and more. Parents and kids spend about thirty minutes in the pool singing songs, playing games and splashing around. Betsy's and Laura's husbands both took Saturday morning classes with the boys, which was a great father-son activity for them (and gave Betsy and Laura a few extra hours of sleep!). Although classes are offered at many community centers and health clubs year-round, just make sure you want to be braving the winter temperatures with a damp head and a squirming child. And be forewarned: in most cases even heated pools can often feel pretty chilly, although the children seem to mind a lot less than the parents. During the summer you can also find swimming classes at many of the state, county and municipal swimming facilities, which we listed in the "Pools & Beaches" section of Chapter 8.

Briarcliff Manor

Club Fit for Kids
584 N. State Rd.
(914) 762-3444
www.clubfit.com

Classes for kids age 4 months and older. Parent/Infant and Parent/Tot classes focus on interactive water play, fun and songs. For ages 3 and up, classes focus on basic techniques and water safety skills.

Jefferson Valley

Club Fit for Kids
1 Lee Blvd.
(914) 245-4040
www.clubfit.com

See the listing under Briarcliff Manor for information.

Montrose

Premier Athletic Club
2127 Albany Post Rd.
(914) 739-7755
www.premierathletic.com

They offer kids' programs that are available to the general public, including swimming, tennis, raquetball, fitness, soccer and basketball. Members' children can also enjoy free programs such as supervised gym, yoga, swimming, ballet and creative movement.

Mount Kisco

Saw Mill Club
77 Kensico Dr.
(914) 241-0797
www.sawmillclub.com

Classes for children from 6 months to 12 years that are age- and level-appropriate. The focus is on improving stroke techniques, acquiring safety skills and increasing water comfort while gaining strength and endurance.

Purchase

Purchase College SUNY Department of Physical Education
735 Anderson Hill Rd.
(914) 251-6546
www.purchase.edu

Classes for kids ages 6 months to 12 years. Infant and preschool lessons are taken with a parent or caregiver. The classes for older children focus on primary skills and stroke development.

Tarrytown

Marymount College of Fordham University
100 Marymount Ave.
(914) 332-7445

This "Learn to Swim Program" includes Saturday classes for kids ages 5-10, focusing on primary swim skills, strokes, and life saving techniques. There are Sunday morning "Family Swims" year-round.

White Plains

New York Sports Club for Kids
4 City Center
(914) 946-0404
www.nysc.com

These learn-to-swim programs, for kids ages 6 months to 14 years, integrate safety skills with fun activities. They also offer classes that prepare your children for swim team participation like "Swim Team Conditioning" (ages 6-14) and "Stroke & Turn" (ages 7-14).

YOGA

Unlike gymnastics classes, which have a more frenetic pace, yoga classes offer your child the opportunity to create a positive mind/body connection in a more relaxed setting. Yoga is a great way for children to become aware of their breathing, their muscles and their limbs while having lots of fun. Whether turning their bodies into windmills or slithering like snakes, kids in these classes will learn the beauty of slowing things down just a beat.

Irvington

Yoga Works
50 S. Buckhout St.
(914) 591-YOGA (9642)
www.yogaworks.com

Kids' yoga classes for ages 3-5 and 6-9. Pre- and postnatal yoga are also offered.

Katonah

Little Buddha
260 Katonah Ave.
(914) 232-2732

Classes include family yoga, Mommy & Me, pre- and postnatal yoga, yoga for special needs

Mamaroneck

The Yoga Sanctuary
One Depot Plaza
(914) 381-9642
www.yogasanctuary.net

Prenatal, kids' yoga, Mommy & Me, and "Yoga for Teens" programs are offered. For grown-ups, there are Pilates mat classes, Reiki healing circles, nutritional health counseling, meditation and even massage rooms.

Mount Kisco

Sonic Kidz
11-13 Main St., 2nd floor
(914) 241-YOGA (-9642)
www.sonicyoga.com

This facility accommodates kids ages 8 weeks to 18 years, as well as parents, caretakers and moms-to-be. "Yogakidz" is a blend of movement, play, empowerment and breathing.

Tuckahoe

Yoga Haven
62 Main St., 2nd fl.
(914) 337-1437
www.yogahaven.com

In addition to a full range of regular yoga classes, Yoga Haven offers prenatal yoga (for women in the second and third trimesters) and postnatal yoga (for new moms and babies under one year of age), as well as prenatal massage.

Valhalla

Yogashine
7-11 Legion Dr. (near Kensico Dam)
(914) 769-8745
www.yogashine.com

Offering yoga classes and Yoga/Movement Therapy for children age 3 and up, including programs for special-needs children and for teens. The classes are an opportunity for kids to enjoy playful, centered movement; learn and create postures; build strength and mental focus; and develop skills in self-calming and cooperation.

Chapter 5

The Grass *Is* Always Greener

Community Playgrounds

County & State Parks

Gardens & Other Gorgeous Places

Nature Centers & Preserves

One of the nicest things about our county is the number of beautiful and diverse outdoor areas for you and your family to enjoy. In exploring them you can start close to home and then work your way further afield as your children (and you) need something new.

So whether you're looking for a wonderful place for a stroll, a fun day at a nature center or just a different swing set and slide, you'll have plenty of options to choose from. We've also included in this chapter information you'll need to know about each location, such as the facilities, the types of activities available and whether there is an admission fee.

COMMUNITY PLAYGROUNDS

It seems that one of the first places every new parent discovers is the local playground. Going to the playground gives you the opportunity not only to get some fresh air but also to meet other moms and dads and, as your children grow, to let them burn off some energy and have a lot of fun. However, at some point both you and your kids will be looking for a little change of pace. The good news is you most likely won't have to go far: Westchester is packed with playgrounds.

The facilities at the following sites vary widely—some have multiple systems of play equipment for different age groups, while others have just a swing set. We've also listed whatever additional features these sites have, whether it's paths for you to walk with your infant in a backpack, fields for your new runner to practice his skills, places to picnic or grill, or ice-skating or swimming facilities. Many of these playgrounds also offer children's programs such as educational events, entertainment and summer camp.

These playgrounds are run by specific municipalities–that is, by cities, towns or villages (hamlets are included within the towns). Virtually all of them are open to the public, but some require a municipal park pass or only admit residents from the specific municipality. For more playgrounds, see other sections of this chapter; almost all of the county and state parks have playgrounds, as do the Blue Mountain and Ward Pound Ridge Reservations (listed in the "Nature Centers & Preserves" section of this chapter).

Ardsley
★ Anthony F. Veteran Park (11 Olympic Ln.)–picnicking/grills, refreshments, swimming
★ Ashford Park (Ashford Ave.)–fields, picnicking
★ McDowell Park (Heatherdell Rd.)–fields, picnicking

Bedford
★ Bedford Hills Park (Haines Rd.)–fields, picnicking, swimming
★ Bedford Memorial Park (Greenwich Rd., Bedford Village)–fields, ice-skating, picnicking, swimming
★ Katonah Memorial Park (North St., Katonah)–fields, hiking/walking, picnicking, sledding, swimming

Briarcliff Manor
★ Chilmark Park (Macy Rd.)–fields
★ Jackson Road Park (Jackson Rd.)
★ Law Memorial Park (Pleasantville Rd.)–swimming, wading pool
★ Neighborhood Park (Whitson & Fuller Rds.)–fields

Bronxville
★ Dogwood Park (Garden Ave.)
★ Sagamore Park (Sagamore Rd.)
★ School Field (Bronxville Public School)–fields

Buchanan
★ Recreation Site (West Ave.)–fields, swimming

Cortlandt
★ Buchanan/Verplanck Elementary School (Westchester Ave., Verplanck)
★ Charles J. Cook Recreation Center (Furnace Dock Rd.)–fields, picnicking/grills, swimming
★ Frank G. Lindsey Elementary School (Trolley Rd., Montrose)–fields
★ Lake Allendale Playground (Allen Rd.)
★ Maple Avenue Playground (Lafayette & Maple Aves.)
★ Muriel H. Morabito Community Center (Westbrook Dr.)
★ Sprout Brook Park (Sprout Brook Rd.)–picnicking/grills, swimming

✶ Sunset Park (Montrose Point Rd., Montrose)–fields
✶ Tommy Thurber Playground (Tommy Thurber Ln., off Sunset)

Croton-on-Hudson
✶ Dobbs Park (Maple St., Rte. 129)–fields
✶ Duck Pond Park (Bungalow Rd., off S. Riverside Ave.)–fields
✶ Senasqua Park (on the Hudson River)–picnicking
✶ Sunset Park (Sunset & Lexington Drs.)

Dobbs Ferry
✶ Gould Park (Ashford Ave.)–fields, swimming
✶ Memorial Park (Palisade St.)–fields, wading pool
✶ Waterfront Park (on the Hudson River)–picnicking/grills (open to Dobbs Ferry residents only)

Eastchester
✶ Chester Heights Park (Oregon Ave.)–fields
✶ Cooper Field (Locust Ave.)–fields, tot lot
✶ Garth Road Park (Garth Rd.)–field, picnicking
✶ Joyce Road Park (Joyce Rd.)–fields
✶ Leewood Park (Leewood Dr.)–fields

Elmsford
✶ Massaro Park (50 Cabot Ave.)–fields, picnicking/grills, swimming
✶ Pocantico Park (Saw Mill River Rd.)–picnicking/grills

Greenburgh
✶ Secor Woods Park (Secor Rd., Hartsdale)–fields, picnicking/grills
✶ Webb Park (Central Ave., Hartsdale)–fields, picnicking

Harrison
✶ Bernie Guagnini Brentwood Park (Webster Ave.)–picnicking, swimming, wading pool
✶ Congress Park (Congress St.)–fields
✶ John Passidomo Veteran Park (Lake St., W. Harrison)–fields, picnicking, refreshments, swimming, wading pool
✶ Pettijohn Park (Crotona Ave. & Avondale Rd.)
✶ Riis Park/Station Park (Harrison Ave. & Heineman Pl.)
✶ Rose Avenue Tot Lot (Rose Ave.)
✶ Veterans Memorial Park (Crystal St.)–fields, hiking/walking, picnicking
✶ Wilding Park (Oakland Ave.)–picnicking

Hastings-on-Hudson
★ **MacEchron Waterfront Park** (on the Hudson River)—picnicking
★ **Reynolds Field** (Chauncey Ln.)—fields
★ **Uniontown Field** (Rose St.)—fields, picnicking

Irvington
★ **Halsey Pond Park**—fishing, hiking, play "castle" (residents' permit required)
★ **Matthiessen Park** (Main St. & N. Astor)—bocce ball, playground, picnicking/grills, shuffleboard, spray pool, summertime movies (residents' permit required)
★ **Memorial/Station Road Park** (Station Rd. & Dows Lane Rd.)—fields, picnicking, playground, spray pool, tennis courts (residents' permit required)
★ **Scenic Hudson Park at Irvington** (Bridge St., on the Hudson River)—fields, hiking/walking, picnicking (open to Irvington residents only between Memorial Day and Labor Day, but the guard leaves at 5 pm)
★ **Taxter Road Park** (21 Taxter Rd.)

Larchmont
★ **Flint Park** (Locust Ave. off Thompson St.)—fields, picnicking
★ **Pinebrook Park** (Palmer)
★ **Turtle Park** (Palmer, near train station)
★ **Willow Park** (Willow Ave., off the beach)—fields

Lewisboro
★ **Onatru Farm Park** (99 Elmwood Rd., South Salem)—fields, hiking/walking
★ **Town Park** (Rte. 35, South Salem)—fields, hiking/walking, ice-skating, picnicking, swimming

Mamaroneck
★ **Harbor Island Beach Park** (Mamaroneck Ave. & Boston Post Rd.)—boating, fields, fishing, picnicking, swimming, tennis
★ **Hommocks Park Ice Rink & Swimming Pool Complex** (Hommocks Rd. & Rte. 1)—ice-skating, swimming
★ **Memorial Park** (Myrtle Blvd.)

Mount Kisco
★ **Leonard Park & Memorial Pool** (Main St.)—picnicking, swimming
★ **Mount Kisco Community Center** (Maple Ave.)
★ **Smith Park** (Pineview Rd.)—fields

Mount Vernon
★ **Brush Park** (W. 7th St. between S. 3rd St. & Union Ave.)—fields, picnicking, refreshments
★ **Eddie Williams Playground** (7th Ave. between 3rd & 4th Sts.)

* **Fleetwood Playground** (E. Broad St. & Fleetwood Ave., Fleetwood)
* **Fourth Street Park** (W. 4th St. between S. 7th & 8th Aves.)
* **Grove Street Playground** (Grove St.)
* **Hartley Park** (Gramatan Ave. between Oakley & Lincoln Aves.)
* **Howard St. Playground** (High & Howard Sts.)
* **Hutchinson Field** (Garden Ave. & Sargent Pl.)—fields, miniature golf, refreshments, skating
* **Lorraine Avenue Playground** (Lorraine Ave. & Claremont Pl.)
* **Memorial Field** (Garden Ave. & Sandford Blvd.)—fields, picnicking
* **Nichols School Playground** (High St.)
* **Old 7th Avenue Playground** (7th Ave. between 2nd & 4th Sts.)
* **Purdy Park** (S. 9th Ave. & 2nd St.)
* **Scouts Field** (Midland & Gramatan Aves.)
* **Sophie J. Mee Playground** (S. 3rd Ave. & Sandford Blvd.)

New Castle

* **Gedney Park** (Rte. 133)—fields, hiking/walking, ice-skating, picnicking, sledding
* **Millwood Park** (half a mile north of the Taconic Parkway/Rte. 100 intersection, Millwood)—fields, picnicking
* **Recreation Field/Back of Town Hall** (200 S. Greeley Ave., Chappaqua)—fields

New Rochelle

* **D'Onofrio Park** (Emmet Terr.)—fields, picnicking/grills
* **Eddie Foy Park** (Pelham Rd. at Weyman Ave.)
* **Feeney Park** (7th St. & Washington Ave.)—flower garden, hiking/walking
* **Five Islands Park** (Le Fevre Ln., off Main St.)—hiking/walking, picnicking/grills
* **Flower's Park/City Park** (City Park Rd., off Fifth Ave.)—fields, picnicking, swimming
* **Hudson Park** (Hudson Park Rd., off Pelham Rd.)—refreshments, swimming beach
* **Huguenot Park** (North Ave. & Eastchester Rd.)—hiking/walking, ice-skating
* **Lincoln Park** (Lincoln Ave.)—fields, swimming, wading pool
* **Maplewood Park** (Ralph Rd.)
* **Pinebrook Park** (Pinebrook Blvd. & Tulip Ln.)—fields
* **Roosevelt Park** (Disbrow Ln.)
* **Seacord Park** (Allard Ave. & John St.)
* **Stephenson Park** (Stephenson Blvd.)
* **Sycamore Park** (King's Highway)—fields
* **VFW Tot Lot** (Pelham Rd. & Meadow Ln.)

North Castle

✶ **Clove Road Park** (N. Broadway & Clove Rd., North White Plains)—fields
✶ **John A. Lombardi Park** (85 Cox Ave.)—fields, picnicking
✶ **North Castle Community Park** (205 Business Park Dr., Armonk)—fields, hiking/walking, picnicking
✶ **Quarry Park** (Old Orchard St., Quarry Heights)
✶ **Wallace Pond** (Rte. 22, Armonk)
✶ **Winkler Park** (Greenwich-Banksville Rd.)

North Salem

✶ **Joe Bohrdrum Park** (Sunset Dr. & Daniel Rd.)—fields, picnicking

Ossining

✶ **Buck Johnson Park** (Blue Lantern Rd.)
✶ **Gerlach Park** (Old Albany Post Rd.)—fields, hiking/walking, picnicking
✶ **Louis Engel Waterfront Park** (adjacent to train station parking lot)—picnicking
✶ **Ryder Park** (Morningside Dr.)—fields, hiking/walking, picnicking
✶ **Veterans Park** (Narragansett Ave.)—fields, picnicking

Pelham

✶ **Julien's Playground** (6th St. & 4th Ave.)

Pleasantville

✶ **Nannahagen Park** (Lake St.)—swimming
✶ **Rossell Park** (Rossell St.)
✶ **Soldiers & Sailors Playground** (Clark St. & Manville Rd.)

Port Chester

✶ **Edgewood Park** (Grace Church St.)
✶ **Lyon Park** (Putnam Ave. & King St.)
✶ **Recreation Park** (Locust Ave.)

Pound Ridge

✶ **Town Park** (Rte. 137)—fields, picnicking/grills, swimming

Rye

✶ **Disbrow Park** (Oakland Beach Ave.)—fields
✶ **Gagliardo Park** (Nursery Ln.)—fields, picnicking
✶ **Recreation Park** (281 Midland Ave.)—fields, picnicking

Rye Brook

✶ **Crawford Park** (Ridge St.)—fields, picnicking
✶ **Garibaldi Park** (Garibaldi Pl.)—fields
✶ **Pine Ridge Park** (Pine Ridge Rd.)—fields

Scarsdale
* Aspen Park (Aspen Rd.)—fields
* Corell Park (East of Corell Rd., at Sycamore Rd.)—fields
* Crossway Field (Mamaroneck Rd. & Crossway)—fields
* Davis Park (Lyons Rd. & Grand Blvd.)—fields
* Greenacres Playground (Huntington Ave. & Montrose Rd.)
* Hyatt Field (Boulevard & Potter Rd.)—fields
* Municipal Pool (Mamaroneck Rd.)—refreshments, swimming
* Scout/Butler Field (Wayside Ln.)—fields

Sleepy Hollow
* Barnhart Park (Barnhart Ave.)
* Devries Park (Devries Ave.)—fields, hiking/walking, picnicking/grills, refreshments
* Douglas Park Greenway Trail (New Broadway)—picnicking
* Margotta Courts (Valley St.)
* Reverend Sykes Park (Valley St.)

Somers
* Reis Park (Rte. 139)

Tarrytown
* Glenville Woods (Benedict Ave.)—hiking/walking
* Patriot's Park (Next to the Warner Library)—picnicking

Tuckahoe
* Fisher Avenue Park (Fisher Ave.)
* Main Street Park (Main St. & Marbledale Rd.)
* Parkway Oval (Consulate Dr.)—fields
* Pleasant Place Park (Pleasant Pl.)

White Plains
* Battle-Whitney Park (Chatterton & Battle Aves.)—fields
* Chatterton Playground (Chatterton & Harmon Aves.)
* Church Street School (Church St.)—swimming
* Delfino Park (Lake St.)—fields, picnicking/grills, refreshments, skating
* Druss Park (Bryant. & Prospect Aves.)—picnicking
* Gardella Park (Ferris & Park Aves.)—fields, picnicking/grills, swimming, wading pool
* George Washington School (Orchard St.)—fields
* Gillie Park (Mamaroneck Ave. & Gedney Way)—fields
* Kittrell Park (Bank St. & Fisher Ave.)—swimming, wading pool
* Liberty Park (Lake St. at Silver Lake)—boating, fishing, hiking, picnicking
* Mamaroneck Avenue School (Mamaroneck Ave.)—fields
* Mattison Playground (Quinby Ave. & Lynton Pl.)—picnicking
* Mitchell Place Tot Lot (Mitchell Pl.)

* **Old Tarrytown Road Park** (Old Tarrytown Rd.)—picnicking/grills
* **Post Road School** (Post Rd.)—fields, swimming
* **Ridgeway School** (Ridgeway Ave.)—fields
* **Slater Center** (Fisher Ct.)
* **Travis Hill Park** (Lincoln Ave.)—fields, hiking/walking, picnicking/grills
* **Turnure Park** (Main St.)—picnicking/grills
* **Washington Avenue Park** (Washington Ave.)—picnicking/grills
* **Yosemite Park** (40 Yosemite Ave.)—fields, picnicking/grills

Yonkers

* **"Boo" Wilson Playground** (Tuckahoe Rd.)
* **Bregano Park & Playground** (Rigby St. & Brandon Rd.)
* **Bronx River Road Playground** (Bronx River Rd. & Winfred Ave.)
* **Buena Vista Playground** (107-109 Vista Ave.)
* **Caryl Avenue Playground** (Caryl & Saratoga Aves.)
* **Cedar Place Playground** (20 Cedar Pl.)
* **Cerone Avenue Playground** (Cerone Ave.)
* **Clemens Park & Playground** (Leighton Ave.)
* **Cochran Park & Playground** (Oliver Ave.)
* **Columbus Park & Playground** (Park Hill Ave.)
* **Coyne Park & Playground** (McLean & Old Jerome Aves.)
* **Culver Street Playground** (Culver St. & Livingston Ave.)
* **Doyle Park & Playground** (Walnut St. & Ashburton Ave.)
* **Dunn Park & Playground** (Glenwood & Vineyard Aves.)
* **Fay Park & Playground** (Abeel St.)
* **Ferme Park & Playground** (Brewster & Dunston Aves.)
* **Fleming Park & Playground** (Prescott St.)
* **Georgia Avenue Playground** (Georgia & Louisiana Aves.)
* **Gramatan Hills Playground** (Palmer Rd. & Little John Pl.)
* **Grant Park & Playground** (Park Ave.)
* **Irving Park & Playground** (View St. & Bartholdi Pl.)
* **Kinsley Park & Playground** (Park & Chase Aves.)
* **Lennon Park & Playground** (Lake & Park Aves.)
* **O'Boyle Park & Playground** (Hawthorne Ave.)
* **Pelton Park & Playground** (McLean & Van Cortlandt Park Aves.)
* **Pickett Park & Playground** (Knowles St. & Hawthorne Ave.)
* **Pitkin Park & Playground** (87 Locust Hill Ave.)
* **Post & Elliott Playground** (Post St. & Elliott Ave.)
* **Richter Park & Playground** (Nepperhan Ave. & Reade St.)
* **Ruebo-Cieslinski Park & Playground** (Edwards & Frederick Pls.)
* **Schultze Park & Playground** (St. Eleanoras Ln.)
* **Smith Park & Playground** (Nepperhan & Lake Aves.)
* **Stillwell Park & Playground** (1018 McLean Ave.)
* **Sullivan Oval Park & Playground** (Van Cortlandt Park Ave. & Spruce St.)
* **Tansey Park & Playground** (184 Stanley Ave.)

* Trenchard Street Playground (Trenchard St.)
* Trevor Park & Playground (Ravine Ave.)
* Vark Street Park & Playground (Vark St.)
* Washington Park (S. Broadway)
* Welty Park & Playground (Mile Square & Barton Rds.)
* Wilson Park & Playground (Alexander Ave.)

Yorktown

* Blackberry Woods (Marcy St., Shrub Oak)
* Chelsea Park (Gomer St., Yorktown Heights)—fields
* Downing Park (Rte. 202/Crompond Rd., near Rte. 132)—fields, picnicking/grills
* George Washington Elementary School (Lexington Ave., Mohegan Lake)—fields
* Hanover East (Wellington Rd., Yorktown Heights)
* Ivy Knolls Park (Ivy Rd. & Spring St., Shrub Oak)—ice-skating
* Junior Lake Park (Edgewater St., Yorktown Heights)—ice-skating, picnicking/grills, swimming
* Lincoln Titus Elementary School (Lincoln Ave., Crompond)—fields
* Railroad Station Park (Commerce St., Yorktown Heights)
* Shrub Oak Park (Sunnyside St., off of Rte. 6, Shrub Oak)—fields, swimming
* Sparkle Lake (Granite Springs Rd., Yorktown Heights)—ice-skating, picnicking/grills, swimming beach
* Walden Woods (Curry St., Yorktown Heights)
* Willow Park (Curry St., Yorktown Heights)—fields, ice-skating
* York Hill Park (Hawthorne Dr., Yorktown Heights)—fields
* Yorktown Community and Cultural Center (Commerce St., Yorktown Heights)—fields

COUNTY & STATE PARKS

The Westchester County Parks system maintains over fifty recreational facilities set on more than 17,000 acres. The county is also home to two New York State Parks. In addition to beautiful scenery, these places offer opportunities to hike, bike, swim, ice-skate, picnic and, in some cases, even play miniature golf.

Some of the county parks require a Westchester County Park Pass for admission. Passes cost $45 and are valid for three years; first-time buyers receive a coupon at the point-of-purchase that will allow them to purchase a Park Pass for only $35. Your Park Pass provides you with access to all county-owned parks, golf courses, pools, beaches, nature centers, and historic sites. Each pass allows free admission for the pass holder and two adults; children under the age of twelve are admitted for free. Passes are available at many of the county park information centers, as well as at the Westchester County Center (in White Plains) and the Westchester County Parks Department (in Mount Kisco). The Park Pass also provides some discounts in user and parking fees. The passes are available to all residents of Westchester County over the age of twelve; proof of county residency is required (either a driver's license or two other valid forms of identification, one of which must be a photo ID). Park Passes are not transferable and cannot be used by anyone but the holder. For more information on the Park Pass, and for information on any of the parks listed below, call the **Westchester County Parks Department at (914) 864-PARK or visit www.westchestergov.com/parks**. You can also register with that website to get automatic e-mail updates of events at the various county parks.

Ardsley

V.E. Macy Park
Saw Mill River Rd.
(914) 946-8133

This centrally-located 172-acre park is a perfect spot for group picnics. There are bathroom facilities available.

Hours: Daily 8 am to dusk

Activities: Picnicking, playground

Admission: County Park Pass required

Cortlandt

Croton Gorge Park
Rte. 129
(914) 827-9568

This ninety-seven-acre property at the base of the Croton Dam is a popular spot for fishing, picnicking and hiking, with direct trail access to New York State's Old Croton Aqueduct. The park is also available in winter for cross-country skiing and sledding. There are bathroom facilities.

Hours: Daily 8 am to dusk

Activities: Hiking/walking, nature study, picnicking, playground

Admission: Free

Croton-on-Hudson

Croton Point Park
Croton Point Ave.
(914) 862-5290

This 508-acre park offers year-round events and activities in addition to facilities for camping, hiking and swimming. The Croton Point Nature Center has a year-round schedule of interpretive programs. The beach is open on weekends and holidays. There are bathroom facilities and refreshments available.

Hours: Daily 8 am to dusk

Activities: Hiking/walking, nature study, picnicking, playground, swimming beach

Admission: Free

Hartsdale

Ridge Road Park
Ridge Rd.
(914) 946-8133

A 170-acre park offering picnicking facilities, ball fields and playgrounds. There are bathroom facilities.

Hours: Daily 8 am to dusk

Activities: Fields, nature study, picnicking, playground

Admission: County Park Pass required

Montrose

George's Island Park
Dutch St.
(914) 737-7530

This 208-acre waterfront park contains tidal wetlands, a freshwater pond and wooded trails. It also provides boat access to the Hudson River and areas for nature study and picnicking. There are bathroom facilities.

Hours: Daily 8 am to dusk

Activities: Hiking/walking, nature study, picnicking, playground

Admission: Free

Mount Vernon

Willson's Woods Park
E. Lincoln Ave.
(914) 813-6990

One of the oldest parks in the county, this twenty-three-acre park offers a beautiful swimming pool with an adjacent English Tudor-style bathhouse, as well as areas for picnicking and fishing. There are bathroom facilities and refreshments.

Hours: Daily 8 am to dusk

Activities: Hiking/walking, ice-skating, nature study, playground, picnicking, swimming

Admission: County Park Pass required; Westchester residents only

New Rochelle
Glen Island Park
Pelham Rd.
(914) 813-6720/6721

Located on the Long Island Sound, this 105-acre park offers a variety of recreational facilities, including a beach, an eighteen-hole miniature golf course, a playground, a picnicking area with a pavilion, and magnificent waterfront views. There are bathroom facilities and refreshments available.

Hours: Daily 8 am to dusk

Activities: Hiking/walking, miniature golf, picnicking, playground, swimming beach

Admission: County Park Pass required; Westchester residents only

North Salem
Mountain Lakes Park
Hawley Rd.
(914) 864-7310

Westchester's northernmost county park covers 1,038 acres and is characterized by a rugged landscape and a native hardwood forest with miles of trails. Located on the property is Mt. Bailey, the highest point in Westchester, which affords breathtaking vistas in every season. There are bathroom facilities.

Hours: Daily 8 am to dusk

Activities: Boat rentals, hiking/walking, ice-skating, nature study, swimming

Admission: Free

Sleepy Hollow
Kingsland Point Park
Palmer Ave.
(914) 631-1068

Home of the Historic Tarrytown Lighthouse, this eighteen-acre park has ball fields, picnic areas and kayaking. There are bathroom facilities.

Hours: Daily 8 am to dusk

Activities: Hiking/walking, nature study, playground

Admission: County Park Pass required

Somers

Lasdon Park, Arboretum & Veterans Memorial

Rte. 35

(914) 864-7268

www.co.westchester.ny.us/parks/ParksLocations02/Lasdon.htm

This 234-acre property consists of a bird and nature sanctuary, woodlands, open grass meadows and formal gardens with flower and shrub specimens from all over the world. Lasdon is also the site of the Chinese Friendship Pavilion, a gift from the People's Republic of China to the citizens of Westchester. The park also houses four inspirational memorials and a museum honoring Westchester veterans. There are bathroom facilities.

Hours: Daily 8 am to dusk

Activities: Hiking/walking, nature study

Admission: Free

Valhalla

Kensico Dam Plaza

Bronx River Parkway

(914) 328-1542

At the base of the Kensico Dam, this property covers ninety-eight acres. The park hosts a wide variety of activities, including ethnic celebrations, concerts, antiques shows and arts and crafts shows. There are bathroom facilities and refreshments available.

Hours: Daily 8 am to dusk

Activities: Hiking/walking, nature study, picnicking, playground

Admission: Free

White Plains

Saxon Woods Park

Mamaroneck Ave.

(914) 995-4480

www.westchestergov.com/parks/parkslocations02/SaxonWoods.htm

This 700-acre property offers a variety of recreational facilities, including a pool, picnic areas and an eighteen-hole miniature golf course. It is also the site of the county's only playground that is accessible to the disabled. There are bathroom facilities and refreshments available.

Hours: Daily 8 am to dusk

Activities: Hiking/walking, miniature golf, nature study, picnicking, playground, swimming (County Park Pass required for swimming)

Admission: Free

Yonkers

Sprain Ridge Park
Jackson Ave.
(914) 231-3450/3452

Located on a ridge between the northbound and southbound lanes of the Sprain Brook Parkway, this park's 278 acres include a developed portion with a pool complex and picnic areas. The remainder of the park is heavily wooded, with a variety of hiking and mountain bike trails. There are bathroom facilities and refreshments available.

Hours: Daily 8 am to dusk

Activities: Hiking/walking, nature study, picnicking, playground, swimming

Admission: County Park Pass required

Tibbetts Brook Park
Midland Ave.
(914) 231-2865

One of the first parks developed by the county, this 161-acre park contains a mammoth 412 x 125 foot pool. The park offers many recreational activities throughout the year and hosts ethnic celebrations, fairs and festivals during the summer months. There are bathroom facilities and refreshments available.

Hours: Daily 8 am to dusk

Activities: Biking, hiking/walking, ice-skating, miniature golf, picnicking, playground, swimming

Admission: County Park Pass required; Westchester residents only

Yorktown Heights

Franklin D. Roosevelt State Park
2957 Crompond Rd.
(914) 245-4434
http://nysparks.state.ny.us/parks/info.asp?parkID=139

This park encompasses spacious picnic areas and a huge pool that accommodates several thousand people at one time. Fishing and boating are allowed in Mohansic Lake and Crom Pond; rowboat rentals are also available in season. There are bathroom facilities and refreshments available.

Hours: Weekdays 9 am to dusk, weekends 8 am to dusk; the pool is open in season, weekdays 10 am-5 pm, weekends 10 am-6 pm

Activities: Biking, boating, hiking/walking, ice-skating, picnicking, playground, and swimming

Admission: Free; Parking, $5; Pool use, $2 for adults and $1 for children

NEW JERSEY

Van Saun County Park

216 Forest Ave., Paramus

(201) 262 3771

www.co.bergen.nj.us/parks/Parks/Van%20Saun%20Park.htm

The park has four age-appropriate playgrounds—one for infants, one for toddlers, one for young children and another for slightly older kids—as well as a carousel and a ride-on train that circles a small zoo. There is also a farm-yard that has chickens, geese, sheep, goats, pigs and cows. In the summer months there is a sprinkler spiral for children to run through. There are picnic tables and refreshments are available.

Hours: Zoo: daily 10 am-4:30 pm; Carousel: daily 10 am-6 pm; Train: daily 10 am-5 pm

Activities: Biking, hiking/walking, picnicking, playground

Admission: Free; May-October, Fridays-Sundays and holidays-zoo admission is $2 per adult and $1 for children over 12; November-April, zoo admission is free

What to Know Before You Go: Like any family attraction, this park is more crowded on the weekends or on a holiday, which can translate into long lines for the zoo, the train ride or even the snack bar. If you find yourself there on a crowded day with an excited toddler, we encourage the tag team approach: one parent gets in line while the other occupies the child. Be sure to bring a change of clothes as the sprinklers may prove too tempting to avoid. Simon once rode home in nothing but a diaper as everything else he'd had on was soaked.

GARDENS & OTHER GORGEOUS PLACES

In addition to playgrounds and parks, Westchester is home to a number of beautiful gardens. In the past, prominent residents-including celebrities, business tycoons and other notable some-bodies built mansions and castles that still dot the county, most with scenic gardens, fountains and beautiful Hudson River vistas. Some of these places have become historic sites and museums, so you can pack your infant in a snuggly and catch up on some culture or begin teaching your older child about past aristocracy. And, of course, many of these are lovely places just for strolling and picnicking.

Savvy Suggestion

Catch a wave at Willson's Waves Water Park at Willson's Woods Park in Mount Vernon. Three-foot waves, a cool 18-foot-high water slide, and even a water playground with cascades and lots of spouts on the spray deck is a great summertime outing.

Croton-on-Hudson

Van Cortlandt Manor
S. Riverside Ave.
(914) 271-8981
www.hudsonvalley.org/vancortlandt

The eighteenth-century stone manor house and reconstructed tenant house host cooking, spinning, weaving, brick manufacturing and blacksmithing demonstrations. The grounds include orchards as well as ornamental herb and heirloom vegetable gardens.

Hours: April-October, Wednesday-Monday 10 am-5 pm; November-December, weekends 10 am-4 pm; Closed January-March

Admission: House tours: $10 adults, $6 children 5-17, free for children under 5; Grounds only: $5 adults, $3 children 5-17, free for children under 5

Katonah

Caramoor Center for Music and the Arts
Rte. 137
(914) 232-5035
www.caramoor.org/html/museumgardens.htm

You can tour this Mediterranean-style house museum or just enjoy strolling and picnicking in the magnificent gardens, which include a butterfly garden. On Thursdays and Fridays from May to December, afternoon tea is served at 3 pm. In addition to classical music and jazz performances, Caramoor also has concerts for children and families.

Hours: May-October, daily 10 am-5 pm; Guided house tours are available Wednesday-Sunday, 1-4 pm

Admission: $9 adults, free for children under 16

North Salem

Hammond Museum & Japanese Stroll Garden
Deveau Rd.
(914) 669-5033
www.hammondmuseum.org

Stroll through three acres of Japanese gardens, enjoy the changing exhibits and eat in an outdoor café. The museum also sponsors Saturday children's programs for ages 6-12, including "Make a Bonsai Garden" and "Origami Mobile."

Hours: May-June, Wednesday-Sunday 12-4 pm; July-August, Sunday 11 am-3 pm; September-November, Wednesday-Sunday 12-4 pm; Closed December-April

Admission: $5 adults, free for children under 12

Purchase

Donald M. Kendall Sculpture Garden at PepsiCo
Anderson Hill Rd. (PepsiCo World Headquarters)
(914) 253-2900
www.hudsonrivervalley.com/index.cfm?section_id=6&page_id=169

This is a world-renowned garden and sculpture collection. The collection contains some forty pieces of twentieth-century art and features works by masters such as Auguste Rodin and Alexander Calder. But more importantly for parents, the 168 acres are open to the public, and there are walking trails, flower gardens, picnic tables and a fish-stocked pond. Free maps are available at the information center. There is a no-touch policy; nevertheless, this is a great place to take children.

Hours: Daily 9 am-5 pm

Admission: Free

What To Know Before You Go: There is no café, so if you plan to picnic you need to bring food with you.

Tarrytown

Lyndhurst
635 S. Broadway
(914) 631-4481
www.lyndhurst.org

This site has over sixty-five acres of manicured lawns, unusual trees and shrubs, and winding paths. Highlights include The Rose Garden, developed in the early 1990s, and great views of the Hudson River and the Tappan Zee Bridge. The Carriage House Café is open May-October, Wednesday-Sunday 11 am-3 pm

Hours: April-October, Tuesday-Sunday and holiday Mondays (Memorial Day, Labor Day, Columbus Day) 10 am-5 pm; November-

April, weekends and holiday Mondays (Martin Luther King Day and Presidents' Day) 10 am-4 pm

Admission: $10 adults, $4 students 12-17, free for children under 12

Sunnyside
Sunnyside Ln., off Rte. 9
(914) 591-8763
www.hudsonvalley.org/sunnyside

The nineteenth-century home of author Washington Irving ("The Legend of Sleepy Hollow" and "Rip Van Winkle") includes plantings, walkways and picnic grounds.

Hours: March, weekends 10 am-4 pm; April-October, Wednesday-Monday 10 am-5 pm; November-December, Wednesday-Monday 10 am-4 pm; January-February, hours vary, call for times

Admission: House tours: $10 adults, $6 children 5-17, free for children under 5; Grounds only: $5 adults, $3 children 5-17, free for children under 5

Yonkers
Untermyer Park and Gardens
945 N. Broadway
(914) 377-6450

Developed in the early 1900s, this grand Beaux Arts garden offers a Greek-style amphitheater, fountains, canals and Hudson River views.

Hours: Daily dawn to dusk

Admission: Free

MANHATTAN & THE BRONX
The Cloisters
Fort Tryon Park, Manhattan
(212) 923-3700
www.metmuseum.org/Works_of_Art/department.asp?dep=7

Located on four acres overlooking the Hudson River in northern Manhattan, this branch of The Metropolitan Museum of Art is devoted to the art and architecture of medieval Europe. The building incorporates elements from medieval southern France, including cloisters and other monastic architecture. There are reproduction gardens, as well as approximately 5,000 works of medieval art such as tapestries and stained-glass windows. Gallery workshops for kids ages 4-12 and their families are held at held at 1 pm on the first Saturday of every month.

Hours: March-October, Tuesday-Sunday 9:30 am-5:15 pm; Novem-

Savvy Suggestions

Strap on your helmets and head to the Bronx
River Parkway for Bike, Skate & Scooter Sundays.
The Parkway is closed to cars between North
White Plains and Bronxville (a sixteen-mile
stretch) from 10 am to 2 pm every Sunday during
May, June and September (except holiday
weekends). Bike from the Westchester County
Center south to Scarsdale Road in Yonkers. Skate
or scooter from the Westchester County Center
north to Fisher Lane in North White Plains.

ber-February, Tuesday-Sunday 9:30 am-4:45 pm; Closed New Year's
Day, Thanksgiving Day, Christmas Day

Admission: $15 adults, $10 students and senior citizens, free for
children under 12

What to Know Before You Go: The Trie Café serves continental
breakfast, light lunch and dessert May-October, Tuesday-Sunday,
10 am-4:30 pm. Free city parking is available in Fort Tryon Park.
Strollers are not permitted on Sundays; back carriers are available
for borrowing at the coat check.

New York Botanical Garden—
Everett Children's Adventure Garden
Bronx River Parkway at Fordham Rd., Bronx
(718) 817-8700
www.nybg.org/family/ecag.html

This twelve-acre indoor/outdoor science exploration center for
kids features forty hands-on nature discovery activities, including
mazes, galleries, microscopes, topiaries, treasure hunts, a sparkling
waterfall and glorious gardens. The Garden also hosts Family
Events, such as the Special Summer Storytelling Series, Scarecrow
and Harvest Weekend, and Goodnight Garden and Goblin. Other
programs, such as The Holiday Train Show (a perennial favorite!)
and Garden Sprouts, a gardening program for kids ages 3-5 with
parent or caregiver, require additional fees.

Hours: April-June, weekdays 1-6 pm, weekends and Memorial Day
10 am-6 pm; July-August, Tuesday-Sunday 10 am-6 pm; September-
October, weekdays 1-6 pm, weekends and holiday Mondays (Labor
Day and Columbus Day) 10 am-6 pm; November-March, weekdays

1-4 pm, weekends and holiday Mondays (Martin Luther King Day and Presidents' Day) 10 am-4 pm

Admission: $3 adults, $1 children 2-12, free for children under 2. Admission to the NYBG grounds is free; some exhibits require additional fees

What to Know Before You Go: Lunch and snacks are available in the Garden Café year-round. Picnic tables are located near the Everett Children's Adventure Garden, the Snuff Mill and on the Snuff Mill River Terrace.

Wave Hill
675 W. 252nd St., Bronx
(718) 549-3200
www.wavehill.org

Stroll through the various gardens, such as the wild flower garden, herb garden or aquatic garden (which has a small pond filled with large goldfish). Or just snag one of the many Adirondack chairs and take in the spectacular public garden overlooking the Hudson River. The drop-in "Family Art Project" (Kerlin Learning Center, Saturdays and Sundays 1-4 pm) is free with admission to the grounds; your child will learn to make paintings, prints, collages and sculptures out of paper, clay, mud, twigs and other natural materials. There are also storytellers, singers, dancers and musicians, as well as special events. The Wave Hill Café serves light fare with outdoor seating Tuesday-Friday 11 am-4:30 pm; Saturday and Sunday 10 am-4:30 pm; Wednesdays in June and July 10 am-8 pm. There is also a picnic area.

Hours: April 15-October 14, Tuesday-Sunday 9 am-5:30 pm; open until 9 pm on Wednesdays in June and July. October 15-April 14, Tuesday-Sunday 9 am-4:30 pm. Open on Memorial Day, Labor Day, Columbus Day; Closed New Year's Day, Martin Luther King Day, Presidents' Day, Thanksgiving, Christmas Day.

Admission: March-November, free Tuesday all day and Saturday 9 am-12 pm; Wednesday-Sunday, $4 adults, free for children under 6; free December-February

What to Know Before You Go: There is a very small members-only parking lot. You will probably have to park along the road outside the gardens, so you may have a little hike before you begin your leisurely stroll. For this reason, and because the grounds are so vast, we suggest you bring a stroller for toddlers who may get tired. But be aware that some areas, like the aquatic garden, are only accessible by steps, making strollers a somewhat cumbersome proposition.

PUTNAM COUNTY

Boscobel Restoration
Rte. 9D, Garrison
(845) 265-3638
www.boscobel.org

The grounds of this historic house museum comprise a formal rose garden with over 140 varieties of roses, fountains, an apple orchard and an herb garden. The one-mile Woodland Trail winds through twenty-nine acres of wooded landscape and features vistas of the Hudson River, as well as a gazebo, bridge and benches. Christmas Candlelight Tours and other special events are held seasonally.

Hours: April-October, Wednesday-Monday 9:30 am-5 pm; November-December, Wednesday-Monday 9:30 am-4 pm; Closed Thanksgiving and Christmas

Admission: House tours: $10 adults, $7 children 6-14, free for children under 6; Grounds only: $7 adults, $5 children 6-14, free for children under 6.

NATURE CENTERS & PRESERVES

Here's one way of teaching your kids about the birds and bees, literally. If you or your child is into bird-watching, butterflies or reptiles, there are a lot of great places in Westchester to suit your needs. Filled with trails, these places are perfect for a leisurely stroll, a brisk outdoor walk or a vigorous hike. While you're there, you can immerse yourself in nature study and help your child learn to identify trees, plants and wildflowers. At the nature centers kids can pet and hold live animals and take classes on nature, animals and crafts.

Bedford

Mianus River Gorge Preserve
167 Mianus River Rd.
(914) 234-3455
www.mianus.org

Over 700 acres and five miles of walking trails along Westchester's only old-growth forest.

Hours: April-November, daily 8:30 am-5 pm

Admission: Free

Savvy Suggestions

Summer Fun

* ✴ Invite the neighborhood kids over to run in the sprinkler
* ✴ Saxon Woods Park for miniature golf, playground and swimming
* ✴ Hudson Valley Shakespeare Festival at Boscobel
* ✴ Van Saun County Park–there's something here for everyone!
* ✴ Organize a small picnic at a local playground or park
* ✴ Feed the animals at The Children's Zoo at the Bronx Zoo
* ✴ Create temporary masterpieces with colorful chalk or sidewalk paint
* ✴ Head to Rye Playland for rides and relaxation
* ✴ Enjoy the books and A/C at your local library

Westmoreland Sanctuary
260 Chestnut Ridge Rd.
(914) 666-8448
www.westmorelandsanctuary.org

This 625-acre nature preserve has eight miles of trails, a museum and a variety of activities and educational programs. Activities for children include a Children's Nature Hike, Exploring Insects & Spiders, and an Annual Fall Festival with a petting zoo, arts & crafts projects and more.

Hours: Trails: daily dawn to dusk; museum: Monday-Saturday 9 am-5 pm, Sunday 10:30 am-5 pm. Holiday schedules may vary.

Admission: Free

Chappaqua

Pruyn Sanctuary Butterfly & Hummingbird Garden
275 Millwood Rd. (Rte. 133)
(914) 666-6503
www.sawmillriveraudubon.org/Pruyn.html

Over ninety acres with more than 125 types of annual and perennial flowering plants, over twenty-five species of butterflies and moths, and two dozen species of birds.

Hours: Daily dawn to dusk

Admission: Free

Cross River

Ward Pound Ridge Reservation
Rtes. 35 & 121 S.
(914) 864-7317
www.westchestergov.com/Parks/brochures/Wardbrochmain.htm

Westchester County's largest park offers a variety of activities in all seasons, including a playground, miles of wooded trails, and areas for picnicking, fishing and cross-country skiing. The park is home to the Trailside Nature Museum, which hosts weekend nature programs year-round. There are bathroom facilities and refreshments available.

Hours: Daily 8 am to dusk

Admission: Free

Croton-On-Hudson

Brinton Brook Nature Preserve
Albany Post Rd.
(914) 666-6503

This is a wooded nature preserve with trails, a stream, a lake and ruins.

Hours: Daily dawn to dusk

Admission: Free

Katonah

James Ramsey Hunt Sanctuary
N. Salem Rd., off Rte. 35
(914) 666-6177

Rich in birds and wildlife, this sanctuary covers over 200 acres of land. Its extensive trail system is complemented by a network of small bridges and boardwalks.

Hours: Daily dawn to dusk

Admission: Free

Marian Yarrow Nature Preserve
Mt. Holly Rd.
(914) 244-3271

This preserve features extensive trails, a thirty-foot waterfall and Hidden Lake, a favorite watering hole for migratory birds.

Hours: Daily dawn to dusk

Admission: Free

Mount Kisco

Butler Sanctuary and Meyer Preserve
Chestnut Ridge Rd.
(914) 244-3271

Boasting hundreds of acres of forest, streams, fields, scenic views and a well-marked trail system, this preserve is home to over 140 species of birds, 110 species of trees, shrubs and vines, and 250 species of wildflowers.

Hours: Daily dawn to dusk

Admission: Free

Marsh Sanctuary
114 South Bedford Rd.
(914) 241-2808

This is a 120-acre sanctuary with a wildflower garden, a boardwalk for bird watching, a 350-seat Greek-style amphitheater, hiking trails and a boardwalk into the marsh.

Hours: Daily dawn to dusk

Admission: Free

North White Plains

Cranberry Lake Preserve
Old Orchard St.
(914) 428-1005
http://westchesterny.com/Parks/NatureCenters05/Cranberry.htm

A nature preserve with 165 acres of forest, wetlands and a lake. Three miles of trails, including a loop around the lake, make for good strolling and hiking. The Nature Center offers interpretive programs every weekend throughout the year.

Hours: Trails: daily dawn to dusk; Nature Center: Tuesday-Saturday 9 am-4 pm

Admission: Free

Ossining

Teatown Lake Reservation
1600 Spring Valley Rd.
(914) 762-2912, ext.10
www.teatown.org

This 759-acre nature preserve and education center has over fourteen miles of walking and hiking trails; a Nature Center with live animals, including snakes, birds of prey, turtles, amphibians, rabbits and a porcupine; and a Nature Store with a broad selection of children's science materials, toys and nature-related books, as well as adult gifts, cards and stationery. The reservation also offers

Environmental Education Programs for children and adults (additional fees apply and pre-registration is required).

Hours: Nature Center: Tuesday-Saturday 9 am-5 pm, Sunday 1 pm-5 pm; Trails: dawn to dusk

Admission: Free

What to Know Before You Go: No bikes are allowed on the trails.

Peekskill

Blue Mountain Reservation

Welcher Ave.
(914) 862-5275
www.westchestergov.com/parks/parkslocations02/BlueMountain.htm

A 1,500-acre reservation that features miles of trails for strolling and nature study as well as more challenging hikes to the tops of two large peaks, Mt. Spitzenberg and Blue Mountain. There's a playground, as well as ice-skating and picnicking. There are bathroom facilities.

Hours: Daily 8 am to dusk

Admission: Free

Rye

Rye Nature Center

873 Boston Post Rd.
(914) 967-5150
www.ryenaturecenter.org

This nature center has forty-seven acres of grounds, with two-and-a-half miles of nature trails. Trail maps are available outside the main building. The center offers a series of programs where kids ages 3-5 can explore the outdoors as well as participate in games, crafts, and songs. There is a summer camp for kids ages 3 and up.

Hours: Grounds: daily 9 am-5 pm; Building: Monday-Saturday 10 am-4 pm

Admission: Free

Scarsdale

Greenburgh Nature Center

99 Dromore Rd.
(914) 723-3470
www.townlink.com/community_web/gnc

A thirty-three-acre woodland preserve that offers trails, a museum, a hands-on discovery room and live animals. There are seasonal programs, such as maple-sugaring, and the naturalist staff leads classes and programs—like "Nature Bugs and Critters" and "Crafts & Kids"—that involve nature discovery for kids ages 3-5 with a parent or caregiver. No need to sign up: you can take these classes on an ad hoc basis (additional fees apply).

Hours: Grounds-daily dawn to dusk; Manor House: Saturday-Thursday 9:30 am-4:30 pm; Animal Museum (inside the Manor House): weekdays 9:30 am-noon and 1-4:30 pm, weekends 10 am-4:30 pm

Admission: Free admission to the grounds; Manor House: $4 adults, $2 children 2-12; Greenburgh residents with Unicard pay half-price; members enter for free

What to Know Before You Go: The trails are unpaved and can be bumpy. Watch running toddlers, and if you use a stroller make sure it has big tires.

Weinberg Nature Center
455 Mamaroneck Rd.
(914) 722-1289
www.scarsdale.com/weinberg.asp

A ten-acre sanctuary with live animals, a meadow, a fruit orchard, an apiary for bees, and a butterfly and hummingbird garden. Stroll the trails, visit the Trailside Nature Museum for nature-related exhibits, meditate in the Japanese-style Zen Garden and lunch in the picnic area. A Native American Village explores the history of the Lenape and Iroquois Tribes. Special events and programs for toddlers include hands-on sensory awareness, exploration and discovery sessions, storybook time and live animals (additional fees apply).

Hours: Grounds: dawn to dusk; Interpretive Center: September-June, Wednesday-Sunday 9 am-5 pm; July-August, Monday-Friday 9 am-5 pm

Admission: Voluntary donation

Tarrytown
Rockefeller State Park Preserve
Rte. 117, 1 mile east of Rte. 9 (Between Sleepy Hollow & Pleasantville)
(914) 631-1470
http://nysparks.state.ny.us/parks/info.asp?parkID=60

This park has a wide variety of habitats, including wetlands, woodlands, meadows, fields and a lake. Carriage paths that traverse the park are ideal for strolling and jogging. The Visitor Center hosts exhibits of local and historical interest. There are bathroom facilities.

Hours: Daily 8 am to dusk

Admission: Free; Parking is $5 (April-October, Wednesday-Sunday 9 am-4:30 pm; November-March, weekends and holidays only)

And Don't Forget...

Bronx River Parkway Reservation
Yonkers to Valhalla
(914) 723-4058
www.westchestergov.com/parks/parkslocations02/BronxRiver.htm

Westchester's oldest park, this 807-acre paved "linear park" was created as an adjunct to the Bronx River Parkway, which opened in 1925. The reservation features miles of paths for biking, walking and nature study, as well as ponds, wooden footbridges and hundreds of varieties of native trees and shrubs.

Hours: Daily 8 am to dusk

Admission: Free

Savvy Suggestion

Here's a cheap thrill. Go to your local fire station. The fireman will happily show you around and often will let children sit in the fire trucks and see the flashing lights. Many stations give kids plastic fireman's helmets to take home so they'll never forget their visit.

Chapter 6

The Great Indoors

Indoor Play

Libraries

Stores with Story Times

Arts & Crafts Walk-Ins

Wonderful Websites

When it's too hot (or too cold) to go to your neighborhood play-ground, rest assured that there is an abundance of indoor activities to keep you and your child amused and engaged—from letting their imaginations run wild at the local library to letting their bodies run wild at an indoor play space. One point to keep in mind: if you decided that one of these activities would be the perfect thing to do on a rainy day, chances are so did lots and lots of other parents. Our advice—particularly for play spaces and walk-in facilities—is to go as soon as they open. It'll get more crowded as the day goes on, but you can get in a good hour or two of fun before it gets uglier than a one-day clearance sale at Loehmann's.

One of the things we like best are the number of free options when it comes to entertaining our kids. Local libraries are a goldmine of cool activities from snuggling up on a couch with a great book to picking out new DVDs to watch when you get home. And, many stores offer story times and free activities that can make great impromptu outings.

Lastly, instead of buying video games, turn to one of the websites we've listed—they will engage kids of all ages, and will tap into their special interests. And when it comes to answering questions like "Why is the sky blue?" now we have a place to turn instead of having to shrug and say "Go ask your father."

INDOOR PLAY

Not long after the little creatures begin walking do you find your-self desperately searching for places they can go running. Luckily, there are many indoor play spaces in and around Westchester. Most are well-equipped with climbing structures, sandboxes, ride-on toys, train sets and more.

Generally, there is an admission fee for the kids, but grown-ups enter for free. Before celebrating what a good deal that is, remember, it's a deal with the devil. When they're climbing up the habitrail-for-humans, so are you. When they're sprinting through the 10,000 square feet of floor space, so are you. Some parents get away with blithely reading a magazine or chatting with friends while their little ones try to disprove the laws of gravity, but most parents are keeping a close eye on their kids. This is a great way to spend a morning or an afternoon when you don't want to be outside. Remember, weekends and inclement weather can make indoor play spaces a bit of a mob scene, but if you and your child can handle it, God bless.

Elmsford

Sportime USA
380 Saw Mill River Rd., #1
(914) 592-2111
www.sportimeusa.com

Over 40,000 square feet of indoor sports and amusements, includ-ing over 200 video/arcade games, sports activities, wall climbing, laser tag, billiards, batting cages, bowling, bumper cars and more. They also have a special area set aside for the younger kids, with climbing tubes, a ball pit and suitable rides.

Hours: Sunday-Thursday 11 am-10:30 pm, Friday 11 am-12:30 am, Saturday 10 am-12:30 am

Cost: Varies, depending on activity

Ages: 3 and up

Mahopac

A Kids Castle
288 Rte. 6
(845) 628-1166
www.kidscastleonline.com

A Kids Castle offers things that will entertain infants, toddlers and grade-school children. The play structure has been designed by Little Tikes and features two slides and activity tunnels. Kids can also enjoy the eight-foot rock wall, a make-believe house area and a Dinosaur Dig that will capture the minds of young paleontologists. There is a separate, self-contained infant/toddler area with a soft play setup, ride-on toys and an "activity tree" that allows young ones to explore at their level. For the older set they also have the latest video games, air hockey and foosball tables.

Hours: Tuesday 10 am-4 pm, Saturday & Sunday 10 am-5 pm

Admission: $8 per child, $6 per sibling. (On "Terrific Tuesdays" admission is $6 for everyone.)

Ages: 1–12

What to Know Before You Go: In addition to offering birthday party facilities, A Kids Castle also has several different types of class offerings ranging from cooking to karate. Check their website for up-to-the-minute class information and cost.

Jumpin' Jeepers
926 Rte. 6 (DeRaffele Plaza)
(845) 621-4922
www.jumpinjeepers.net

Join "Jumpin' Jack," the friendly kangaroo mascot at this 5,000-square-foot indoor play space. There are kiddie rides, games, tunnel systems, a super slippery yellow slide and a bumping, jumping bounce house. "Jumpin' Joey's" is an area just for toddlers and offers age-appropriate ride-on toys and hideaways.

Hours: Monday-Saturday 11 am-8 pm, Sunday 11 am-5 pm

Admission: $6 Monday-Thursday, $8 Friday-Sunday

Ages: 1-10

What to Know Before You Go: There is a sit-down lunch and dinner area where they serve pizza, chicken wings and thirteen flavors of ice cream. (There's also a salad bar, if you want something a bit healthier.) The snack bar has plenty of other snacks and drinks to fill up and cool down excited kids. They also have private rooms for birthday parties.

New Rochelle
New Roc City
33 Lecount Pl. (Exit 16 off I-95)
(914) 637-7575
www.newroccity.com

Imagine an entertainment and retail megaplex that's over a million square feet of fun. New Roc City, located right in the heart of downtown New Rochelle, offers entertainment for all ages. There is the Regal Cinema IMAX theater, in addition to a "regular" eighteen-screen movie theater, and the New Roc Fun House

Arcade, a play center for all ages. There is an NHL-size skating arena and the New Roc Speedway, Westchester's only Indy Go-Kart Track, featuring a 700-foot course with over twenty Go-Karts. New Roc City is also home to New Roc n' Bowl, which has forty-eight fully computerized automatic bowling lanes with bumpers that go up and down so parents and children can play together, as well as lightweight balls and ramps to make it a fun and easy experience for children as young as 3. The newest attraction is "The Putting Edge," a glow-in-the-dark miniature golf course. There are two large, family-friendly eateries—Applebee's and Zanaro's.

Hours: Monday-Thursday 11 am-10:30 pm, Friday 11 am-1 am, Saturday 10 am-1 am, Sunday 11 am-11 pm

Cost: Varies, depending on activity

Ages: All ages

Port Chester

Leapin' Lizards
421 Boston Post Rd., 3rd fl. (Kohl's Shopping Center)
(914) 937-JUMP
www.leaplizards.com

Here your children can climb, bounce, crawl, jump and slide through tunnels, mazes, slides, ball baths, foam forests, obstacle courses and more. There is a special area for toddlers and those children who are not yet comfortable with the climbing tubes. Be aware, however, that once your kids enter the maze of tubes and tunnels you may find yourself having to crawl in after them if they get lost. Leapin' Lizards also has a game room with arcade games and toddler rides. They offer several value-packs and memberships that will save you money if you plan to go frequently.

Hours: Daily 10 am-4 pm

Admission: $8.99 children children 5 and over, $7.99 for children 5 and under on weekdays before 3 pm

Ages: 1-12

What to Know Before You Go: There is a snack bar with seating available at a central location, so you can keep an eye on your kids. You cannot bring meals from the outside, but they do have standard "kid's fare" if you want to feed your kids there. We recommend calling ahead to find out if there are any birthday parties scheduled for when you plan to be there, as it can get pretty crowded on days when multiple parties are taking place.

Shrub Oak

Jolly Amusements
1414 E. Main St.
(914) 526-9094
www.jollyamusements.com

Jolly Amusements is open to the public from Monday though Saturday for free play and recreation. Young children will have fun in the Jolly Zone play center and dress-up station. There is a separate infant/toddler area as well. Parents can sit and relax at the "juice bar" or find a spot in the play area near their child. The concession stand offers coffee, juice and water as well as plenty of snacks.

Hours: Monday-Thursday 10 am-4 pm, Friday 10 am-3 pm, Saturday 8:30 am-12 pm

Admission: $8 children over 1, $4 children under 1, and free for children in car seats

Ages: 1-5

What to Know Before You Go: Jolly Amusements also offers birthday parties as well as several classes for children 1-8 years old in things like arts & crafts, music, cooking and even scrapbooking.

Tuckahoe

Locomotion
95 Lake Ave.
(914) 337-4722

A small but cozy indoor play space that's great for younger toddlers. They have toys, trains, a dress-up area, some ride-on or push toys and a large sandbox as well as a climbing structure. Locomotion is also accessible by train (Metro North's Harlem line, across from the Tuckahoe Station) so it's perfect for non-driving babysitters.

Hours: It varies depending on classes and party schedules, but the general schedule is: Monday, Tuesday, Thursday and Friday 10 am-5 pm, Wednesday 11 am-5 pm, Saturday 11 am-6 pm, Sunday 12-6 pm

Admission: $11 for half a day (10 am-1 pm or 1 pm-5 pm); $10 for the second child

Ages: 1-5

What to Know Before You Go: Call ahead to make sure the space is open for general play as it is sometimes closed for private birthday parties or classes, especially on the weekends. Locomotion does not allow food or drink in the play room and only sells a few snacks. There is a pizzeria next door if you want to grab a slice before or after your outing.

White Plains

Frozen Ropes

55 S. Broadway
(914) 993-6355
www.frozenropes.com

This is part of a national chain of baseball and softball training facilities. They have indoor batting cages and pitchers mounds.

Hours: Weekdays 3-9 pm, weekends 10 am-6 pm

Cost: $20 per 15 minutes

Ages: 6 and up

Yonkers

Kid-o-Robics

Cross County Shopping Center (Upper Mall, near Macy's)
(914) 965-2000

This play space boasts one of the largest soft play areas around, including five ball pits, a zipline, a trapeze and two giant slides. They also have an arcade with over thirty ticket-redemption games and rides. Some admission packages include a meal pass (a slice of pizza, small popcorn and a small soda). Or, when they're ready, your kids can go from the ball pit to a pit stop at the snack bar, which has a few other kid-friendly offerings.

Hours: Monday-Thursday 9 am-8 pm, Friday-Saturday 9 am-9 pm, Sunday 10 am-8 pm

Admission: $5-12 per child, depending on admission package and time

Ages: All ages

What to Know Before You Go: Since there is really just one big play area, younger, tentative children may be intimidated by the running and jumping "big kids". Because Kid-o-Robics is located in the massive Cross County Shopping Center, there are tons of stores, casual restaurants, several department stores and a movie theater nearby.

Savvy Suggestion

Keep a container filled with pennies in your car for when you need an impromptu activity. Head to The Westchester or Stew Leonard's and let your child toss pennies into the fountains while "making a wish."

ROCKLAND COUNTY

Krazy City
1000 Palisades Center Dr. (The Palisades Center Mall), West Nyack
(845) 353-5700
www.krazycity.com

This indoor family amusement park (formerly Jeepers) has rides, attractions and games, including a haunted roller coaster, laser tag bumper cars, miniature golf and Thunder Bowl. There is a "Gemstone Mining Adventure," where kids can uncover treasure; a "Prehistoric Fossil Dig," for junior archeologists; and a "Wild Earth Safari Simulator," for budding adventure photographers. There is also a "Toy Factory" for making K'Nex creations and a "Glam Parlor" for designing fashion jewelry, as well as "Big Apple Ball Play," an interactive soft play area. Celebrations restaurant offers sandwiches, salads, wraps and pizzas.

Hours: Monday-Thursday 11 am-9 pm, Friday 11 am-10 pm, Saturday 10 am-10 pm, Sunday 11 am-8 pm

Cost: You can pay for points or for time. Rides/attractions are 12-20 points each; points start at $0.25 each, and the per-point price goes down as you buy more points. One hour of rides and games (no attractions) starts at $19.99. If it's crowded and you'll need to wait in line, paying by points makes more sense.

Ages: 2-12

New York Sports Club (for kids)
1000 Palisades Center Dr. (The Palisades Center Mall), West Nyack
(845) 358-1818
www.mysportsclubs.com/clubsched/nyscclubs.htm

This idea made us slap our foreheads and exclaim, "Why didn't anyone do this sooner?!" NYSC has initiated a "Drop & Shop" program where children ages 3-10 can spend time enjoying kid-friendly activities like sports, games, music, gymnastics, arts & crafts and even kickboxing while the grown-ups shop, take in a movie or have a leisurely cup of coffee. You don't even have to be a member of NYSC to take advantage of this opportunity. And, just when you thought it couldn't get any better, twice a month (on Friday nights) they offer a "Kids Night Out" program from 6:30-9:30 pm.

Hours: Monday, Wednesday, Friday and Saturday 9:30 am-1 pm; Tuesday-Thursday 4 pm-7 pm.

Cost: Members $5 per hour; nonmembers $6 per hour. The "Kids Night Out" program is $17 per hour for members, $18 per hour for nonmembers.

Ages: 3-10

Wee Play
33 Rte. 304, Nanuet
(845) 624-0114
www.weeplayusa.com

This indoor play facility features a play village with a make-believe pizzeria, supermarket and play house, a sand play area, and an indoor track for tricycles and Little Tikes cars. They also have an enclosed tot area for the very young and a multi-level climbing structure with slides and tunnels for slightly older kids.

Hours: Monday-Friday 9:30 am-5:30 pm, Saturday 10:30 am-6:30 pm, Sunday 10:30 am-5:30 pm.

Admission: $8.50 members, $12.50 nonmembers. A lifetime family membership is $15.

Ages: 1-7

What to Know Before You Go: There is a snack bar with juices, snacks and gourmet coffee.

Savvy Suggestion

Getting Out of the House on a Rainy Day

* Play with creepy crawlers and cuddly critters at the Greenburgh Nature Center.
* Visit your local library to read, play on the computer and meet other families.
* Go to the pet store and look at the animals.
* Head to Cosi and make some s'mores.
* Go to the Palisades Mall and ride the ferris wheel.

LIBRARIES

The only thing better than keeping your child entertained is doing it for free.

The local libraries in Westchester offer a wide range of story hours and events for the little ones—including Story Times, Music, Arts & Crafts, and more—primarily for ages 6 months and up. For some programs, you must be a resident of that town or village, and certain programs may require advance registration. Usually all you'll need is a library card to attend. Many of the libraries also have

Savvy Suggestion

"Test drive" books or videos from the library on your kids before buying your own copies.

wonderful Children's Rooms that are great places to just hang out in. The librarians are incredibly helpful and don't mind putting away the stacks of books you and your child discovered on your visit.

Seriously, this is the best bargain going in Westchester. In addition to books, you can check out videos and DVDs (for you or your children), which you get to keep for a week. Libraries also lend out CDs and audiobooks, and most have high-speed internet access. Get a free library card at your local branch, which will also give you borrowing and return privileges at any branch. (The library in White Plains requires you to go through a special authorization process for non-residents, but once that's completed you can borrow to your heart's content.) Each library posts its own hours, which may change from summer to winter. For information on the Westchester Library System, as well as on individual libraries, go to **www.westchesterlibraries.org**.

We have to mention here that several libraries have gone through or are planning major renovations that will make visiting an even more pleasant experience. For a truly spectacular example of what's to come, check out "The Trove" at the White Plains public library. This multi-million dollar renovation not only expanded the space considerably, but the beautiful design and magical décor— including a pirate ship reading nook in the back and a cave with a flat screen TV showing children-friendly videos throughout the day—will enchant children of all ages.

Ardsley
9 American Legion Dr.
(914) 693-6636

Armonk
19 Whippoorwill Rd. East
(914) 273-3887

Armonk/North White Plains
10 Clove Rd.
(914) 948-6359

Bedford
On the Village Green
(914) 234-3570

Bedford Hills
26 Main St.
(914) 666-6472

Briarcliff Manor
Library Rd.
(914) 941-7072

Bronxville
201 Pondfield Rd.
(914) 337-7680

Chappaqua
195 S. Greeley Ave.
(914) 238-4779

Croton-on-Hudson
171 Cleveland Dr.
(914) 271-6612

Dobbs Ferry
55 Main St.
(914) 693-6614

Eastchester
11 Oak Ridge Pl.
(914) 793-5055

Greenburgh
300 Tarrytown Rd.
(914) 993-1600

Harrison
Downtown (Main) Library
Bruce Ave.
(914) 835-0324

Harrison/West Harrison Branch
2 Madison St.
(914) 948-2092

Hastings-on-Hudson
Maple Ave.
(914) 478-3307

Irvington
12 S. Astor St.
(914) 591-7840

Katonah
26 Bedford Rd.
(914) 232-3508

Larchmont
121 Larchmont Ave.
(914) 834-2281

Mamaroneck
136 Prospect Ave.
(914) 698-1250

Montrose
Hendrick Hudson Free Library
185 Kings Ferry Rd.
(914) 739-5654

Mount Kisco
100 Main St.
(914) 666-8041

Mount Vernon
18 S. First Ave.
(914) 668-1840

New Rochelle
1 Library Plaza
(914) 632-7878

Huguenot Children's Library
794 North Ave.
(914) 632-8954

North Salem
Titicus Road/Rte. 116
(914) 669-5161

Ossining
53 Croton Ave.
(914) 941-2416

Peekskill
Field Library
4 Nelson Ave.
(914) 737-1212

Pelham
530 Colonial Ave.
(914) 738-1234

Pleasantville
*Mount Pleasant
Public Library*
350 Bedford Rd.
(914) 769-0548

Port Chester
1 Haseco Ave.
(914) 939-6710

Pound Ridge
*The Hiram Halle
Memorial Library*
271 Westchester Ave.
(914) 764-5085

Purchase
3093 Purchase St.
(914) 948-0550

Rye
1061 Boston Post Rd.
(914) 967-0480

Scarsdale
54 Olmsted Rd.
(914) 722-1300

Somers
Rte. 139/Reis Park
(914) 232-5717

South Salem
15 Main St.
(914) 763-3857

Tarrytown
The Warner Library
121 North Broadway
(914) 631-7734

Tuckahoe
71 Columbus Ave.
(914) 961-2121

Valhalla
Mount Pleasant Branch
125 Lozza Dr.
(914) 741-0276

White Plains
The Trove
100 Martine Ave.
(914) 422-1476

Yonkers
Crestwood Branch
16 Thompson St.
(914) 337-1500

Getty Square Branch
7 Main St.
(914) 337-1500

Grinton I. Will Branch
1500 Central Park Ave.
(914) 337-1500

Yorktown/Shrub Oak
John C. Hart Memorial Library
1130 Main St.
(914) 245-5262

STORES WITH STORY TIMES

If you're looking for a great free activity for you and your little one, check out one of the story times offered at the county's many bookstores and other kid-oriented stores. (And if there's one thing we're big fans of, it's free entertainment.) In addition to simple story reading, other events may include author readings, costumed character story times and children's performers, just to name a few. While you're certainly never obligated to buy anything, once they've got you there they know there's a decent chance that you'll buy a few of the titles you and your child have been reading. After all, children make very persuasive salespeople, do they not? Most of the big bookstores also have cafés or coffee shops, so you can grab a much-needed jolt of caffeine after thirty-seven consecutive recitations of *The Very Hungry Caterpillar*. Check the stores' websites or stop by one of the locations listed below to find out about upcoming events.

Croton-on-Hudson

Wondrous Things
4 Old Post Rd. S.
(914) 271-3044
www.wondrousthings.com

Hartsdale

Barnes & Noble
111 S. Central Ave.
(914) 948-1002
www.barnesandnoble.com

Mount Kisco

Borders Books
162 E. Main St.
(914) 241-8387
www.bordersstores.com

Scarsdale

Borders Books
680 White Plains Rd.
(914) 725-4637
www.bordersstores.com

The Scholastic Store
450 Central Park Ave., Scarsdale
(914) 725-7201
www.scholastic.com/scarsdalestore

White Plains

BabyStyle
125 Westchester Ave., (The Westchester Mall)
(914) 948-9511
www.babystyle.com

Barnes & Noble
230 Main St., (City Center)
(914) 397-2420
www.barnesandnoble.com

Borders Books
60 S. Broadway (West Chester Pavilion)
(914) 421-1110
www.bordersstores.com

Yonkers

Barnes & Noble
2614 Central Park Ave.
(914) 771-6400
www.barnesandnoble.com

ARTS & CRAFTS WALK-INS

On a rainy afternoon your child may not be able to run wild, but at least his imagination can. Go to a local arts & crafts studio, where kids can take part in a variety of fun projects, from ceramic painting to sand art. Some places charge an hourly fee and some a project fee, and there is typically a wide range of projects and prices. What grandparent, teacher or other special person in your child's life wouldn't love a hand-made keepsake to proudly display?

Dobbs Ferry

Art In Us
127 Main St.
(914) 591-5377
www.artinusonline.com

Now in a new location, they've also expanded their offerings to include painting your own pottery, a tie-dye bar and build-a-bear.

Hours: Tuesday-Thursday 11 am-5 pm, Friday 1-7 pm, Saturday 11 am-5 pm, Sunday (Fall and Winter only) 12-5 pm. On Fridays from 7 to 9 pm you can drop your kid(s) off so you can get dinner while your kids create something fabulous; call for a reservation.

Cost: $10 and up depending on the piece

Hartsdale

Michaels Arts & Crafts
319 North Central Ave.
(914) 946-1872
www.michaels.com

On Saturdays between 11 am and 1 pm, you can swing by with your child for a free arts & crafts project. Michaels also offers a lot of classes ranging from jewelry making to cake decorating. A fee may apply.

Larchmont

Children's Creative Corner
7 Addison St.
(914) 833-2880

Sixty-five different projects for ages 2-14. There is also a drop-off program for children 2-5 where preschoolers either pick their own craft or enjoy the preselected activity; parents can feel free to run a few errands while their little ones have a ball. Snack, story time and free play are also included.

Hours: Weekdays 9:30 am-5:30 pm, Weekends 10 am-7 pm

Cost: $14 per hour

Paint Your Art Out
2005 Palmer Ave.
(914) 833-2321
www.paintyourartout.com

Ceramic painting.

Hours: During the school year—Wednesday 1:30-6 pm, Thursday 1:30-8 pm, Friday 1:30-6 pm, Saturday 11 am-6 pm, Sunday 12-5 pm; summer hours—Wednesday and Saturday 11 am-6 pm, Thursday and Friday 11 am-9 pm

Cost: $7-$66, depending on the piece (includes firing fee)

Savvy Suggestion

Make Friday night a date night and drop your kids off from 7-9 pm at Art in Us in Dobbs Ferry. They can use their imaginations doing fun and creative thing—and so can you . . . *wink wink*.

Savvy Suggestion

Looking for something fun to break up the weekend blahs? Check libraries, craft stores and educational stores like The Lakeshore Learning Company and The Scholastic Store for free weekend activities. You may even get lucky and find a puppet show or performance at a nearby library.

Mohegan Lake

Let's Be Creative
1950 E. Main St.
(914) 528-7888

Ceramic painting.

Hours: Tuesday-Sunday 12-5 pm

Cost: $11-$200, depending on the piece (includes 1 1/2 hours of studio time, glazing and firing fee)

Scarsdale

Fun Craft
590 Central Park Ave.
(914) 472-1748

Ceramic painting and sand art.

Hours: Daily 10 am-6 pm

Cost: $9-$13, depending on the piece

Lakeshore Learning Store
969 Central Park Ave. (Midway Shopping Center)
(914) 472-1820
www.lakeshorelearning.com

Enjoy free craft activities for kids ages 3 and up, every Saturday from 11 am to 3 pm.

Paint Your Own Pottery
838 Scarsdale Ave.
(914) 472-7281

Ceramic painting (with non-toxic glazes that are food-safe). There's no time limit, and you pay by the piece.

Hours: Tuesday-Friday 11 am-6 pm, Saturday 11 am-4:30 pm, Sunday 1-4:30 pm

WONDERFUL WEBSITES

Many of our kids no doubt know computers better than we do. These great sites provide fun, distraction and education for a variety of age groups—including coloring, arts & crafts, games, puzzles, stories, science, recipes and more. They make helpful diversions for a rainy afternoon!

www.enchantedlearning.com – An easy-to-use family of websites that emphasize imagination, creativity and learning

www.familyfun.com – Arts & crafts, games, mazes, puzzles and more for ages 2-12

www.funbrain.com – Educational games for K-8th grade

www.funschool.com – Educational games for ages 3-11

www.kidsclick.org – A web search engine for kids

www.kidsgames.org – Games, coloring, stories and songs for kids 0-10

www.littleclickers.com – A directory of educational websites for kids 3-12, from Children's Technology Review magazine

www.nasa.gov/audience/forkids – Information on space travel, as well as games, art, stories and activities

www.nationalgeographic.com/kids/– Science experiments, a cartoon factory, and information on animals and geography

www.nickjr.com – Games, crafts, recipes and more, based on Nickelodeon television shows

www.pbskids.org – Games, stories, coloring and music based on your favorite PBS characters

www.puzzlemaker.com – Create and print customized word search crossword and math puzzles

www.sciencenewsforkids.org – Science articles, puzzles, games and experiments for kids 9-13

www.storiestogrowby.com – Stories from around the world for ages 6-12

www.superb.net/cardtric/tricks.htm – Step-by-step card tricks for beginners on up

www.zeeks.com – Arcade-style games and moderated message-boards for ages 9-14

Savvy Suggestion

Stay-at-Home Activities

* Thread Cheerios on string for an edible necklace (mini pretzels work too).
* Cook something fun—whether it's baking cookies or English muffin pizza-faces.
* Start a book club with your kid: read a story, do related activities and have a discussion about what you've read.
* Practice measuring, pouring, counting and sorting with dried beans and pasta.
* Buy "Window Markers" (Crayola makes them) and let your kids create temporary masterpieces on your windows or mirrors.
* Keep some extra games, toys or arts & crafts materials in your "gift closet" just in case you get snowed in and need something new and different to play with.
* Buy a science kit for hours of experimenting fun. Don't have one? Baking soda and vinegar will give you lots of fizzy fun.
* Drape a sheet or blanket over a table and have an indoor camp-out.

Chapter 7

Culture Club

Museums

Art Tours & Classes

Theaters, Concerts & Children's Performances

There comes a time in your child's life when you have to accept that those classical music tapes you've been playing since pre-birth will only get her so far. Now it's time to begin the next phase of your child's cultural education. In Westchester and nearby areas, there are great cultural institutions to share with your kids—so plan a trip to one of these fantastic children's museums or theaters. The listings here are specifically for children or feature children's programs. Obviously New York City is the center of the world when it comes to culture—and being just a short train ride away from the center of the world isn't too shabby.

MUSEUMS

A new children's museum is coming to Westchester! The Campaign for the Westchester Children's Museum, formed in March 2001, is working to build a facility at the Bathhouses at Historic Rye Playland; they expect to break ground in 2006. The museum is envisioned as a place where children can experience the cultural diversity of Westchester, explore the history and environment of Long Island Sound and the Hudson River, and examine the development of the Westchester communities through science, technology and the arts. **If you'd like more information on this effort, visit www.discoverwcm.org.**

In the meantime, cast the net a bit wider and you'll find numerous places where kids can explore art, science, natural history and much, much more. There are a number of children's museums in surrounding counties that have great activities for kids—some places can keep them busy all day! Also, several of the "grown-up" museums in the area have special children's areas or programs for children. These places are worth the trek.

Katonah

Katonah Museum of Art
Rte. 22 at Jay St.
(914) 232-9555
www.katonahmuseum.org

The museum has six major exhibitions each year, as well as a sculpture garden. The Children's Learning Center—an interactive art exploration area—hosts a variety of exhibitions, programs and drop-in activities, including "Tuesday for Tots." In addition, there are several three-session parent/child courses, such as "Create a Memory Box" and "See-and-Do Art Activities."

Hours: Tuesday and Thursday-Saturday 10 am-5 pm, Wednesday 10 am-8 pm, Sunday 12-5 pm

Admission: $3 adults, free for members and children under 12, free on Wednesdays after 5 pm

Yonkers

Hudson River Museum/Andrus Planetarium
511 Warburton Ave.
(914) 963-4550
www.hrm.org

Westchester's oldest and largest museum features events for kids. Recent special attractions have included "Funny Fish," with live creatures from the Hudson River, and "At the Turning of Time," a mask and puppet show dramatizing the history of the Hudson River. The Andrus Planetarium has a variety of shows on the constellations, planets and sky.

Hours: May-September—Wednesday-Sunday 12-5 pm, Friday 12-9 pm; October-April—Wednesday-Sunday 12-5 pm

Admission: Museum—$5 adults, $3 seniors and children, free for members; Planetarium—$5 adults ($4 on weekend afternoons), $3 children 12 and under

What to Know Before You Go: Friday Star Nites (7 pm show) are free.

CONNECTICUT

Bruce Museum of Arts & Sciences
1 Museum Dr., Greenwich
(203) 869-0376
www.brucemuseum.org

The art collection may not excite your child, but she may be interested in the museum's natural history exhibits, which include reptiles, fish, butterflies, minerals, fossils, and bird and mammal displays. The museum also offers a variety of children's programs, including "Look and See: For Young Museum Visitors," a class for kids 3-5 (with parents or caregivers) that explores the museum's galleries through hands-on experiences, crafts and stories.

Hours: Tuesday-Saturday 10 am-5 pm, Sunday 1-5 pm; closed on major holidays.

Admission: $7, $6 for students ages 5-22, free for children under 5, members free on Tuesdays

What to Know Before You Go: There is a great park outside the museum with picnic tables, a terrific playground for toddlers and one for older kids. The Bruce Museum is only a five-minute drive from downtown Greenwich, a town filled with great restaurants, stores and two movie theaters. You can really make this trip an all-day event.

Danbury Railway Museum
120 White St., Danbury
(Former New Haven RR Danbury Station)
(203) 778-8337
www.danbury.org/drm/Museum.htm

Located in the historic station and rail yard in downtown Danbury, the museum offers indoor toy train exhibits, a hands-on play area with train sets and outdoor train rides on real trains. The seasonal themed rides—haunted train, Santa train, Easter Bunny train, etc.— are a big hit with the kids, and the gift shop is loaded with train-related merchandise and books.

Hours: January-March, Wednesday-Saturday 10 am-4 pm, Sunday Noon-4 pm; April-December, Tuesday-Saturday 10 am-5 pm, Sunday Noon-5 pm

Admission: $6 adults, $4 children 3-12, free for children under 3

Savvy Suggestion

Are you a children's museum member? Then you may be able to get into others for free, too. About 140 children's museums in the U.S. and Canada have reciprocal agreements, providing members with free admission.

For a list of participating museums go to: www.childrensmuseums.org/visit/reciprocal.htm

Stepping Stones Museum for Children

303 West Ave., Norwalk
(203) 899-0606
www.steppingstonesmuseum.org

Exhibits at this museum encourage hands-on exploration and discovery for children age 10 and under, incorporating the themes of Science and Technology, The Arts, and Culture and Heritage. Exhibits include "Toddler Terrain" (for ages 3 and under), "Waterscape" (an interactive water exhibit), "Express Yourself" (an art center), "In the Works" (a motion center) and an exhibit on Connecticut.

Hours: Wednesday-Sunday 10 am-5 pm, Tuesday 1 pm-5 pm; closed on major holidays.

Admission: $8 per person, free for children under 1

What to Know Before You Go: The museum has a café featuring child and adult-friendly breakfast (cereals, omelets, etc.), lunch (wraps, salads, pizzas, hot dogs, etc.), and snack offerings (yogurts, puddings, healthy snacks) for visitors. You can also bring your own food and enjoy it at the indoor eating area or the larger outdoor picnic area. Smocks are provided at the Waterscape area, but energetic kids can still get drenched; you may want to bring an extra set of clothes.

MANHATTAN & QUEENS

American Museum of Natural History

79th St. & Central Park West
(Enter on Central Park West at 81st St. or 77th St.)
(212) 313-7278
www.amnh.org

Kids interested in dinosaurs, birds or fish will love exploring this museum. The Hall of Ocean Life reopened after its renovation, and the ninety-four-foot-long female blue whale model (originally installed in 1969) is back. In addition, the Butterfly Conservatory has become a popular annual event, and the Discovery Room offers a hands-on look at the museum through puzzles and games, artifacts and specimens, scientific challenges and investigations. The museum also offers a variety of programs for kids, and the Space Show at the Rose Center/Hayden Planetarium is fun for all ages.

Hours: Daily 10 am-5:45 pm; the Rose Center is open on Fridays until 8:45 pm; closed Thanksgiving and Christmas Day

Admission: $14 adults, $8 children 2-12, free for members and children under 2; additional fees apply for the Rose Center, Space Show and IMAX theater.

What to Know Before You Go: The Museum Food Court (lower level) has sandwiches, pizza, a grill, a salad bar and more. Strollers are not allowed in the Space Theater, but you can leave them outside. Children under 2 are admitted to the theater free and must sit on their parents' laps.

Children's Museum of the Arts
182 Lafayette St.
(212) 941-9198
www.cmany.org

This is a hands-on art museum for children ages 1-12, with activities that include painting, sculpting, building and imagining in many different media. Special exhibits and activities include the "Monet Ball Pond"; "Preschool Creative Play Area"; "Lines and Shapes," where kids use computer sketch pads to create shapes on a giant color-form wall; and the "Wonder Theater," where children are given a theme and encouraged to design a set, costume and props, which they then use to produce and perform vignettes. The museum has many programs, both registered and walk-in, for young children.

Hours: Wednesday-Sunday 12-5 pm, Thursday 12-6 pm

Admission: $8 per person, free on Thursday 4-6 pm

Children's Museum of Manhattan
The Tisch Building
212 W. 83rd St.
(212) 721-1234
www.cmom.org

This museum offers five floors of exhibits such as "Alice's Wonderland: A Most Curious Adventure," "Little West Side," and "Art Inside-Out." The museum also offers parent/child classes for kids 6 months to 3 years, as well as after-school classes for kids 4-12.

Hours: Wednesday-Sunday 10 am-5 pm; closed Thanksgiving Day, Christmas Day and New Year's Day.

Admission: $8 per person, free for children under 1 and members

What to Know Before You Go: Strollers must be left at the coat check. No food or beverages are permitted in the museum.

Museum of Biblical Art
1865 Broadway at 61st St.
(212) 408-1500
www.mobia.org

The Museum of Biblical Art showcases the connection between art and religion in the Jewish and Christian traditions. The museum collection includes some of the first printed editions of the Bible in Hebrew, ancient Greek and English. Programs for children ages

4-13 include crafts workshops based on the museum's art as well as holiday craft workshops.

Hours: Tuesday-Wednesday 10 am-6 pm, Thursday 10 am-8 pm, Friday-Sunday 10 am-6 pm. Closed Independence Day, Thanksgiving Day, Christmas Day and New Year's Day.

Admission: Free

New York Hall of Science
47-01 111th St., Queens
(718) 699-0005
www.nyhallsci.org

NYHS features more than 400 hands-on exhibits focused on biology, chemistry and physics. There is an outdoor park with refurbished rockets and a climb-in capsule that is the same size as the original Mercury capsule. In Preschool Place children under the age of 6 can operate a multi-ethnic market, use cranes and a conveyor system, and build structures. March through December, weather permitting, the Science Playground provides an out-door laboratory where children can experience science through giant slides, windmills, a water play area, a light-activated kinetic sculpture, a 12-kid teeter-totter, and more (additional fees apply).

Hours: Tuesday-Thursday 9:30 am-2 pm, Friday 9:30 am-5 pm, Saturday-Sunday 10 am-6 pm. Holiday weeks and July-August, weekdays 9:30 am-5 pm, weekends 10 am-6 pm. Closed Labor Day, Thanksgiving Day and Christmas Day.

Admission: $11 adults, $8 children 2-17, free for children under 2

ROCKLAND COUNTY
Lower Hudson Valley Challenger Learning Center
225 Rte. 59, Airmont
(845) 357-3416
www.lhvcc.com

Be an astronaut for a day in a NASA-designed spacecraft simulator! Public Missions to the Moon, to Mars and to a comet are offered on a rotating basis on the third Sunday of every month.

Hours: Third Sunday of every month. Missions begin at 2 pm and last approximately three hours.

Admission: $15 per person for ages 9 and up

What to Know Before You Go: They recommend that participants be at least 9 years old; however, younger children may participate if accompanied by an adult. Reservations are recommended.

DUTCHESS COUNTY
Mid-Hudson Children's Museum
75 North Water St., Poughkeepsie
(845) 471-0589
www.mhcm.org

MHCM has over fifty interactive exhibits on topics such as dinosaurs, trains, virtual reality, art and more. There's also a rock climbing wall, a water table, free art and science activities every day, structured playgroups for kids ages 0-5 and summer camp for ages 4-12.

Hours: Tuesdays-Sundays 11 am-5 pm. Closed New Year's Day, Memorial Day, Fourth of July, Labor Day, Thanksgiving Day and Christmas Day.

Admission: $6.50 per person for ages 1 and up

NEW JERSEY
Liberty Science Center
251 Phillip St., Liberty State Park, Jersey City
(201) 200-1000
www.lsc.org

At the time of this writing, Liberty Science Center is undergoing a major expansion. The museum is temporarily housed at Riverside, the historic Central Railroad of New Jersey Terminal (still within Liberty State Park), and features a single 4,000-square foot exhibition, "Eat and Be Eaten," which focuses on predator-prey relationships—it's a sneak preview of a larger exhibition that will be part of the museum when it reopens.

When LSC reopens (scheduled for Summer 2007), it will be double its former size, with new interactive exhibits focusing on skyscrapers, communications and the Hudson River, among other subjects. It will also feature a Young Learners Exhibition for children 1 1/2 to 5 years old as well as improved visitor amenities. All exhibit areas— focused on the museum's themes of invention, health and technology—will be renewed, and the 3D Laser Show and the IMAX theater will reopen.

Hours: Weekdays 10 am-4 pm, weekends 10 am-5 pm

Admission: $3 per person, while housed at Riverside

What to Know Before You Go: From Liberty State Park, you can catch the Circle Line ferry to the Statue of Liberty and Ellis Island. There is also waterfront picnicking and a large children's play area. Visit www.libertystatepark.org for more information.

New Jersey Children's Museum
599 Valley Health Plaza, Paramus
(201) 262-5151
www.njcm.com

With over thirty exhibits in 15,000 square feet, this museum will keep your little ones busy no matter what their interests or ages. Exhibits include the "Baby Nook," "Housekeeping," and "Science and Technology." In the fire truck, your children can dress in real fire gear, sit in the truck and steer and ring the bell. In the "Kid-Sized Grocery," they can shop, fill their carts and check out at the register. At the "Kid-Sized Pizzeria," they can "cook" and serve everything from pizza to fish and broccoli. And in "The Medieval Castle," they can dress as kings, queens, knights and princesses.

Hours: Weekdays 10 am-6 pm; weekends October-April 10 am-6 pm, May-September 10 am-5 pm; closed Thanksgiving and Christmas Day.

Admission: $8 per person, free for children under 1

What to Know Before You Go: No strollers are permitted in the museum.

Savvy Suggestion

Family memberships at museums generally cost around $100 and pay for themselves within four visits. They often come with discounts, invitations to special events and other bonuses.

ART TOURS & CLASSES

We'd be remiss if we didn't mention these two organizations which offer group programs for you and your child to explore museums and galleries. After all, it couldn't hurt to expose them to fine art while they're still young!

ARTKIDS
(646) 201-9168
www.artmuseny.com

ARTKIDS exposes children ages 3-12 to New York City museums, art galleries and auction houses. Age-grouped small classes meet for one hour each week (or 75 minutes for older kids) at a designated museum to visit exhibits and do related art projects. Classes are purchased in a series (there are 5-14 classes in a series, depending on the season) and average about $45 per class; this might sound pricey but it includes museum admission costs, which can run up to $20 per visit. Children under 5 must be accompanied by a parent or guardian. This organization also runs ARTDATE, series of 75-minute morning or evening classes for adults that include a lecture, discussion and tour of one of New York's museums or galleries.

Metropolitan Moms
(212) 206-7272
www.metropolitanmoms.com

Metropolitan Moms offers museum tours, gallery walks, artist studio visits, culinary adventures and historical neighborhood explorations such as a walking tour of the architecture of Greenwich Village. "Metropolitan Mix with Babies" is an educational class for moms with babies up to 1 year old; activities are designed for easy navigation of strollers, tours are kept small and there are babysitters on hand to help out. "Metropolitan Toddlers" introduces toddlers (1-3 years old) to the Metropolitan Museum while educating their moms on the various exhibits; classes include art projects and other activities. There are also "Moms-only" classes and special events. Prices vary: phone or e-mail for details.

Savvy Savings

Check to see if your or your spouse's companies participate in a corporate cultural savings program. You may be able to get in free to many museums, zoos and other locations that require admission.

THEATERS, CONCERTS & CHILDREN'S PERFORMANCES

Once your children are old enough to sit through a show, you'll find that there are many to choose from, whether you're looking for an adaptation of a classic story, an original production, a puppet show or a kid's concert. Now that Sam and Simon are older and their attention spans can handle it, we're eager to expose them to as many different experiences as possible so that they can begin to build an early appreciation for music and theater (hopefully!).

Bronxville

The Corner Store
1428 Midland Ave., 2-J
(914) 237-8680
www.thecornerstoredancecompany.org

Modern dance productions including live original music, story-telling, poetry, humor and a variety of musical instruments. Children participate from their seats, learning movements, words and songs. A different show is offered each year.

Cost: Varies

Ages: 3-12

Musical Adventures for Children
Concordia Conservatory
171 White Plains Rd.
(914) 395-4507

A subscription series of three Saturday-morning concerts for children.

Cost: $35 adults, $20 children (for the series)

Ages: 3-7

Elmsford

Westchester Broadway Theater
75 Clearbrook Rd
(914) 592-2222
www.broadwaytheatre.com

Unlike the performances for adults, there is no food service for Children's Theatre productions. Also, since seating is at tables, all tables are potentially shared tables. Previous productions have included *Charlie and the Chocolate Factory*, *The Wizard of Oz* and *'Twas the Night Before Christmas*.

Cost: Varies

Ages: Varies

Irvington

Irvington Town Hall Theater
85 Main St.
(914) 761-7463

This venue puts on tried-and-true shows as well as original pro-ductions. Previous shows include *The Life and Rhymes of Fiona Gander*, *The Prince and the Pauper*, and the "All Star Broadway Holiday Concert."

Cost: Varies

Ages: Varies

Mamaroneck

Emelin Theater
153 Library Ln.
(914) 698-0098
www.emelin.org

In addition to a repertoire of grown-up shows, the Emelin Theater offers a wide range of children's theater pieces. Past shows include *Charlotte's Web, Alice in Wonderland, Raggs Kids Club* and *The Paper Bag Players.* Most children's events are general admission, and people are seated on a first-come, first-served basis.

Cost: Varies

Ages: 3 and up

Ossining

Blueberry Pond Arts Center
Shine House
Cedar Lane Park, 235 Cedar Ln.
(914) 923-3530
www.blueberrypond.org

Westchester's only professional theater company dedicated solely to developing and producing new plays. The Young People's Theatre program offers workshops for aspiring actors and playwrights, encouraging new works for young audiences.

Cost: Varies

Ages: Varies

Pleasantville

Jacob Burns Film Center
364 Manville Rd.
(914) 747-5555
www.burnsfilmcenter.org

Originally named The Rome Theater, this beautiful Spanish Mission style cinema, built in 1925, was one of the first movie theaters in Westchester County. It closed its doors in 1987 due to competition from neighboring multiplexes until a group, led by founder Stephen Apkon, bought it with hopes of restoring it to its former glory. The JBFC opened its doors to the public in June 2001 and has featured films ranging from human rights documentaries to Shakespeare. They also show classic films for kids like *The Wizard of Oz, A Little Princess* and *Charlotte's Web.*

Cost: Varies

Ages: Varies

Purchase
The Performing Arts Center
735 Anderson Hill Rd.
(914) 251-6200
www.artscenter.org

A five-theater complex on the Purchase College campus. Previous children's programming has included Maurice Sendak's *Little Bear*, *Zoppe Family Circus*, *The Red Balloon* and *The Giving Tree*.

Cost: Varies

Ages: 3-9

Scarsdale
Bendheim Performing Arts Center
JCC of Mid-Westchester
999 Wilmot Rd.
(914) 472-3300

In addition to grown-up shows, the Bendheim offers a variety of children's performances. Previous shows include *The Magic Land of Peter Pan* and *Mixed Up Mother Goose*.

Cost: Varies

Ages: Varies

Tarrytown
The Tarrytown Music Hall
13 Main St.
(914) 631-3390
www.tarrytownmusichall.org

The Music Hall offers "Shows for Young Audiences on Weekdays." Past shows have included *The Lion, The Witch, and The Wardrobe*, Judy Blume's *Otherwise Known as Sheila The Great*, and *Bravo, Amelia Bedelia*.

Cost: Varies

Ages: Varies

White Plains
Westco Productions
9 Romar Ave.
(914) 761-7463
www.westcoprods.com

Westco puts on three traditional holiday performances in November and December for kids: *Frosty the Snowman*, *The Wizard of Oz*, and a hospital tour of *The Frog Prince*. The theater has expanded its scope to include other musical adaptations of well-known classics such as *The Diary of Anne Frank*, *Hair*, *Annie* and various Shakespeare plays. Shows are performed at the Rochambeau School's theater, Westchester Broadway Theater and the Irvington Town Hall. Westco also offers children's theater workshops: an introduction to theater for kids ages 3-4 (with parent or caregiver) and a workshop for kids 5-12 that culminates with the performance of a show.

Cost: Varies

Ages: 2-12

White Plains Performing Arts Center
11 City Pl. (City Center)
(888) 977-2250
www.wppac.com

In addition to grown-up shows, WPPAC produces tried-and-true children's favorites like *Jack and the Beanstalk*, *Snow White* and *The Frog Prince*. They also put on special events, such as performances by The Russian American Kids Circus and Dance Asia.

Cost: Varies

Ages: Varies

Yorktown

Yorktown Stage
Yorktown Community Cultural Center
1974 Commerce St. (entrance off Veterans Rd.)
(914) 962-0606
www.yorktownstage.com

Past productions include *Annie*, *The King and I*, *The Nutcracker*, and *Snow White*.

Cost: Varies

Ages: Varies

CONNECTICUT

Quick Center for the Arts
Fairfield University
1073 N. Benson Rd., Fairfield
(203) 254-4190
www.fairfield.edu/quick/quick.htm

Previous shows for children include *Little Red Riding Hood*, *Jack and the Beanstalk*, *The Pied Piper*, and *Just So Stories*.

Cost: $12 adults, $10 children

Ages: Varies

Stamford Center for the Arts
307 Atlantic St., Stamford
(203) 325-4466
www.onlyatsca.com

In addition to old favorites like *The Nutcracker*, the center has special shows such as "My First Orchestra Concert," in which the music director of the Stamford Symphony Orchestra introduces kids to classical music. Performances take place at the Rich Forum and The Palace Theater.

Cost: Varies

Ages: Varies

Stamford Theater Works/ Purple Cow Children's Theater
200 Strawberry Hill Ave., Stamford
(203) 359-4414
www.stamfordtheatreworks.org

Children's shows are performed May through July and during the winter holiday season. Performances include stories, music, dance, puppetry, magic and lots of audience participation.

Cost: Varies

Ages: 3-8

MANHATTAN
13th Street Repertory Company
50 West 13th St. (at 6th Ave.)
(212) 675-6677
www.13thstreetrep.org

Weekend performances of original children's shows. Past shows include *Rumple Who?* and *Wiseacre Farm*.

Cost: $7 (cash only, at box office)

Ages: Varies

Jazz for Young People
Rose Theater
Time Warner Center, Columbus Circle (60th St. and Broadway)
(212) 258-9800
www.jalc.org/04_05/e_f_jazz4yp.html

Wynton Marsalis, Artistic Director of Jazz at Lincoln Center, hosts this series of Saturday afternoon family concerts featuring the Lincoln Center Jazz Orchestra.

Cost: $40-120 for series of four concerts

Ages: 6 and up

Literally Alive

(212) 866-5170

www.literallyalive.com

A production company that specializes in bringing classic children's literature to life on the stage through music, art, dance, puppetry and storytelling. In addition to watching the productions, families can participate in pre-show workshops. Previous productions include *Beauty and the Beast* and *The Velveteen Rabbit*.

Cost: Varies

Ages: Varies

The Little Orchestra Society

Avery Fisher Hall at Lincoln Center

(66th St. and Broadway)

The Kaye Playhouse at Hunter College

(695 Park Ave. at 68th St.)

(212) 971-9500

www.littleorchestra.org

Lolli-POPS concerts teach kids the ABCs of music with the help of "Bow" the Panda, "Toot" the Bird, "Buzz" the Bee and "Bang" the Lion, each representing a different section of the orchestra. Happy Concerts for Young People produces performances such as *Peter and the Wolf* and *Amahl and the Night Visitors*.

Cost: $99 for a Lolli-POPS 3-show subscription; $10-50 for each Happy Concert

Ages: Lolli-POPS, 3-5; Happy Concerts, 6-12

Manhattan Children's Theater

52 White St.

(212) 226-4085

www.manhattanchildrenstheatre.org

Weekend performances for kids and families. Previous shows include *Rikki Tikki Tavi, Aesop's Fables* and *Alice in Wonderland*.

Cost: $15 adults, $10 children

Ages: Varies

New Victory Theater

209 W. 42nd St. (just west of Broadway)

(212) 382-4000

www.newvictory.org

A beautifully restored landmark Broadway theater just for kids, with afternoon, early evening and weekend performances. Past shows include *A Year with Frog and Toad, The New Shanghai Circus* and *Twinkle Twinkle Little Fish*.

Cost: $7-28 members, $10-40 non-members; membership is automatic when you order tickets to three or more shows.

Ages: Varies

Papageno Puppet Theater
Ray's Pizza
Columbus Ave. and 82nd St.
(212) 874-3297

Various children's shows (pizza not included!).

Cost: $7

Ages: 0-10

Paper Bag Players
225 W. 99th St.
(212) 663-0390
www.thepaperbagplayers.org

Original theater for children performed at The Kaye Playhouse at Hunter College, as well as at Symphony Space and Kingsborough and LaGuardia Community Colleges. Performances are on weekends, January-March.

Cost: $10-25

Ages: 4-9

Symphony Space
2537 Broadway (at 95th St.)
(212) 864-5400
www.symphonyspace.org

This theater hosts family programs that acquaint children with live performances, including film, plays, musicals, dance and more—some performed by kids for kids, some by adults for kids.

Cost: Varies

Ages: Varies

TheatreworksUSA
121 Christopher St.
(212) 279-4200
www.theatreworksusa.org

Theaterworks USA is a not-for-profit theatre for young audiences. From November through April the group produces shows such as *Phantom of the Opera*, *A Christmas Carol*, and *The Adventures of Huckleberry Finn*. All performances are matinees at the Lucille Lortel Theatre in Greenwich Village.

Cost: $35 ($25 if you purchase four performances)

Ages: Ages 4 and up

Vital Theatre Company

2162 Broadway (at 76th St.)
(212) 579-0528
www.vitaltheatre.org

Original childrens' theatre at weekend matinee performances. Past shows include *Animal of the Year* and *History Time Henry*.

Cost: $15 per ticket, $65 for a Family Pass (5 tickets you can use at multiple performances)

Ages: Varies

PUTNAM COUNTY

Hudson Valley Shakespeare Festival

Boscobel Restoration
Rte. 9D
(845) 265-3638
www.hvshakespeare.org

An energetic, inventive cast performs Shakespeare under a big yellow-and-white striped tent on the grounds of this historic house museum. Productions are usually comedies and are extremely accessible and entertaining, even for young children. HVSF performs June-August. You can picnic on the grounds before the show; either bring your own meal or order one though the box office.

Cost: $20-35 per ticket, depending on performance

Ages: 0 and up

Chapter 8

Family Fun For All Seasons

Summer
Pools & Beaches
Boating
Miniature Golf
Amusement & Water Parks

Fall/Spring
Apple-Picking & Pumpkin Patches
Bowling

Winter
Ice-Skating (Indoor & Outdoor)
Sledding
Skiing, Snowboarding & Tubing

Here's the stuff you really moved to Westchester for. Things that make your city friends green with envy (that is, in addition to not having to cram everything you own into two tiny closets). Pools, beaches, boating and miniature golf in the summer. Picking your own apples and pumpkins in the fall. And, in the winter, lots of choices when it comes to cold-weather fun, like ice-skating, skiing, snowboarding and sledding. So no matter what the season, easy access to all this and more is what suburbia is all about.

SUMMER
Pools & Beaches

When the temperature heats up, it's time to head for the water. In addition to cooling you down, some pools and beaches also offer entertainment to bring out the kid in anyone, including giant pool toys, face painting and deejay music.

While there are plenty of municipal swimming pools in West-chester, most are restricted to town or village residents. We've listed them here for your information; check your local recreation department for hours and opening and closing dates. Fortunately, there is a state park in Westchester with swimming facilities, and the Westchester County Parks system has four beaches and five pools available to all county residents; we've included those list-ings here as well. Most require a Westchester County Park Pass, which is available at many of the county park information centers, as well as at the Westchester County Center (in White Plains) and the Westchester County Parks Department (in Mount Kisco). They cost $45 and are good for up to three years. Each pass allows free admission to county-owned park facilities for the pass holder and up to two guests; children under 12 are also admitted for free. With a pass you get to use all county-owned park facilities and you also receive some discounts in user and parking fees. **For more information, call the Parks Department at (914) 864-PARK (-7275) or visit www.westchestergov.com/parks.**

Hours at all county swimming areas are 10 am to 6:30 pm, but opening and closing dates vary. For kids over 3, there are summer "Learn-to-Swim" classes at Sprain Ridge, Saxon Woods and Tibbetts Brook (children 3-5 must be accompanied by an adult). Registration is required; for more information, call (914) 864-7056.

Bedford
✱ Bedford Hills Park (Haines Rd.)
✱ Bedford Memorial Park (Greenwich Rd., Bedford Village)
✱ Katonah Memorial Park (North St., Katonah)

Briarcliff Manor
✱ Law Memorial Park (Pleasantville Rd.)

Buchanan
✱ Recreation Site (West Ave.)

Cortlandt
✱ Charles J. Cook Recreation Center (Furnace Dock Rd.)
✱ Sprout Brook Park (Sprout Brook Rd.)

Croton-on-Hudson
✱ Croton Point Park Beach (Croton Point Ave.)—County Park, no pass required; open weekends and holidays only

Dobbs Ferry
✱ Gould Park (Ashford Ave.)
✱ Memorial Park (Palisade St.)

Elmsford
✱ Massaro Park (50 Cabot Ave.)

Greenburgh
✱ Anthony F. Veteran Park (11 Olympic Ln., Ardsley)

Savvy Suggestion

Tired of the community pool?
Go to www.swimmingholes.org to find local spots
where you can take a dip. The site lists more than
900 spots in the U.S. and Canada, and rates them
for kid-friendliness.

Harrison

✱ Bernie Guagnini Brentwood Park (Webster Ave.)
✱ John Passidomo Veteran Park (Lake St., W. Harrison)

Lewisboro

✱ Town Park (Rte. 35, South Salem)

Mamaroneck

✱ Hommocks Park Ice Rink & Swimming Pool Complex (Hommocks
Rd. & Rte. 1)

Mount Vernon

✱ Willson's Woods (E. Lincoln Ave.)—County Park Pass required;
Westchester residents only

New Rochelle

✱ Flower's Park/City Park (City Park Rd. off Fifth Ave.)
✱ Glen Island Park Beach (Pelham Rd.)—County Park Pass required;
Westchester residents only
✱ Hudson Park (Hudson Park Rd. off Pelham Rd.)
✱ Lincoln Park (Lincoln Ave.)

North Salem

✱ Spruce Lake at Mountain Lakes Park (Hawley Rd.)—County Park,
no pass required; open weekends and holidays only

Pleasantville

✱ Nannahagen Park (Lake St.)

Pound Ridge

✱ Town Park (Rte. 137)

Rye
★ Playland (Playland Parkway) (See Amusement Parks listing on page 169 for more information)—County Park, no pass required
★ Oakland Beach (Dearborn & Forest)

Scarsdale
★ Municipal Pool (Mamaroneck Rd.)

White Plains
★ Church Street School (Church St.)
★ Gardella Park (Ferris & Park Aves.)
★ Kittrell Park (Bank St. & Fisher Ave.)
★ Post Road School (Post Rd.)
★ Saxon Woods Park (Mamaroneck Ave.)—County Park Pass required for swimming

Yonkers
★ Sprain Ridge Park (Jackson Ave.)—County Park Pass required
★ Tibbetts Brook Park (Midland Ave.)—County Park Pass required; Westchester residents only

Yorktown
★ Franklin D. Roosevelt State Park (2957 Crompond Rd.)
★ Junior Lake Park (Edgewater St., Yorktown Heights)
★ Shrub Oak Park (Sunnyside St. off of Rte. 6, Shrub Oak)
★ Sparkle Lake (Granite Springs Rd., Yorktown Heights)

Savvy Suggestion

"Twilight Swim," from 4 pm until closing, offers reduced admission fees at all county swimming areas, so that residents who work during the day have an opportunity to enjoy the swimming facilities.

Boating

Whether you are looking for a lazy late-summer rowboat outing, a fishing afternoon followed by the traditional "one that got away" story, or maybe an active kayaking excursion, you can find it here. The Westchester County Parks Department permits fishing everywhere except in the nature preserves and where "No Fishing" signs are posted.

You'll need a New York State fishing license; to get one, visit the New York State Department of Environmental Conservation website www.dec.state.ny.us/website/dfwmr/fish/fishregs/fishlicense.html, or call the Westchester County Clerk's office at (914) 995-3080 for more information.

Self-launching sites (where you can access the Hudson River or Long Island Sound with your own boat) require a Parks Pass. Most of the boat rental sites listed below are seasonal; call for more information.

Armonk

Wampus Pond
Rte. 128
(914) 273-3230

Rowboat rentals.

Croton-on-Hudson

Croton Point Park
Croton Point Ave.
(914) 862-5290

Access to the Hudson River for sailboards, canoes and car-top carried boats.

Montrose

George's Island Park
Dutch St.
(914) 737-7530

Access to the Hudson River for boats up to twenty-one feet in length.

New Rochelle

Glen Island Park
Pelham Rd.
(914) 813-6720 (-6721)

Access to Long Island Sound for boats up to twenty-one feet in length.

Rye

Playland Park
Playland Parkway
(914) 813-7000
www.ryeplayland.org

Pedal boat rentals, lake cruises, and self-launching access to Long Island Sound for car-top carried boats and kayaks.

White Plains

Liberty Park
Lake St. at Silver Lake

Paddle boat and rowboat rentals; access to lake for kayaks and rowboats.

Yorktown Heights

Franklin D. Roosevelt State Park
2957 Crompond Rd.
(914) 245-4434

Rowboat rentals

Miniature Golf

Whether it's due to the fun of the game or the pure silliness of hitting a ball into a clown's open mouth, it seems to be a universal truth that kids love miniature golf. It's a great activity for kids as young as 2 or 3, and most grown-ups love it too. Most of these courses are open seasonally, so be sure to check with them before heading out.

Elmsford

Golden Bear Golf Center
300 Waterside Dr.
(914) 592-1666

Cost: $7 adults, $5.50 children

Hours: Weekdays 8 am-10 pm, weekends 7 am-11 pm

Mohegan Lake

Family Golf Center at Yorktown
2710 Lexington Ave.
(914) 526-8337

Cost: $5 adults, $4 children

Hours: April-October, daily 8 am-10 pm; November-May, weekdays 9 am-8 pm, weekends 8 am-8 pm

New Rochelle

Glen Island Park
Pelham Rd.
(914) 813-6720 (-6721)
County Park Pass required for parking.
Cost: $3 adults, $2 children
Hours: Memorial Day–Labor Day, 12-6 pm

Rye

Playland
Playland Parkway
(914) 813-7000
www.ryeplayland.org
Cost: $3.50 per person
Hours: Daily 10 am until one hour before park closing

White Plains

Saxon Woods Park
Mamaroneck Ave.
(914) 995-4480 (-4481)
Cost: $3 adults, $2 children
Hours: Sunday-Thursday 12-8 pm, Friday-Saturday 12-9 pm

Yonkers

Tibbetts Brook Park
Midland Ave.
(914) 231-2865
Cost: $3 adults, $2 children
Hours: Daily 11 am-7 pm

Savvy Suggestion

There's something for everyone at Harbor Island Park—a playground, a beach, a marina, boat launching area, docks and fishing floats, tennis courts, ball fields and picnic tables. There are also restrooms and showers.

Harbor Island Park
Intersection of Mamaroneck Ave. & Boston Post Rd.
Mamaroneck

Amusement & Water Parks

If you're looking for all-day amusement, here are three spots that will keep your family busy for hours. From roller coasters to water rides, bumper boats to games and entertainment, these sites offer something for everyone.

Fishkill

SplashDown Water Park
Adventure Island Family Fun Center
2200 Rte. 9
(845) 896-6606
www.splashdownpark.com

SplashDown features a beach, a wave pool, three large water slides, a pirate ship with five kiddie slides, a large activity pool, a water spray area and a water balloon game. If you don't feel like getting wet, there is also miniature golf, mini basketball and a large picnic area. Adventure Island is an indoor facility with a soft play area with tunnels, tubes, chutes and a ball pit, in addition to a giant slide, bumper cars, bumper boats and games.

Hours: Memorial Day Weekend-Labor Day Weekend, daily 10 am-7 pm; Adventure Island is also open Labor Day Weekend-Memorial Day Weekend, Saturdays and Sundays 11 am-5 pm.

Admission: $17.95-22.50 (depending on height) 10 am-closing, $13.95-17.95 (depending on height) 3 pm-closing; Adventure Island games and activities are extra; for children 2 and younger, you must purchase a SplashDown swimsuit that goes over a diaper.

What to Know Before You Go: Coolers are allowed for picnicking but glass containers and alcoholic beverages are not. Swim attire should not have any rivets, buckles or metal.

Jefferson Valley

Osceola Beach & Picnic Grounds
399 E. Main St.
(914) 245-3246
www.osceolabeach.com

In addition to a beach, this destination spot on Lake Osceola features miniature golf, bumper boats, paddle boats, kayaks, pony rides, a kiddie play park with an air castle, and people dressed up as cartoon characters and clowns. You can buy food from the snack bar, bring your own lunch or cook on their grills. They also offer facilities for hosting birthday parties.

Hours: Open on weekends from Memorial Day through Father's Day, and seven days a week from Father's Day through Labor Day. Park hours are weekdays 9 am-6 pm, weekends and holidays 8 am-6 pm.

Swimming hours are (weather permitting) weekdays 10 am-5 pm, weekends and holidays 10 am-6 pm. The snack bar opens at 11 am.

Admission: Weekdays, $6 adults, $4 children 3-10; weekends and holidays, $10 adults, $6 children 3-10. Price includes parking, admission and beach access. Additional fees apply for miniature golf, pony rides, boating and some other activities.

Rye

Playland
Playland Parkway
(914) 813-7000
www.ryeplayland.org

This amusement park offers over fifty rides for children and adults, including roller coasters, vertical thrills and water rides. Kiddyland has rides for kids ages 2 and over. Playland also has a swimming pool, lake boating and pedal boats, miniature golf, indoor ice-skating, a picnic area, free entertainment, arcade games, and a beach, boardwalk and pier on Long Island Sound. You'll find traditional amusement park foods and snacks, such as pizza, cotton candy, etc., as well as chains such as Burger King, Nathan's, Carvel and Captain Hook's seafood restaurant.

Hours: Hours vary, depending on season, activity and weather—call or check the website for details.

Admission: Tickets cost $1.25 (the per-ticket price is lower if you buy multi-ticket books) and rides cost 2-4 tickets each. Parking is $5 on weekdays, $7 on weekends and $10 on holidays.

What to Know Before You Go: Some Kiddyland rides have height restrictions and many do not allow adults to ride with the children. Use caution when visiting with the weekend mobs—keep an eye on your child at all times.

Savvy Suggestion

A great way to cool off on hot days is to have a family car wash. Kids love the soapy water and spraying the hose. For younger kids put a container of soapy water outside and let them wash their toy cars and rinse them with a hose or water bucket.

FALL/SPRING

Apple-Picking & Pumpkin Patches

There's really nothing like being outside on a beautiful, sunny fall day with fresh air and colorful foliage. But it's even better if you can combine your outdoor time with a fun family activity like apple-picking. Many of the orchards and farms listed here have farm stands featuring their own products, including produce, cider, doughnuts, pies, fresh breads, maple syrup, fudge and various crafts and gift items. Most of them have great fall activities for the kids. After a fun day outdoors, you can return home and make a wonderful apple crisp or pie from your just-picked apples.

There are only three such farms in Westchester, so we've included spots in Dutchess, Orange and Ulster Counties, along with some in Connecticut and New Jersey. In season, Westchester farms are often swarming on weekends; the farther you travel, the more you'll avoid the crowds (and you'll also have a better pick of produce!).

But don't limit your farm visits to autumn—a number of these spots offer fun for other seasons, including pick-your-own berries, peaches and flowers in spring and summer, and choose-your-own Christmas trees in the winter. And some have barnyard animals or zoos, playgrounds and other attractions. Orchards and farms are open seasonally and hours vary; call for more information.

WESTCHESTER COUNTY

Granite Springs

Stuart's Fruit Farm
Granite Springs Rd.
(914) 245-2784
www.farmy.com/stuartsfarm.html

Here you can pick your own pumpkins as well as twenty varieties of apples.

North Salem

Outhouse Orchards
Hardscrabble Rd.
(914) 277-3188

Pick-your-own apples. They have a small zoo of geese, ducks, goats, chickens and rabbits. On fall weekends, they have events such as pony rides, pumpkin picking, farmers market, face painting and hayrides. They also do birthday parties.

Savvy Suggestion

Easy Apple Crisp

Peel and thinly slice ten Macintosh apples. Layer them 3/4 of the way up a baking dish (with or without pie crust). Pour 1/2 cup apple juice over the apples. Combine 3/4 cup flour, 3/4 cup brown sugar and 1 tsp. cinnamon. Cut in 1 stick of butter or margarine. Sprinkle mixture over the apples and pat down. Bake in a preheated 325° F oven for 45 minutes.

Yorktown

Wilkens Fruit and Fir Farm
1335 White Hill Rd.
(914) 245-5111
www.wilkensfarm.com

Pick-your-own apples, raspberries and pumpkins, as well as several acres of "Choose-N-Cut Christmas Trees." A wagon ride takes you to and from the orchard, and two farm markets sell cider, freshly baked pies and doughnuts.

CONNECTICUT

Blue Jay Orchards
125 Plumtree Rd., Bethel
(203) 748-0119
www.bluejayorchards.com

Pick-your-own apples, pears, peaches and pumpkins. In September and October there are hayrides and a maze.

Savvy Suggestion

For more on New York pick-your-own farms and apple festivals, go to **www.nyapplecountry.com.**

Silverman's Farm
451 Sport Hill Rd., Easton
(203) 261-3306
www.silvermansfarm.com

Pick-your-own apples, peaches, plums, nectarines, flowers and pumpkins. There is a cider mill, where you can watch apple cider being made, and an animal farm with buffalo, llamas, sheep, pigs, exotic birds and more. In the fall, there are tractor rides and hayrides. The farm market offers eighteen varieties of freshly baked pies, New England farm-style preserves, jams, jellies, honeys and syrups.

Warrup's Farm
51 John Reed Rd., Redding
(203) 938-9403
www.localharvest.org/listing.jsp?id=4687

Pick-your-own peaches, pumpkins, vegetables, flowers and herbs. There are also maple syrup demonstrations, barnyard animals and, in season, hayrides.

Jones Family Farm
266 Israel Hill Rd., off Rte. 110, Shelton
(203) 929-8425
www.jonesfamilyfarm.com

Pick-your-own strawberries, blueberries and pumpkins, and choose-your-own Christmas trees. In the fall, there are hayrides and horse-drawn wagon rides.

ORANGE COUNTY
Applewood Orchards & Winery
82 Four Corners Rd., Warwick
(845) 986-1684
www.applewoodorchards.com

Pick-your-own apples and pumpkins. In addition to the orchards and winery, there are barnyard animals, including ducks, horses, bunnies and sheep. In the fall, there are hayrides, music and puppet shows.

Pennings Farm Market
161 Rte. 94 S., Warwick
(845) 986-5959
www.penningsfarmmarket.com

Pick-your-own apples. Pennings also features "Barnyard Buddies Feeding Corral," "Pennings Express 'Play-Train'" and a playground. In season, there are hayrides, a haunted house, live music, story telling, pony rides and other activities.

ROCKLAND COUNTY

Dr. Davies Farm
306 Rte. 304, Congers
(845) 268-7020
www.drdaviesfarm.com

Pick-your-own apples and pumpkins, as well as hayrides and a farm market with cider, fresh baked apple pies and chocolate chip cookies. Perhaps most importantly, there are wagons to pull the kids in as you walk through the orchard.

DUTCHESS COUNTY

Keepsake Farm Market & Country Bake Shop
9 Fishkill Farms Rd., Hopewell Junction
(845) 897-2266
www.keepsakeorchards.com

Pick-your-own apples, strawberries, raspberries, blackberries, blueberries, peaches, cherries and pumpkins. There is also a petting zoo and seasonal activities, including hayrides, live music and live wood carving demonstrations.

Dykeman's Farm
231 West Dover Rd., Pawling
(845) 832-6068
www.bestcorn.com

Pick-your-own raspberries, apples, flowers, winter squash, pumpkins and a wide variety of other vegetables, including tomatoes and peppers. During pumpkin season, there are hayrides, refreshments, face painting and other events.

Barton Orchards
63 Apple Tree Ln., Poughquag
(845) 227-2306
www.bartonorchards.com

Pick-your-own strawberries, raspberries, blueberries, peaches, apples and pumpkins. There's also a petting zoo and a playground. In the fall, enjoy weekend Harvest Festivals, with live entertainment, pony rides, hayrides and a corn maze.

ULSTER COUNTY

Apple Hill Farm
141 Rte. 32 S., New Paltz
(845) 255-1605
applehillfarm.com

Pick-your-own apples, pumpkins and gourds. You can buy home-grown fruit, fresh apple cider and apple cider donuts in their restored 1859 barn.

NEW JERSEY

Abma's Farm
700 Lawlin's Rd., Wyckoff
(201) 891-0278
www.abmasfarm.com

In addition to a large pumpkin patch, this farm offers a small petting zoo, pony rides and hayrides. There is also an eighteenth-century barn where you can buy fresh produce, eggs, poultry and specialty products.

Bowling

What is it about bowling that kids love so much? The crash when the ball hits the pins? The sense of mastery when they knock down some pins? We're not sure, but now that our kids are a little older, we've found it's the perfect thing for turning a boring, late autumn Sunday afternoon into a fun time for the whole family. Even younger children, with a little luck (and a little help), can propel the ball down the lane and knock down a few pins—something that is sure to fill them with glee.

All of the bowling centers listed below have bumpers for small children. Many offer other activities, such as video games and billiards, and most have a snack bar. League play takes up most lanes on evenings and weekends, so be sure to call for hours and availability before you go. Also, the costs listed below do not include shoe rentals.

Jefferson Valley Bowl
3699 Hill Blvd., Jefferson Valley
(914) 245-7771

Twenty-four lanes, a snack bar, video games, billiards, foosball and air hockey.

Cost: Weekdays $3.25 per person, evenings and weekends $4 per person

New Roc 'n Bowl
New Roc City, 33 LeCount Pl. (Exit 16 off I-95), New Rochelle
(914) 637-7575
www.newroccity.com

In addition to seventeen lanes of bowling, this site has glow-in-the-dark bowling, air hockey, virtual bowling, foosball and a deejay on Friday and Saturday nights.

Cost: $3-7 per game, depending on day of week and time of day

Savvy Suggestion

Delight your child with a train ride. Pick a destination on your local train route that you'd both like to explore. Most towns have plenty of stores, casual restaurants or diners, and places of interest near the train station.

Cortlandt Lanes

2292 Crompond Rd., Peekskill

(914) 737-4550

Thirty-eight lanes, a restaurant, a bar and a snack bar.

Cost: Weekdays $4 per person, evenings and weekends $4.50 per person

AMF White Plains Lanes

47 Tarrytown Rd., White Plains

(914) 948-2677

www.amfcenters.com

Fifty-six lanes, a snack bar and video games.

Cost: Weekdays $5.50 per person, evenings and weekends $6.50 per person

Cross County Lanes

790 Yonkers Ave., Yonkers

(914) 423-2088

Twenty lanes, a bar, a snack bar and video games.

Cost: Weekdays $3.50 adults, $2.50 children; evenings and weekends $4.75 per person

Homefield Bowl

938 Saw Mill River Rd. Yonkers

(914) 969-5592

Thirty-two lanes, a bar, a snack bar and video games.

Cost: Weekdays $3.50 adults, $2.50 children; evenings and weekends $4.75 per person

Savvy Suggestion

Bowl-At-Home

Decorate empty soda bottles or cardboard paper towel tubes with paint, markers or stickers and arrange them as "bowling pins." You and your child can "bowl" by rolling or tossing a rolled-up pair of socks or a small, soft ball at the "pins."

CONNECTICUT

Bowlarama III
109 Hamilton Ave., Stamford
(203) 323-1041

Twenty lanes, a snack bar and video games.

Cost: $5 per person

WINTER

Ice-Skating

For all you parents out there who have dreams of one day seeing your little ones in an "Ice Spectacular" or recruited by the NHL, you'll be glad to know that there are many places to ice-skate in Westchester.

Below we've listed a selection of both indoor and outdoor ice rinks. For more skating spots, check out "Community Playgrounds" and "County & State Parks" in Chapter 5. Outdoor facilities are, of course, seasonal, as are some of the indoor facilities. Call for specific opening and closing information, since many rinks open and close throughout the day and have specific times set aside for lessons, hockey clubs and free skate/public skating sessions. All of the indoor facilities listed here offer figure skating, hockey, free skate and lessons; some have skate rental, and most offer birthday parties. At the outdoor sites ice-skating is permitted seven days a week during the daylight hours, weather permitting and when the sign "Skating Today" is posted.

INDOOR SKATING

Elmsford

Westchester Skating Academy
91 Fairview Park Dr.
(914) 347-8232
www.skatewsa.com
Cost: $8.50 adults, $7.50 children

Katonah

Harvey School Rink
260 Jay St. (Rte. 22)
(914) 232-3618
Cost: $5 per half hour

Larchmont

Hommocks Park Ice Rink
Boston Post Rd. & Weaver St.
(914) 834-3164
Cost: $6 adults, $5 children (non-residents); $4 adults, $3.50 children (Mamaroneck residents)

Mount Vernon

The Ice Hutch
655 Garden Ave.
(914) 699-6787
Cost: $6 per person

New Rochelle

New Roc Ice at New Roc City
33 LeCount Pl. (Exit 16 off I-95), New Rochelle
(914) 637-7575
www.newroccity.com
Cost: $8 per person

Rye

Playland Ice Casino
Playland Parkway
(914) 813-7010
www.ryeplayland.org/IceCasino
Cost: $6 adults, $4 children under 12

Yonkers
Edward J. Murray Memorial Skating Center
348 Tuckahoe Rd.
(914) 377-6469

Cost: $5 adults, $3.50 children

CONNECTICUT
Stamford Twin Rinks
1063 Hope St., Stamford
(203) 968-9000
www.icecenter.com

Cost: $7 adults, $5 children 12 and under

ROCKLAND COUNTY
Palisades Center Ice Rink
1000 Palisades Center Dr. (The Palisades Center Mall), West Nyack
(845) 353-4855
www.palice.com

Cost: $7 adults, $5 children

OUTDOOR SKATING

Bronxville
Bronxville Lake at Bronx River Reservation
(914) 723-4058

Peekskill
Blue Mountain Reservation
Welcher Ave.
(914) 862-5275

Valhalla
The Reflecting Pool at Kensico Dam Plaza Park
(914) 328-1542

Yonkers
Tibbetts Brook Park
Midland Ave.
(914) 864-7275

There's also a great hill for sledding!

Savvy Suggestion

Here's what to do when your child outgrows his ice skates in just one season: trade them in towards a new pair of skates for next year at Bob Peck's Skate and Sport Shop, 31 Lake St., 2nd floor, White Plains, (914) 949-0579. The trade-in value is generally $15-35, depending on the condition of the skates.

Sledding

Nothing brings back the memories of childhood winters like sledding. We remember using trashbags and lunch trays when a "proper" sled or toboggan was not on hand—and how good the hot chocolate tasted after our adventures—but, most of all, we remember the fun. You may have already found your favorite slope in a neighbor's back yard or on your local school grounds— or, like us, (discreetly) on the nearby golf course—but if not, check out the following sledding locations. For more information on sledding spots, call the Westchester County Parks Department at (914) 864-PARKS or visit www.westchestergov.com/parks.

Cortlandt

Croton Gorge
Rte. 129
(914) 827-9568

Cross River

Ward Pound Ridge Reservation
Rtes. 35 & 121 S.
(914) 864-7317

Somers

Lasdon Park, Arboretum & Veterans Memorial
Rte. 35
(914) 864-7268

Yonkers

Tibbetts Brook Park
Midland Ave.
(914) 231-2865

Skiing, Snowboarding & Tubing

For grown-ups, winter brings such enjoyable activities as digging out the car before work or shoveling the driveway, but for kids it's a chance for some *real* outdoor fun. Even before he learned the cause-and-effect of snow and snow days, Sam got excited when it would snow and, at age six, he took to skiing like he'd been born in the Alps. For younger kids, tubing (with a parent) is a great option. Many of the places listed below have kid-friendly bunny slopes, lessons for new skiers (some even offer free lessons for first-time skiers) and on-premise nurseries for those not yet slope-ready. For your little snow bunnies, here's a selection of mountains where you can take advantage of the white stuff this winter. Some of these sites can be done as daytrips, while others require at least an overnight stay; check the resort websites for recommendations on lodging.

HUDSON VALLEY

Holiday Mountain
Monticello
(845) 796-3161
www.holidaymtn.com

Skiing, snowboarding, tubing

Savvy Suggestion

Enjoy high tea with Madeline, as her favorite dishes—including Bemelmans Teany Burgers and Fries, Pepitos Crudités and Dips, Petite Banana Splits Fontainebleau, and Eiffel Tower Hot Fudge Sundaes—are served on linen and china. Bemelmans Bar is named for the author of the children's book series, who covered the walls with painted illustrations of his characters in 1947 in order to pay for 18 months of room and board at the hotel. High tea is held Fridays, Saturdays and Sundays, 12-4 pm. ($20 minimum per person; reservations are required.)

The Madeline Tea Party
Carlyle Hotel, Bemelmans Bar
35 E 76th St (at Madison), New York
(212) 744-1600
www.thecarlyle.com

Mount Peter Ski Area
Warwick
(845) 986-4992
www.mtpeter.com

Skiing, snowboarding

Thunder Ridge Ski Area
Patterson
(845) 878-4100
www.thunderridgeski.com

Skiing, snowboarding

CONNECTICUT

Mohawk Mountain Ski Area
Cornwall
(860) 672-6100
www.mohawkmtn.com

Skiing, snowboarding

Mount Southington Ski Area
Plantsville
(860) 628-0954
www.mountsouthington.com

Skiing, snowboarding

Powder Ridge Ski Area
Middlefield
(860) 349-3454
www.powderridgect.com

Skiing, snowboarding, tubing

Ski Sundown
New Hartford
(860) 379-7669
www.skisundown.com

Skiing, snowboarding

Woodbury Ski Area
Woodbury
(203) 263-2203
www.woodburyskiarea.com

Skiing, snowboarding, tubing, cross-country skiing, sledding

NEW JERSEY

Campqaw Mountain
Mahwah
(201) 327-7800
www.skicampgaw.com

Skiing, snowboarding, tubing

Hidden Valley
Vernon
(973) 764-4200
www.hiddenvalleynj.com

Skiing, snowboarding, tubing

Mountain Creek
Vernon
(973) 827-2000
www.mountaincreek.com

Skiing, snowboarding, tubing

CATSKILLS AREA (NEW YORK)

Belleayre Mountain
Highmount
(800) 942-6904
www.belleayre.com

Skiing, snowboarding

Bobcat Ski Center
Andes
(845) 676-3143
www.mcintoshauction.com/bobcat.html

Skiing, snowboarding

...Savvy Suggestion

Westchester County Park Pass holders can receive discounts on lift tickets and ski rentals at over a dozen nearby ski areas, including Catamount, Hunter, Windham, Berkshire East and Ski Butternut. Discounts on rental packages are also available at Hickory & Tweed in Armonk, Pedigree in White Plains, and Ski, Skate & Board in Tuckahoe.

Savvy Suggestion

For more detailed information on ski areas, including facilities, vertical drop, number of lifts and trails, trail ratings (beginner/intermediate/advanced) and user reviews, organized by state, check out: www.skitown.com/resortguide/usamap.cfm

Cortina Mountain
Haines Falls
(518) 589-6378
www.cortinamountain.com

Skiing, snowboarding, snow skating, tubing

Hunter Mountain
Hunter
(800) 486-8376
www.huntermtn.com

Cross-country skiing, skiing, snow shoeing, snowboarding, tubing

Plattekill Mountain
Roxbury
(800) 633-3275
www.plattekill.com

Cross-country skiing, skiing, snowboarding, tubing

Sawkill Family Ski Center
Kingston
(845) 336-6977
www.sawkillski.com

Skiing, snowboarding, tubing

Titus Mountain
Malone
(800) TITUS-MN
www.titusmountain.com

Skiing, snowboarding, tubing

Villa Roma Ski Area
Callicoon
(845) 887-4880
www.villaroma.com

Skiing, snowboarding, tubing, mini-snowmobiles

Windham Mountain
Windham
(800) 754-9463
www.windhammountain.com

Skiing, snowshoeing, snowboarding, tubing

BERKSHIRES

Berkshire East
Charlemont, MA
(413) 339-6617
www.berkshireeast.com

Skiing, snowboarding

Catamount Ski Area
Hillsdale, NY
(800) 342-1840
www.catamountski.com

Skiing, snowboarding

Jiminy Peak Mountain
Hancock, MA
(413) 738-5500
www.jiminypeak.com

Skiing, snowboarding, tubing

Ski Butternut
Great Barrington, NY
(413) 528-2000
www.skibutternut.com

Cross-country skiing, skiing, snowboarding, tubing

Savvy Superlatives

Our Seasonal Favorites for a Family Saturday

Winter: Skiing at a local slope
Spring: "Meet the Baby Animals" at Muscoot Farm
Summer: A day at Playland, followed by dinner
Fall: Apple-picking at any area orchard

Chapter 9

Surf & Turf

Aquariums

Zoos & Farms

Kids love to watch animals, and trips to the local zoo or aquarium are a fondly remembered part of almost everyone's childhood. Whether it's watching the animals perform at a seal show (or performing for them, as Laura's sons like to do for the gorillas at the Bronx Zoo), or actually feeding and interacting with them at a petting zoo, these trips are wonderful chances for your children to broaden their awareness of other species beyond the family pet. An aquarium visit can be an excellent winter trip when the weather prevents you from doing anything outdoors and, conversely, can also be a cooling indoor respite from hot summer days. Zoo exhibits often vary by season, and their accompanying educational programs can provide your kids with the opportunity to learn about habitats, conservation and more. Who knows? Maybe your child will be inspired to be the next Jacques Cousteau or Jane Goodall.

AQUARIUMS

Although there aren't any aquariums in Westchester, we are well-situated to take advantage of a couple that are nearby. When planning your visit, call ahead or check the website for feeding times or other events; these shows can get very crowded, but they're worth it. Try to get there early to get situated and bring something to distract your child while you're waiting—perhaps a book, a small toy or a snack if they're allowed (we're thinking Goldfish crackers). As with other attractions, aquariums are very crowded on weekends, particularly in the winter; again, getting there early is usually a good idea.

Brooklyn

New York Aquarium
Surf Avenue & West 8th St.
(718) 265-FISH
www.nyaquarium.com

New York Aquarium is part of the Wildlife Conservation Society consortium, which includes the Bronx Zoo, and boasts exhibits featuring over 8,000 animals. Learn about animals living as far away as the Southwest coast of Africa and the Arctic and as close as our own Hudson River. There is an Aquatheater marine mammal demonstration featuring California sea lions, and don't miss feeding time for the sharks, penguins, walruses and sea otters.

Hours: June-August, weekdays 10 am-6 pm, weekends and holidays 10 am-7 pm; September-May, daily 10 am-5 pm

Admission: $12 adults, $8 for children ages 2-12, free for children under 2. Annual memberships are available and are also valid at the Bronx, Central Park, Prospect Park and Queens Zoos.

What to Know Before You Go: It is important to dress for the weather because the Aquarium has both indoor and outdoor exhibits. In terms of eating, there's the SeaSide Cafe (with an ocean view) as well as outdoor vending carts. Picnic tables are available on the Plaza area.

Connecticut

Maritime Aquarium at Norwalk
10 Water St., Norwalk
(203) 852-9700
www.maritimeaquarium.org

A small, "doable" aquarium featuring more than 1,000 marine animals native to the Long Island Sound and its watershed. Exhibits include an indoor-outdoor tank for harbor seals; the 110,000-gallon "Open Ocean" tank, with nine-foot sharks, bluefish, striped bass, rays and other creatures; the sea turtle tank; and the Touch Tank, with sea stars, crabs and other tidal creatures. In "Ocean Playspace," kids up to age 5 can enjoy soft play structures, a Titanic play ship, and dressing up with life jackets, fins and flippers. There are also other special exhibits and an IMAX theater.

Hours: September-June, daily 10 am-5 pm; July-August, daily 10 am-6 pm; closed Thanksgiving and Christmas Day

Admission: $10.50 adults, $9.50 children 2-12; additional charge for IMAX films

What to Know Before You Go: Seal feedings are at 11:45 am, 1:45 pm and 3:45 pm daily. There are good food stands and cafés inside.

No outside food or drink is allowed. The aquarium is located in the historic waterfront neighborhood of South Norwalk ("SoNo"), which has many boutiques, eclectic shops, delis and restaurants.

ZOOS & FARMS

Nothing fascinates preschoolers and young children like a visit with our furry friends—that's the theory at least. When he was younger, Laura's son Sam was far more interested in the school buses in the parking lot than in the "exotic" animals inside the zoo. But as the years went by he became much more intrigued by lions, tigers and bears—and by chasing the chickens and ducks. Honestly, for the first few years of your children's lives, you should probably look at trips to a zoo or farm as something fun and different for you, not them. Your children's abilities to appreciate their surroundings will eventually follow.

Pocantico Hills
Stone Barns Center for Food and Agriculture
630 Bedford Rd.
(914) 366-6200
www.stonebarnscenter.org

A beautiful, non-profit working farm, Stone Barns is home to eighty acres of gardens, pastures and woods, as well as an educational center for sustainable, ecological farming. Explore the farm on your own (pick up a self-guided brochure or audio tour in the Silo Lobby) or join a guided walking tour on weekends to get a close-up look at the produce, cows, sheep, pigs, horses, chickens, ducks and more. Stone Barns also holds family programs that include storytimes, farm activities, tours and craft/science activities. Twice a month, on alternate Sundays at 1 pm, there is a "Family Chore" for young children and parents; check the website for details. There is also a summer camp for kids ages 5-12. This is a relatively new facility and they are introducing activities all the time, so check the website for more information.

Hours: Summer, Wednesday-Sunday 10 am-5 pm; Winter, Wednesday-Sunday 11 am-4 pm

Admission: Free

What to Know Before You Go: The Blue Hill Café has a variety of gourmet and child-friendly foods. If you're bringing a stroller, keep in mind that it can be difficult to maneuver when you're walking around the farm.

Sleepy Hollow
Philipsburgh Manor
Rte. 9
(914) 631-3992

This stone manor house was once owned by the Philipse family, one of the wealthiest families in New York and one of the largest slaveholders in the region. Now a living history museum, the site features a 1680s Manor House, a working eighteenth-century barn and water-powered grist mill, and a reconstructed tenant farmhouse. The grounds are home to historic breeds of cattle, sheep and chickens. There are hands-on exhibits and tours featuring scripted vignettes. Picnic facilities overlook the mill-pond, and the Greenhouse Café is open from May through October. Tours of Kykuit, the Rockefeller Estate, leave from here, but they're not appropriate for children under 10.

Hours: March, weekends 10 am-4 pm; April-October, Wednesday-Monday 10 am-5 pm; November-December, Wednesday-Monday 10 am-4 pm

Admission: $9 adults, $5 children 5-17, free for children under 5

Somers
Muscoot Farm
Rte. 100
(914) 864-7282
www.co.westchester.ny.us/parks

Owned by Westchester County, Muscoot Farm covers 777 acres. Visitors can walk through the Dairy Barn, Milk House, Ice House, Blacksmith Shop and several other barns and buildings. There are more than seven miles of hiking trails; trail maps are available in the Reception Center. Popular annual events for families include "Meet the Baby Animals," "Tractor Day" and pumpkin picking. Muscoot offers other events, as well as a variety of Saturday work-shops throughout the year. Hayrides are offered from May through October on Sunday afternoons, weather permitting.

Hours: Daily, 10 am-4 pm

Cost: Hayrides-$2 per person

What to Know Before You Go: On weekends from May to October a variety of foods and beverages are available. Visitors are not allowed to pet or feed the farm animals. Dogs are not allowed.

Yonkers

Stew Leonards
1 Stew Leonard Dr.
(914) 375-4700
www.stewleonards.com

Hailed as the "Disneyland of Dairy Stores" by the New York Times, Stew Leonard's has a petting and feeding zoo, as well as animatronics throughout the store. A big plus: you can get your shopping done at the same time! They also have two locations in Connecticut.

Hours: Daily, 8 am-10 pm

Cost: Free

MANHATTAN, THE BRONX & QUEENS

Bronx Zoo
Fordham Rd. & Bronx River Parkway (Exit 6), Bronx
(718) 367-1010
www.bronxzoo.com

The largest metropolitan zoo in the nation, The Bronx Zoo has more than 6,000 animals. There are many wonderful exhibits, including JungleWorld, the Himalayan Highlands, and the Congo Gorilla Forest, where you can get nose-to-nose with Western lowland gorillas. The Children's Zoo has a petting and feeding zoo for the little ones and offers other programs for families, preschoolers and older kids (additional fees apply). Food is available at several cafes and snack stands, some with seating. One last thing: the Zoo is massive, so even if you have a child who loves to walk it's a good idea to bring or rent a stroller.

Hours: April-October, weekdays 10 am-5 pm, weekends and holidays 10 am-5:30 pm; November-March, daily 10:30 am-4:30 pm

Admission: $8 adults, $6 children 2-12, free for children under 2, $6 seniors (65+); free on Wednesday (but the suggested donation is the same as the general admission price); Children's Zoo—$2 per person; parking—$8; additional entry fees apply for some exhibits, such as the Congo Gorilla Forest. Annual memberships can be purchased and are good for admission to The Central Park, Prospect Park, and Queens Zoos, as well as the New York Aquarium.

What to Know Before You Go: For the Children's Zoo, go to Parking Lot C (Corona)—take Exit #7 off the Bronx River Parkway. Strollers must be collapsed on rides and checked or left outside at some exhibits. Rental strollers are available ($6/day for a single, $10/day for a double).

Central Park Zoo
830 Fifth Ave., Manhattan
(212) 861-6030
www.wcs.org/home/zoos/centralpark

Made even more popular with the younger set because of the movies *Madagascar* and *The Wild*, children are sure to love this attraction. Here you can visit a rain forest and an Antarctic habitat, and see more than 1,400 animals—right in the middle of Manhattan. The new Tisch Children's Zoo lets kids see animals up close. And don't forget the sea lion feedings! The zoo also offers a variety of education classes, programs and special events. Snacks and beverages are available in The Café.

Hours: November-March, daily 10 am-4:30 pm; April-October, weekdays 10 am-5 pm, weekends and holidays 10 am-5:30 pm

Admission: $8 adults, $3 children 3-12, free for children under 3, $4 seniors (65+)

What to Know Before You Go: Enter Central Park at 65th St. & 5th Ave. and walk south one block. Other attractions within walking distance are Wollman Rink, a little further west in Central Park, and the FAO Schwartz flagship store at 59th St. & 5th Ave.

Savvy Suggestion

When you consider admission costs, parking and extra fees for some attractions, becoming a member of the Wildlife Conservation Society can make sense even if you use it just a few times a year. You can join online at **www.wcs.org**. Membership packages, which start at $75, entitle you to free admission to The Bronx, Central Park, Prospect Park and Queens Zoos as well as the New York Aquarium, and provide you with certain discounts and the opportunity to attend several free members-only events.

Savvy Suggestion

Are you a member of a local zoo? When traveling, check reciprocal agreements—more than 100 zoos around the country have agreements that provide members free admission.

Queens Zoo

53-51 111th St., Flushing Meadows Corona Park, Queens
(718) 271-1500
www.queenszoo.com

The Queens Zoo is a tribute to American animals, including bison, mountain lions, California sea lions and bald eagles. With the feel of a small national park, the zoo's paths meander from the Great Plains to the California coast to a Northeast forest.

Hours: November-March, daily 10 am-4:30 pm; April-October, weekdays 10 am-5 pm, weekends and holidays 10 am-5:30 pm

Admission: $6 adults, $2 children 3-12, free for children under 3, $2.25 seniors (65+)

CONNECTICUT

Beardsley Zoo

1875 Noble Ave., Bridgeport
(203) 394-6565
www.beardsleyzoo.org

Located on fifty-two acres of Beardsley Park, this zoo has more than 300 animals, including some endangered species. Exhibits include: a South American rain forest; a New England Farmyard with goats, cows, pigs, sheep and more; and a Victorian Carousel Museum with restored antique horses and rides. There is a restaurant, a snack bar and a picnic grove.

Hours: Daily, 9 am-4 pm; closed Thanksgiving, Christmas Day and New Year's Day; New World Tropics Building—daily 10:30 am-3:30 pm; Carousel Museum—seasonally 10:30 am-4 pm

Admission: $9 adults, $7 children 3-11, free for children under 3

Heckscher Farm at Stamford Museum & Nature Center

39 Scofieldtown Rd., Stamford

(203) 322-1646

www.stamfordmuseum.org/farm.html

This traditional working farm encompasses ten acres, with pigs, cows, goats, chickens and more. Walkways are paved, so strollers have easy access. Special seasonal events include spring planting, summer picking, fall apple cidering and winter crafts. A big draw: Nature's Playground, where kids can scale a spider's web, zoom down an otter slide or climb into a hawk's nest to survey their territory. The playground also has a picnic area.

Hours: Heckscher Farm—daily 9 am-4 pm; Nature's Playground—daily 9 am-5 pm; closed July 4th, Thanksgiving, Christmas Day and New Year's Day.

Admission: $6 adults; $5 children 3-14; free for children under 3 and for members

What to Know Before You Go: Visit from 10 am-noon or 3-5 pm to interact with the farm staff as they do their chores: feeding the animals, cleaning the barns, milking cows or goats, or collecting eggs.

DUTCHESS COUNTY

Trevor Zoo at Millbrook School

290 Millbrook School Rd. (off Rte. 44), Millbrook

(845) 677-3704

www.millbrook.org/oncampus/zoo.asp

Founded in 1936 by Frank Trevor, Millbrook School's first biology teacher, who wanted to share his passion for wildlife with all people, especially students. Today the zoo is an integral part of Millbrook School and holds more than 120 exotic and indigenous animals. In 1989 the zoo was accredited by the AZA (American Zoo and Aquarium Association). Because The Trevor Zoo is part of a college preparatory school, its educational mission extends to all zoo visitors, who will gain a greater understanding of wildlife and the natural world during their time at this very unique (and manageable) zoo.

Hours: Daily 8 am-5 pm

Admission: $4 adults, $2 children. Note that admission for groups other than families is by appointment only.

Chapter 10

Whining & Dining

"Restaurant Readiness"
(For Your Child & You)

Restaurant Tips

Hibachi, Mariachi & More:
Our Top Picks for Family-Friendly Restaurants

When we wrote the first edition of KidSavvy, our perspective was naturally molded by Sam and Simon, our toddlers. Our experiences of taking the children to restaurants were often focused on wanting to grab a bite and praying that we would leave with both the restaurant and our dignity relatively intact. So we offered lots of suggestions about the "how" of eating out with your kids and less about the "where."

As kids get older, they begin to make their tastes and preferences known. That doesn't automatically mean that you are doomed to a future of fast-food burgers and pizza. Research shows that exposing kids to a wide variety of foods is a good thing for them, so if you can, get them to try different things. Who knows? Your child may turn out to be a sushi maven or have a passion for gnocchi— but just to be safe, it can't hurt to have a small stash of crackers or something you know they'll eat if your attempt at feeding them exotic cuisine is a flop.

Laura's sons Sam and Ben are "good eaters" and enjoy a wide range of foods that are not breaded and deep-fried or reconstituted (but, of course, they like lots of foods that are). Betsy's son, on the other hand, has a very limited repertoire made all the more difficult by his dislike of typical "kid food." And trust us, it's not for lack of exposure or attempts to broaden his horizons. Betsy reassures herself that Simon will probably not go off to college still eating only bacon and cereal, but until then their dining options are limited to the most family-friendly of restaurants.

"RESTAURANT READINESS"
(For Your Child & You)

There are a few things to keep in mind when evaluating how "restaurant ready" your little one is.

First, Let's Talk About What "Family-Friendly" Means

Do you mean the hostess won't give you the hairy eyeball when you request a high chair? Do you mean you can leave a pile of half-eaten french fries and Cheerios under your child's chair without fear of being banned for life? Or do you mean that the other diners in the restaurant won't cluck their tongues and roll their eyes when you are seated next to them? While your odds are likely better at more informal spots, the truth is that any and all of these things can happen at any place from the most casual to the most formal restaurant.

What Is My Child's Temperament?

Can he sit quietly playing with a spoon for hours or will he squirm and scream after five minutes of restricted mobility? Temperament is important, and age has a lot to do with it. Once, Betsy was sitting in a restaurant with Simon, then eighteen months old and screaming his head off. A woman sitting at the next table looked over and smiled sympathetically. "Now I remember why I don't do this often," Betsy said, feeling miserable. "Oh, I've been taking Tyler to restaurants since she was born," the mother responded smugly. "I wanted her to get used to them." It turned out Tyler was only nine months old—a much easier age for restaurant visits (assuming they're not walking yet!). "Just wait six months," Betsy said with a grin.

On the one hand, your children will certainly never get used to restaurants if you never take them to one, on the other, at a certain age some kids discover that crawling under the table is much more interesting than sitting at it. Although Laura has a friend who swears that her impeccable table manners are the result of frequent childhood visits to the likes of Le Cirque, only you know how much "table time" your child can tolerate, so do yourself and every diner a favor: follow your kid's lead.

What Can I Put Up With?

Will you mind if your child crawls under the table? Will you be embarrassed if he pulls the "table cloth trick"? Do you have the energy and patience to simultaneously entertain her and eat a

Caesar salad? Ben will sit quietly on Laura's lap for hours if she sings "The Itsy Bitsy Spider" over and over—but that's no way to spend dinner. (Although after a couple of glasses of wine, it's not so bad.) Here's the thing: particularly in the case of toddlers, don't expect more than they can give. If you can keep the volume down, minimize disruptions to other diners and have a relatively pleasant outing, call it a success. Don't be too hard on yourself—or your children, if they act a little like children. And remember, practice makes (almost) perfect, so even if one outing doesn't go exactly the way you imagined it would (and what meal with kids ever does?), give it another shot.

What Is the Purpose of This Meal?

Are you trying to catch up with a girlfriend you haven't seen since you had the baby? Are you attempting to have a much-needed romantic night out with your husband? Do you just want to get out of the house? Whatever the situation, know that if you bring your child, at a certain point you may be required to give the little one sitting next to you more attention than the grown-up seated across from you. Take Betsy's thirtieth birthday, for example. A close friend took her to lunch at the restaurant in the upscale store Barney's. As soon as the food arrived they had to send it back to be wrapped up to go, then ate their meal in the bathroom so that her friend could comfortably breast-feed.

If you really want to be able to relax and enjoy your friend's company, try doing it over coffee. That way, no one is waiting for a waitress to reappear and if you have to leave abruptly you haven't ruined a perfectly good meal. The less pressure you put on yourself and your child, the more relaxed you'll be.

If you're trying to reconnect with your spouse over a nice meal, we strongly suggest that you take up your parents or in-laws on their offer to babysit. If you don't have any friends or family nearby, bite the bullet and hire someone for a few hours. Skipping dessert or choosing a slightly less expensive place will make the cost of the babysitter easier to swallow.

RESTAURANT TIPS

Ok, ready to go out to eat? Here are a few tips to chew on.

Choose your place wisely. Yes, you can get nasty, withering looks at a diner just as easily as you can at an exclusive French restaurant, but somehow it's easier to deal with when you're in jeans rather than formalwear and the entrees cost less than $25. So choose wisely. If your child spills strained peas all over the tray at a fast-food restaurant, it's really no big deal. Old-fashioned diners—which are ubiquitous in Westchester—generally have speedy service and a high tolerance for messiness, which is critical when you venture out with young children.

Go at off-hours. When a restaurant is slower, the service is faster. Go to dinner at 5 or 5:30 pm, before the place fills up. This is also a great end-of-the-day activity, leaving you only bath and bedtime to deal with when you get home.

Line up your requests like dominoes. When your child is very young, order something for them as soon as you are seated—that plate of french fries may buy you valuable time as you wait for the rest of the food to arrive. Ask for the check before you're ready for it, so you're not stuck searching for a waiter as your toddler— ready to go—dissolves into hysterics. If they require that you pay at the register (which is always a little annoying) it's helpful to have a few singles in your wallet for the tip so that you don't have to return to the table once you've packed up all your paraphernalia.

Don't forget your bag of tricks. Bring along some age-appropriate toys for your children, like paper and crayons, matchbox cars or dolls, Legos, stickers and a small book or two. Add a few new things to the bag every now and again; not only will the toys occupy the kids before or after they've eaten, but they'll look forward to playing with toys that they don't see that often. Another benefit is that you'll always have the bag ready and waiting, saving you valuable time as you're trying to get out the door. For lighter travelers, keep a small box or Ziploc of crayons in your purse.

Be creative with your environment. Look around: kid-friendly activities may be right at your fingertips. When Sam was younger, Laura often kept him occupied until the food came by building a house with sugar packets (by the way, she says sugar substitutes work best), identifying letters on the ketchup bottle, or counting the people in the restaurant. Now that he's older, practicing reading with the menu helps pass the time. And on a trip to Spain, she kept him placated at late-night tapas feasts with dinner table readings of *James and the Giant Peach.*

B.Y.O. Always bring a stash of food you know your child will eat: Goldfish, cereal, yogurt, baby food, whatever. Even if your child is typically a really good eater, it never hurts to have a back-up plan just in case.

Make eating out a special event. Let your child know that going on this and future outings depends on their good behavior. As an added incentive, have certain foods, drinks, or desserts be "restaurant only" items—things your child can have only outside the home. This will not only reinforce good behavior but will also make the trip seem more special.

HIBACHI, MARIACHI & MORE: OUR TOP PICKS FOR FAMILY-FRIENDLY RESTAURANTS

Hibachi: Japanese Restaurants

Now this is hot. Everyone can enjoy watching the chef turn out mouthwatering masterpieces with theatrical flair as the shrimp go flying and a tower of onions form an edible volcano. There are several hibachi restaurants in Westchester and the surrounding area. Many have wonderful atmospheres and added features like koi ponds and excellent sushi.

Abis Japanese Traditional Cuisine
www.abisrestaurant.com

Abis has three locations:
406 Mamaroneck Ave.
Mamaroneck, NY
(914) 698-8777

14 Marble Ave. (Chestnut St.)
Thornwood, NY
(914) 741-5100

381 Greenwich Ave.
Greenwich, CT
(203) 862-9100

Edo Japanese Steak House
4787 Boston Post Rd. (between Fowler & Pelhamdale Aves.)
Pelham, NY
(914) 738-1413

Gasho of Japan
2 Saw Mill River Rd. (Skyline Dr.)
Hawthorne, NY
(914) 592-5900

Ichiro Hibachi Sushi & Bar
875 Saw Mill River Rd.
Ardsley, NY
(914) 478-8588

Kang Suh
2375 Central Park Ave. (Jackson Ave.)
Yonkers, NY
(914) 771-4066

Kira Sushi
575 Main St. (School St.)
Armonk Town Center
Armonk, NY
(914) 765-0800

Mt. Fuji Sushi
176 North Bedford Rd.
Mount Kisco, NY
(914) 666-2348

Noda Restaurant
200 Hamilton Ave.
White Plains, NY
(914) 949-0990
www.nodarestaurant.com

Mariachi: Mexican Restaurants

Most Mexican restaurants are fun and friendly, and these three
spots are no exception: they even have wandering Mariachi bands.
These restaurants are noisy enough to not mind lively children, and
Tequila Sunrise has a separate bar area too, so you can keep a safe
distance from the tequila shooters (or discretely pop over for one
of your own).

Tequila Sunrise
145 Larchmont Ave.
Larchmont, NY
(914) 834-6378

Casa Maya
706 Central Park Ave. (Army Rd.)
Scarsdale, NY
(914) 713-0771

Gusano Loco
1137 W. Boston Post Rd. (Richbell Rd.)
Mamaroneck, NY
(914) 777-1512

And More: Diners, Pizzerias & Other Kid-Friendly Finds

Bellizzi

One side of the restaurant is a pizzeria and Italian restaurant, the other has two playrooms for children of all ages. For the younger kids (ages 4 and under) there are tunnels and lofts to climb through, as well as age-appropriate rides and games. For the older kids (4-10 years old), there is a large slide and tunnel adventure to chase their friends through, non-violent video games, and other games they play for tickets to redeem for prizes. There are also two private rooms for birthday parties. The kids' menu includes food choices that you (and your kids) will love—like butterfly pasta, ravioli, homemade chicken tenders and, of course, pizza. All kids' meals include a child-size soda, milk or juice and a child-size gelato for dessert.

Bellizzi has two locations:
1272 Boston Post Rd.
Larchmont, NY
(914) 833-5800

153 Main St.
Mount Kisco, NY
(914) 241-1200

Café Nordstrom
The Westchester Mall (3rd fl.)
125 Westchester Ave.
White Plains, NY
(914) 946-1122

When getting a seat in City Limits looks unlikely, and the food court is jammed, head into this enjoyable eatery tucked away in Nordstrom's gift department on the third floor. They offer great soups, salads and sandwiches for grown-ups as well as four basic staples of kid cuisine: mac & cheese, hot dogs, chicken fingers and grilled cheese. These are all under $4 and come with a drink and chips. It's very rarely crowded and they have large windows so you and your child can enjoy the view of the hustle and bustle below.

California Pizza Kitchen
365 Central Park Ave.
Scarsdale, NY
(914) 722-0600

When your child is given a kids' menu that's also a coloring book, you know you've come to the right place. Spacious booths and a wide variety of food make this a popular place. So popular, in fact, that if you pull up on a Saturday at noon you shouldn't be surprised if you're in for a long wait. However, the attentive staff, yummy food and friendly atmosphere make the waiting worth it.

Candlelight Inn
519 Central Ave. (Old Army Rd.)
Scarsdale, NY
(914) 472-9706

The best burgers in the county, along with sandwiches, salads and other fare. And, if your baby refuses to sleep, they're open until 3 am. Needless to say, they don't take reservations; run in to see if there's a wait before you bother to park and get your kids out of the car.

Chuck E. Cheese's
255 W. Rte. 59
Nanuet, NY
(845) 627-2788

This national emporium of kid's fun and food opened just across the bridge in 2005. If your kids are like ours, chances are they've been tempted by the siren song of the Chuck E. Cheese's commercials (yes, even on PBS). In addition to all the food kids love (and some salads and sandwiches for the adults) they also have stage shows, play zones, rides, games and prizes.

City Limits Diner
This "haute" diner is a constant family favorite because of its funky décor, extensive menu and infinite patience in dealing with their youngest patrons. The food is miles above traditional diner fare, which makes it a very popular—and often crowded—destination. It's worth going on slightly off-hours, particularly on the weekends. Hitting the mall location when it first opens is also a good idea since the waits can be considerable at the other White Plains location. (Plus it's a great way to check out every model of baby stroller, since they're parked outside the restaurant like Harleys at a biker bar.)

City Limits Diner has three locations:
200 Central Ave.
White Plains, NY
(914) 686-9000

The Westchester Mall (3rd fl.)
White Plains, NY
(914) 761-1111

135 Harvard Ave.
Stamford, CT
(203) 348-7000

Cosi

The s'more the merrier at these comfy chain eateries, located throughout Westchester. They have a wide variety of delicious and healthy sandwiches and salads along with their incredible freshly made bread. They also have a huge range of drinks, from coffees to ciders and smoothies. For kids, all the locations offer at least three perennial favorites: turkey with lettuce and mayo, gooey grilled cheese, and tuna, each served with chips and a drink. But the piéce de rèsistance is make-your-own s'mores: mini-camp-fires come fully loaded with all the necessary goodies—a great treat for kids of all ages. The Cosi in Rye also has ice cream.

Cosi has four locations:
1298 Boston Post Rd.
Larchmont, NY
(914) 834-9797

15 S. Moger Ave.
Mount Kisco, NY
(914) 242-5408

77 Quaker Ridge Rd.
New Rochelle, NY
(914) 637-8300

50 Purchase St.
Rye, NY
(914) 921-3322

Global Gatherings

156 S. Central Park Ave.
Hartsdale, NY
(914) 683-1833

This truly unique eatery is a relative newcomer to Westchester, injecting a little bit of homey but hip ambiance onto Central Avenue. You can stop in for a meal or to shop the exotic and unusual merchandise that the store offers. Check out the Kid's Pu Pu platter, which comes complete with a crust-free PB&J sandwich, mac & cheese, fresh fruit kabobs, chicken fingers and carrot sticks. All kids' selections include a scoop of ice cream. They will even deliver the food to your car if your child is sleeping and you are starving. (A nice alternative to the fast-food drive thru.)

Grandma's of Yorktown
3525 Crompond Rd. (Rte. 202)
Yorktown, NY
(914) 739-7770

Total comfort food, along with the best pies around. There's another location on Central Ave. in Hartsdale, but it focuses mostly on pies and has a limited selection of food.

Mighty Joe Young's
610 W. Hartsdale Ave. (between Central Ave. & Dobbs Ferry Rd.)
White Plains, NY
(914) 428-6868

With all the wild animals already hanging around this place, what's one or two more? But seriously, your kids can check out the trophy animal heads hanging on the walls as you enjoy the decidedly grown-up cuisine. They do have a kids' menu and the place is plenty loud and large enough for "active" eaters.

PT's Country Kitchen
15 East Main St.
Mount Kisco, NY
(914) 244-0602

Figures you'd have to go to Northern Westchester to get some real Southern food. There's fried chicken, ribs, wings, coleslaw, corn and other amazing sides, along with the option to create your own salad. PT's great food also comes in a very kid-friendly atmosphere, with café-style tables and bench chairs as well as high chairs.

Route 22 American Restaurant & Bar
55 Old Rte. 22
Armonk, NY
(914) 765-0022

Located on Old Route 22 in a former 1930's gas station, this restaurant has a décor and ambiance that are a real blast from the past. They have an extensive menu that both you and your kids will love—like a burger served in a three-dimensional "car plate". A signature dish is Danish baby back pork ribs served with Route 22's special barbecue sauce, which is also available to buy in their merchandise shop.

Seaside Johnnie's
94 Dearborn Ave.
Rye, NY
(914) 921-6104

You can sit on or overlooking the beach while you feast on salads and sandwiches for lunch and lots of selections from the sea for dinner. (Don't worry, they have some non-fish options as well.) The kids' menu includes hot dogs, hamburgers, fish and chips, chicken fingers and grilled cheese.

What to Know Before You Go: They do not accept credit cards, but they do have an ATM on the premises. During the summer they have cartoon character appearances on Tuesdays from 6-8 pm and fireworks on Wednesday and Friday nights.

Sports Page Pub
200 Hamilton Ave. (White Plains Mall)
(914) 761-6697

Consistently voted "Westchester's Best Sports Bar and Restaurant," Sports Page has typical pub fare as well as a good array of salads, wraps, and Tex-Mex options. With large booths, a play area for children and dozens of television sets, the atmosphere is perfect for your little league player . . . and Dad will probably like it too.

Sushi Mike's
146 Main St.
Dobbs Ferry, NY
(914) 591-0054

If you're lucky enough to have a child who appreciates sushi (or at least will eat chicken teriyaki) then head to Sushi Mike's. The food is fantastic and inventive. The kids will be mesmerized by the undersea mural that surrounds them and the two tropical fish tanks are great diversions while you wait for the food to be prepared. Mike and his staff are always friendly and attentive; if you're a sushi lover you'll be in heaven.

Wobble Café
21 Campwoods Rd.
Ossining, NY
(914) 762-3459

Wobble is a cheerful, cozy, comfortable neighborhood restaurant with a gourmet chef who studied under Emeril. Art exhibits and children's drawings grace the walls, and children play in an inviting (and carefully cleaned) play area among the tables. The menu is extensive and healthy and sure to please even the pickiest eaters. They serve brunch and lunch six days a week, Tuesday through Sunday, and dinner on weekends.

Chapter 11

Good Car-ma

Vehicle Essentials

Ways to Make Any Trip More Entertaining

Day Trippin'

Whether you're making a trip to the local supermarket or taking an all-day excursion, with a little bit of planning and some of these tried-and-true suggestions no car trip will ever "drive you" insane again.

Most suburban parents' vehicles are more than just a way to get from point A to point B: they're often a combined office, storage bin, hall closet and snack-bar on wheels. And most of us at some point (usually as our car is being driven off the lot at the dealership) have sworn that there will be no eating in, junking up, or any other child-related trashing of *this* car. While it sounds good in theory, we have yet to see this resolution succeed in real life.

To try to keep the car clutter under control, when Simon was a baby Betsy kept a small plastic bin on the floor in front of his car seat. It was a convenient place to store soft rattles, pacifiers, and little toys that might be needed throughout the day. The best part was that when Simon would drop or toss away whatever he was playing with, more often than not it would end up right back in the box. Buy a container that fits snugly in the space between the front and back seats so that it doesn't shift around too much as you're driving. And, of course, if you remember to throw away all the trash and junk each time you fill up the gas tank, you'll cut down on car clutter.

Because life with young children can often take unexpected turns, it helps to be as prepared as possible. Here are some great ways to do just that.

VEHICLE ESSENTIALS

A first aid kit stocked with band-aids, antibacterial ointment, and bandages. You can pick up a prepacked travel kit at most any drugstore or supermarket.

A backup diapering bag with a travel-sized container of diaper ointment, wipes, a changing pad, Purell and, of course, a diaper or two and plastic bags for the dirty ones. If your child is old enough to be out of diapers, it might be a good idea to have a fresh pair of underwear. If you child is a spitter, drooler or messy eater, you might also keep a season-appropriate change of clothes in the car, and perhaps a sweatshirt in case the day turns chilly.

Maps of the county and surrounding areas. For a great Westchester overview be sure to pick up AAA's book of area maps, which includes maps of Manhattan and The Bronx, and parts of New Jersey, Connecticut and Long Island. It's one of our favorites. As a member of AAA you can receive the map book for free, and having the added peace of mind knowing that you are covered in case of an emergency is worth $55 a year. You can also visit a nearby real estate office and ask for copies of local maps; they're detailed and easy to follow.

A small sealed container (mini-coolers are perfect for this) to stash snacks and drinks in. Don't forget to toss in a granola bar or bottle of water for yourself. Laura always keeps store-bought bags of pretzels, Goldfish or crackers in the glove compartment in case Sam or Ben—or husband Andrew—has a sudden "I'm starving!" attack.

A few toys—such as a shovel, pail, ball, etc.—for an impromptu playground visit. Storing them in a mesh bag that allows you to easily shake out the sand before you toss it back in your car will help keep your car clean.

A package of baby wipes. Even if your "baby" is old enough to be the star of his soccer team, these things come in handy in a thousand different ways. From cleaning grimy hands and sticky faces to giving your dashboard a quick detailing, they are invaluable.

Savvy Suggestion

Keep a spare set of children's gloves and a hat in your car, in case a mitten goes missin' or you need to swap out a wet pair for dry ones.

Savvy Sanity Savers

For preschoolers and older children: Cut down on backseat bickering by giving each child a roll of quarters at the beginning of the trip. Every time a fight flares up they have to put a quarter in the piggy bank. Whatever money they're left holding by the time you reach your final destination is theirs to spend.

For long car trips: Laminate a map to give to each child and let them follow along as you drive. Now they'll have their own answer to "Are we there yet?"

Take the show on the road: Bring your Karaoke music with you and take turns being a show-stopper.

WAYS TO MAKE ANY TRIP MORE ENTERTAINING

Here are a few thoughts on great ways to keep your children interested and entertained in the car, no matter how far you're going.

Music. Remember college mix tapes? Well, with modern technology it's easier than ever to put together CDs that both you and your child can enjoy. Download soft, quiet music for lulling your little one to sleep and a mix of fun, silly songs for a sing-along. iTunes and other music sites let you download songs for as little as 99 cents each and they are compatible with both Macs and PCs. And best of all, you won't have to suffer through songs that you can't stand, because you've hand-picked every one.

Audiobooks. Available on tapes, CDs and now even as download-able MP3 files, these are a great way to entertain and educate children, particularly on longer car trips. For a trip to Lake Placid (about five hours from Westchester) Betsy debated buying a portable DVD player to keep Simon amused during the long ride. Stocking up on a bunch of pre-recorded stories and music CDs from the library provided an equally absorbing and significantly cheaper alternative. Attracted to the idea of Sam using his imagination instead of zoning out to a movie, Laura followed Betsy's suggestion and kept him entertained on a trip to Boston—in fact, he didn't want to get out of the car when they arrived at the hotel!

Games. Here's your chance to introduce your child to travel classics like Backseat Bingo and Punch Buggy (although we recommend that children forgo punching the child next to them and instead just shout out "BUGGY!" whenever they see a VW Beetle). Laura has kept Sam entertained in the car by playing a kids' version of Name That Tune (take turns humming a kid's song until the other players guess the name). Simple math games, Twenty Questions and serial storytelling (take turns adding one sentence to a story) are other great boredom busters.

One of our new favorites is a game called NAMEiTS. Available at www.nameits.com, this fun and educational word game gets everybody thinking. Each set consists of twenty-two waterproof, tear-proof cards that require children to score points by spotting different things you might see on your car trip, like a dump truck, an RV and so on. Another set asks each person to name as many things as they can that fly, roll, are hard or round . . . you get the idea. The great thing about that version of the game is that it can occupy your kids anywhere, from sitting in a restaurant to waiting in the checkout line at the supermarket. NAMEiTS games are geared for children ages 4 and up and cost about $10 per set.

Savvy Suggestion

If you have a hard time getting your baby or toddler to stay put during a changing you may find it easier to bring a pull-on training diaper on the road. Once they're cleaned up you can easily pull on a fresh diaper even if it means chasing them around the bathroom to do so.

DAY TRIPPIN'

One of the great things about Westchester is its proximity to so many other family-friendly destinations. Some of the trips listed here are places you can visit in an afternoon, while others may be better for an overnight or weekend stay. We've listed approximate travel times from White Plains to give you an idea of how far each destination is, so take your distance from White Plains into consideration when planning your trips.

NEW YORK

Yankee Stadium Tours
880 River Ave., Yankee Stadium, Bronx
(718) 579-4531
www.yankees.com

This guided tour is guaranteed to be a homerun for your little slugger. This trip includes a tour of the dugout area and field, the press box, Monument Park, scoreboard operations, and clubhouse.

Travel time: 30 minutes

Cost: $12 adults, $6 children ages 14 and under

What to Know Before You Go: The tours are available year-round. Make sure your slugger wears her Yankees T-shirt and hat for a great photo-op in the dugout.

Savvy Suggestion

For longer trips, if you're traveling with your baby or toddler and don't want to bring everything you'll need, there are services to help. Little Travelers will deliver supplies to your destination, including cribs, highchairs, Pack 'n Plays, wagons, bouncy seats, ExerSaucers and strollers. Everything is sanitized and, if you like, they will even set it up for you.

Little Travelers
2890 Rte. 112, #5, Medford, NY 11763
(877) GoBaby-0 / (877) 462-2290
www.little-travelers.com

Rocking Horse Ranch
600 State Route 44-55, Highland
(800) 647-2624 / (845) 691-2927
www.rhranch.com

This "dude ranch" in upstate New York is an all-inclusive resort featuring fun activities for all seasons. Winter activities include skiing and tubing, carriage rides and ice skating; summer activities include swimming, water sports, fishing, miniature golf, and tennis. Year-Round there is horseback riding, pony rides, an indoor pool, spa services, a fitness center, an indoor playspace with a jump-castle and climbing structure, a great outdoor playground, and games and activities such as trivia, bingo and checkers. There is a nursery for younger children and camp for kids ages 4 to 12. The ski slope is very manageable for novice skiers and the instructors are very hands-on and helpful (Sam learned to ski here in an afternoon), and there is also night tubing with a bonfire, hot cocoa and roasted marshmallows. The food is completely satisfactory—not gourmet, but just fine. Room rates vary depending on seasons and occupancy.

Travel time: 1.5 hours

What to Know Before You Go: A two- to three-night stay is enough to experience the Ranch.

New York Waterway Sightseeing Cruises
(800) 53-FERRY (533-3779)
www.nywaterway.com

The Full Manhattan Cruise circumnavigates the Island of Manhattan in just two hours and includes a narrated tour of sights including The Palisades, The Cloisters, The Empire State Building, Yankee Stadium, The United Nations, The Statue of Liberty and other world-famous landmarks. There are two departure locations in Manhattan, at Pier 17 at the South Street Seaport and Pier 78 at West 38th St. and 12th Ave.

Travel time: 30 minutes to NYC location

Full Manhattan Cruise Fare: $25 adults, $12 children

Schedule: May 31-November 7, daily 10:30 am, 1:30 pm and 2:30 pm; November 8-December 31, 10:30 am

Trevor Zoo at Millbrook School

290 Millbrook School Rd. (off Rte. 44), Millbrook
(845) 677-3704
www.millbrook.org/oncampus/zoo.asp

Founded in 1936 by Frank Trevor, Millbrook School's first biology teacher, who wanted to share his passion for wildlife with all people, especially students. Today the zoo is an integral part of Millbrook School and holds more than 120 exotic and indigenous animals. In 1989 the zoo was accredited by the AZA (American Zoo and Aquarium Association). Because The Trevor Zoo is part of a college preparatory school, its educational mission extends to all zoo visitors, who will gain a greater understanding of wildlife and the natural world during their time at this very unique (and manageable) zoo.

Travel time: 1.5 hours

Hours: 8 am-5 pm daily

Admission: $4 adults, $2 children. Note that admission for groups other than families is by appointment only.

Mohonk Mountain House

1000 Mountain Rest Rd., New Paltz
(845) 255-1000
www.mohonk.com

Mohonk Mountain House is a seven-story castle situated on a cliff overlooking glacial Lake Mohonk. This resort opened in 1869 and has 251 guest rooms with 200 balconies where you can soak in the breathtaking view. Offering eighty-five miles of hiking trails, tennis, golf, lake swimming, boating, horseback riding, carriage rides, ice-skating, cross-country skiing, spa services, a fitness center, children's programs and more, it's a great year-round escape. The Kid's Club is complimentary to overnight guests with children ages 2-12. For older kids, there's a "Teen Scene" with activities specially geared towards that age group, from outdoor adventures like mountain biking and rock scrambles to indoor evening interludes of music, movies and games. Mohonk does have a "children under 12 stay free" policy (for up to two children per family) and spacious suites that can accommodate you and your kids comfortably. However, we must warn you, this place is not inexpensive: traditional rooms start at around $370 per night, but that does include three meals a day (although a glass of wine will run you extra). Day passes are also available. Be sure to check the website to see if any specials or packages are being offered.

Travel time: 1.5 hours

CONNECTICUT

The Discovery Museum and Planetarium

4450 Park Ave., (1/2 mile off the Merritt Pkwy., exit 47), Bridgeport
(203) 372-3521
www.discoverymuseum.org

The museum features hands-on science galleries that encourage visitors to manipulate mechanical exhibits on electricity, electronics, computers, sound, light, magnetism and energy. It's also home to the CineMuse Hi-Definition Theater, which shows a variety of movies (usually twenty to thirty minutes long) geared for different age groups, including shows like "Walking With Dinosaurs: Time of the Titans," "Blue Planet: The Deep," "Star Stuff," "Rumpelstiltskin" and "Brer Rabbit." There's also the Henry B. duPont Planetarium, where a realistic and scientifically accurate simulation of the night sky is created on the domed ceiling, with daily presentations for both younger children and general audiences. In the Challenger Learning Center visitors learn about space exploration by becoming part of the team conducting missions to the Moon or Mars. For preschoolers, check out DiscoveryTown, which provides activities for younger explorers such as puppets and a life-sized school bus.

Travel time: 50 minutes

Hours: Tuesday-Saturday 10 am-5 pm, Sunday 12 pm-5pm

Admission: $8.50 adults, $7 children, free for children under 5

What to Know Before You Go: The Planetarium kids' show is Tuesday-Friday 1 pm and Saturday-Sunday 2 pm. The all-ages show is Tuesday-Friday 3:30 pm and Saturday-Sunday 3 pm. The Museum also offers birthday party packages for children ages 3 and up.

Mystic Aquarium and Institute for Exploration

55 Coogan Blvd., Mystic
(860) 572-5955
www.mysticaquarium.org

Step into a re-creation of a Louisiana Bayou in "Swamp Things," a new exhibit filled with baby alligators. Get nose-to-nose with the only Beluga whales in New England and enjoy the California sea lion show, "Lions of the Sea." Kids of all ages can enjoy the new Ray Touch Pool, where they can reach in and touch cownose rays gliding playfully through the water.

Travel time: 2 hours

Hours: July 1-Labor Day: Sunday-Thursday 9 am-7 pm, Friday-Saturday 9 am-6 pm; September-December: daily 9 am-6 pm; December-February: Monday-Friday 10 am-5 pm, Saturday-Sunday and holidays: 9 am-6 pm; February-June: daily 9 am-6 pm; Closed January 1, Thanksgiving and December 25.

Admission: $16 adults, $11 children 3-12, free for children under 2

What to Know Before You Go: Parking is free. You can eat on-premises at The Waterfront Café, adjacent to the Ocean Planet Pavilion, which has a great menu with a variety of foods. There's also a picnic area near the east end of the parking lot if you'd rather bring your own food or dine outdoors on a beautiful day. If you get your hand stamped you can also leave to check out other nearby attractions like the Mystic Carousel and Fun Center and return without having to repay admission.

Mystic Carousel and Fun Center
193 Greenmanville Ave., Mystic
(860) 572-9949

Indoor fun for all with a carousel, games, rides, two restaurants and a gift shop. There are also indoor and outdoor flea markets on Sundays.

Travel time: 2 hours

Hours: Summer: daily 10 am-10 pm; Winter: Thursday and Friday 11 am-10 pm, Saturday 10 am-10 pm, and Sunday 9 am-9pm.

Admission: Free

Children's Garbage Museum of Southwest Connecticut
1410 Honeyspot Road Extension, Stratford
(203) 381-9571
www.crra.org/pages/edu_museums.htm#strtfd

Finally, trash talk that you and your kids can agree on. Here you will get a unique, hands-on, interactive look at how waste is handled and how to work for a better environment. Visit the Trash-o-saurus, walk through a giant compost pile, and observe recycling in action with a "sky box" view of dumping and sorting.

Travel time: 50 minutes

Hours: September-June: Wednesday-Friday 12-4 pm; July-August: Tuesday-Friday 10 am-4 pm

Admission: Free

Savvy Suggestion

Freeze a juice box or pouch, or a bottle of water (only filled up three-quarters of the way, to keep it from bursting), and use it to keep perishable snacks fresh. When it thaws you have a nice cold drink for you or your child.

NEW JERSEY

Medieval Times
149 Polito Ave., Lyndhurst
(888) WE-JOUST or (201) 933-2220
www.medievaltimes.com

Kings, queens, knights, and noble steeds all gathered together inside an 11th-century castle. (This one, however, is climate controlled.) Enjoy the majesty of brave knights on horseback competing at breathtaking speed in daring feats of skill and jousting. Cheer them on to victory as they fight to the finish with swords and weapons! All this, while dining like royalty on a four-course banquet meal. With such a transporting experience you'll almost forget that you're mere minutes from midtown Manhattan. Shows run approximately two hours.

Travel time: 50 minutes

Hours: Fridays at 8 pm, Saturdays at 7 pm, Sundays at 4:30pm

Admission: Normally it's $47.95 for adults and $34.95 for children, but if you order tickets online you'll receive $6 off adult and $3 off child admissions from Sunday to Friday. Parking is included in the admission price.

Savvy Suggestion

Use a plastic laundry basket to pack up anything you might want easy access to while on the road (snacks, towels, toys, etc). Then use it to collect laundry throughout your trip so it'll be ready for the wash when you get home.

PENNSYLVANIA

Sesame Place
100 Sesame Rd., Langhorne
(215) 752-7070
www.sesameplace.com

Located in Bucks County, Sesame Place is about a two-hour drive from mid-Westchester, so you may want to combine it with an overnight visit. It offers over fifty attractions, including a massive water park with water slides for every age, as well as places where you and your kids can stay dry and still have tons of fun. Kids can check out daily shows and parades featuring performances by their favorite characters. Another not-to-miss attraction is the character breakfast, where kids can munch and mingle with the likes of Big Bird and others from 9 am to 10 am. Reservations are required and it costs $12.95 (plus tax) for adults and children, although children under the age of two are admitted for free. While bigger kids will love all the action and adventure, you can let your little ones loose in 1-2-3 Smile With Me—a toddler play area specifically for the five-and-under set.

Travel time: 2 hours

Park Season: May-October

Hours: Opening is generally at 10 am, but closings vary throughout the season, so check the website or call ahead for specific times.

Admission: Elmo's Passport (which gives you two days of admission for the price of one) is $38.95 plus tax per person (children under the age of 2 enter for free). Admission covers all the attractions.

What to Know Before You Go: Sunny day, sweeping those clouds away…If it rains for more than an hour straight during your visit, Sesame Place will give you a free ticket to come back during the same season. There are several places to eat within the park and there is a picnic area outside the park. (If you leave the park get your hand stamped to so that you can reenter at no charge.) Swim attire, including swim diapers or water shoes, can be purchased on site. General parking is $10, preferred parking $13.

New Hope & Ivyland Railroad
32 West Bridge St., New Hope
(215) 862-2332
www.newhoperailroad.com

Only thirty minutes away from both Sesame Place and Philadelphia, this railroad will transport you through beautiful Bucks County and back in time. Take a forty-five minute narrated steam train ride in an antique Passenger Coach, Parlor Car or Open Air Car. The railroad offers specialty trains with historic themes based on local and American history, Stories & Sing-a-longs, and holiday theme rides for Christmas, Easter, or Halloween. You can enjoy a picnic before or after at the station or head to picturesque New Hope for a bite to eat and a stroll down the beautiful main street of the town, which is lined with shops, eateries, and boutiques.

Travel time: 2 hours

Hours: Open at 10:30 am on weekends and at 11 am on weekdays from Memorial Day to the end of October, and at varying times in November and December. Check the website or call for specific times.

Cost: $10 adults, $7 children 2-11, $1.50 children under 2. (Prices for special theme train rides are higher.)

Great Wolf Lodge
1 Great Wolf Dr., Scotrun
(570) 688-9899
www.poconos.greatwolflodge.com

This resort was opened in 2005 and its highlight is a 90-foot-tall, 78,000-square-foot indoor waterpark featuring eleven waterslides, ranging in size from kiddie slides to bigger-kid tube slides, and six pools including an indoor wave pool, a recreation pool, a lazy river and a zero-depth entry pool for the youngest water-fans. There is also a twelve-level treehouse waterfort connected by suspension bridges, cargo nets and web crawls, and a 6,000-square-foot arcade room with more than 100 games. For mom and dad, there is a Starbucks® coffeeshop, a fitness room and Elements™ (an Aveda® concept spa). The waterpark is supervised by nearly 100 lifeguards.

Travel time: 2 hours

Cost: Room rates vary depending on seasons and occupancy.

What to Know Before You Go: A one- or two-night stay will allow you to relax and enjoy. Particularly since Great Wolf is new, it's been quite popular—you'll need to make reservations well in advance.

Savvy Shopping

When you're gearing up for your next trip, be sure to check out Parkers in Rye, NY. They have a wide range of everything you can think of to make your journey a little easier, from a huge variety of travel books to specialty luggage, travel gear, games-on-the-go and more.

Parkers is located at 43 Purchase St., Rye, NY. (914) 921-6400

Chapter 12

The ABCs of Preschool

How to Begin Your Search

Educational Approaches

Taking the Next Step

Preschools in Westchester

Choosing a preschool for your child is a task that may generate the same sort of intense angst as buying a house does. It feels like such a monumental decision: we imagine that it will affect our children's entire educational lives. And while the registration process locally is nowhere near as bad as it is for Manhattan preschools, finding the right preschool in the suburbs poses its own distinct set of challenges.

HOW TO BEGIN YOUR SEARCH

The first thing you need to know is that registration for preschools begins in the fall of the year before you plan on having your child attend. It usually takes place in October or November, so you should plan to start looking at programs after Labor Day. Although not as competitive as schools in New York City, the popular programs in Westchester often fill up quickly, so when you find a program you like put down a deposit to make sure you have a spot come next fall. When Betsy signed up Simon for a "two's program" he wasn't even walking yet! That being said, when Laura heard from friends that she had "missed" the preschool registration window—and then panicked—it turned out that all the places she wanted to look at still had space.

How do you begin your search? First, decide what type of program would be best for your child and narrow down what you're looking for. Do you want your child to go five days a week? Two times a week? Do you want an afternoon program or a morning program? For working parents, finding an all-day program may be a top priority. Other considerations may include the program's hours or whether the facility offers afternoon or enrichment programs.

You'll also want to look at location. For many of us, sending our children to preschool is the first bit of "down time" we've had since they were born, and we want to take advantage of that by hitting the gym, actually reading the paper, freelancing, etc. You may think that driving your daughter twenty-five minutes to the "perfect" preschool is no big deal, but remember: if she's going to school for ninety minutes each day, you'll need to find ways to occupy yourself near her preschool or you'll only be able to go home for a short stint before you need to turn around and pick her up again. For Laura, finding a neighborhood preschool was an absolute necessity since she and her husband work full-time and their nanny needed to be able to walk Sam to school; luckily, there was a great one nearby.

EDUCATIONAL APPROACHES

The next thing to consider when looking at schools is their different teaching approaches. The three most common styles are Developmental, Montessori and Special Needs.

The Developmental Approach

We've all heard the saying "children learn through playing"—this is the fundamental belief behind the Developmental approach to teaching. Children learn the basics of numbers, letters, colors, sizes and shapes through age-appropriate activities, songs, games and stories. This method capitalizes on kids' natural impulses to explore with their senses, to investigate and to integrate learning through play.

Typically, kids can choose among several activities and can play alone or in small groups. The whole group will come together for songs, stories or other "circle time" activities. Although many reading readiness skills may be learned, rote learning, the use of worksheets, and formal early reading lessons are not part of the program.

For example, at Simon's preschool, they brought in bushels of apples and the children measured how many "apples tall" each child was. They voted on which type of apple was their favorite and counted up the votes to determine the winner. They did a cooking project where they learned how to follow a recipe and measure ingredients (and learned a little patience as it cooked). In other words, they were acquiring all the basic building blocks they need to master more complicated skills when they enter kindergarten.

The Montessori Method

These programs place 3-, 4- and 5-year-olds in one large classroom. Dr. Maria Montessori, the founder of this educational method, believed that the best teacher for a child is another child; younger children learn from the older ones, who in turn get satisfaction from being role models.

Montessori is a "child based" program: every child moves at his or her own pace, as opposed to the entire class advancing together. The classroom is designed to facilitate the children's independence and sense of personal empowerment. They move freely within it, selecting work that captures their interest. And they are responsible for the care of their own child-sized environment: when they are hungry, they prepare their own snacks and drinks; they go to the bathroom without assistance; when something spills, they help each other clean up.

The philosophy behind the Montessori Method is that teachers should lead children to ask questions, think for themselves, explore, investigate, discover and, ultimately, learn independently and retain their curiosity and creativity. As a result, since the teacher is not the "focus" of the classroom, there is often a higher student-to-teacher ratio than there is in other programs (although minimum ratios are mandated by the state). Montessori schools usually offer five-day-a-week programs to increase learning consistency and progress.

For more information about the Montessori Method, go to www.montessori.org.

Special Education Programs

For children with special needs, significant delays or other issues, you may want to consider one of the many excellent Special Ed preschools in Westchester. In these schools, special educators and physical, speech or occupation therapists will work with your child to help him develop to the best of his ability. Class size is kept small so that the teachers can give enough attention to all the students. There is a complete listing of preschools for children with special needs in Chapter 18.

TAKING THE NEXT STEP

Once you narrow down your list of preschools based on your personal criteria and the educational approach that feels right to you, you'll want to set up appointments to meet with school directors. Even if you believe you've found the perfect school, it can always help to see more than one in order to give yourself a basis of comparison.

When you meet with the school director, he or she will discuss the school's policies and approach. When Laura looked at preschools for Sam, she was struck by how all the directors described their schools in very similar ways. One area where they did differ is in how they handled separation: some schools insist that you drop off your child and leave, while others will let you stay for the first few weeks. While there's no right or wrong approach, you need to decide what you're comfortable with.

After you meet with the director you'll be given a tour of the school and the classrooms. Make sure you get to observe the school while it's in session; this way you'll get a better sense of how the teachers interact with the children. Take your time and make a second visit if you need to. Going at around the same time as drop-off or pick-up will also give you a chance to check out the other parents. You'll want to envision how your child will fit into the program, but truly, a lot of times the decision where to send your child comes down to where *you* feel most comfortable. Remember, from here on in there will be playdates galore, so make sure that you can envision yourself spending two hours with these parents.

Another thing you'll want to observe is the overall feel of the physical space. Is it bright, cheerful and clean? Are there spaces within the classroom for free play, quiet time and table-top activities? Some of the schools that Laura looked at for Sam were part of community centers, and the buildings were so large she couldn't envision her then 2-year-old son walking through the cavernous hallways (even holding hands in a line with other toddlers). You'll also want to find out how long the teachers have been teaching preschool, and specifically how long they've been at their current positions. One of the big selling features of the preschool Betsy chose was that most of the teachers had been there for over ten years.

Another potential kink in the decision-making process involves the highly charged subject of potty training. Some schools require children to be out of diapers by a certain age. Some will allow children to be in diapers or pull-ups, but they won't change diapers if the need arises, which means you will be "on call". Remember, you are signing your child up nearly a year before she'll be attending school, so you won't know for sure whether she'll still be in diapers. If you love the school, you may be willing to give yourself a deadline for training; however, if you're unsure, you may not want to put yourself (and your child) under pressure by signing up for a program that has a strict no-diapers policy.

Don't forget to find out whether the school you're looking at is licensed by the state, which means it has met the minimum health and safety requirements. You can check with the local Department of Social Services to confirm that the school is currently licensed. Beyond this initial check, you may want to look for a preschool accredited by the National Association for the Education of Young Children (N.A.E.Y.C.). Accreditation by the N.A.E.Y.C. is more stringent than state licensing and is usually a good indication that the school is of high quality. **To find a complete listing of N.A.E.Y.C.-accredited preschools you can go to www.naeyc.org.**

Finally, one of the best pieces of advice we heard on the subject of choosing the right school for your toddler was from an early childhood educator. Speaking to a room full of anxious parents, she reminded them that the people who teach preschools do it because they love children. You are not sending your children to dig ditches. They will be cared for, stimulated and generally have a ball.

PRESCHOOLS IN WESTCHESTER

While we made every attempt to list all the preschools in Westchester, we no doubt missed a few . . . but this is a great starting point for parents looking for preschool programs in their area. In general, preschools (or "nursery schools") accept children who are 3 and 4 years old. We've indicated those programs that also offer a "two's program," a Pre-K program (usually for 5-year-olds with late birthdays), day care, or older grade levels.

Ardsley

Alcott Montessori School
700 Ashford Ave.
Ardsley, NY 10502
(914) 693-4443
Director: Arlene Donegan

Ardsley Community Nursery School
21 American Legion Dr.
Ardsley, NY 10502
(914) 693-4932
Director: Gloria Wolpert
Day care available

Savvy Suggestion

No more listening to the alphabetical listing of school closings and weather delays on the radio ...now you can look them up on the Web! Preschools and daycare centers each follow the calendars, closings and delays of a specific public school district. Bookmark the website for the appropriate school district (a complete list of school district websites is included in Chapter 2, or use the WFAS radio station's website, which also provides information on weather-related closings and delays:
www.wfasstormcenter.com/completelist.asp

Ardsley Methodist Church Nursery School
525 Ashford Ave.
Ardsley, NY 10502
(914) 693-0204
Director: Diana Virrill

Just for Two's
525 Ashford Ave.
Ardsley, NY 10502
(914) 693-5225
Director: Dina Scotto-Reith
2-year-olds only

Lyceum Kennedy
One Cross Rd.
Ardsley, NY 10502
(914) 479-0722
www.lyceumkennedy.com/lkfrench/index.htm
Director: François Heller
3 years old to 5th grade
Note: This is a French bilingual education school.

Armonk

Armonk Childrens Corner
4 Wampus Ave.
Armonk, NY 10504
(914) 273-6224
Director: Nancy Cannella

Armonk Nursery School
Armonk United Methodist Church
3 Bedford Rd.
Armonk, NY 10504
(914) 273-8245
Director: Maryanne Delessio
Babysitting available for children 2 weeks and up; preschool for 2-
to 4-year-olds

Little Sparrows Nursery School of Hillside Church
448 Bedford Rd.
Armonk, NY 10504
(914) 273-9760
Director: Doreen Semple

Montessori Children's Room
67 Old Rte. 22
Armonk, NY 10504
(914) 273-3291
www.armonkmontessori.com
Director: Lynn Coyne
8 weeks to 6 years old

My Nursery School
62 Cox Ave.
Armonk, NY 10504
(914) 273-3114
www.breezemont.com/mynursery.htm
Director: Robin Scott

Timber Ridge Family Center
15 Old Post Rd.
Armonk, NY 10504
(914) 273-4411
Director: Elizabeth Anderson
8 weeks to 12 years old

Bedford

Bedford Discovery School & Infant Centers
190 Harris Rd. (Rte. 117)
Bedford Hills, NY 10507
(914) 666-KIDS (-5437)
Director: Phyllis Lupo

Bedford Village Nursery School
Bedford Village Presbyterian Church
On the Village Green
Bedford, NY 10506
(914) 234-3020
Director: Cathy Lent

For Kids Only
577 North State Rd.
Briarcliff, NY 10510
(914) 923-1889
Director: Wendy Masserman
3 to 12 years old
Preschool and day care

Rippowam Cisqua School
439 Cantitoe St.
Bedford, NY 10506
(914) 244-1204
www.rcsny.org
Director: Kathleen McNamara

Temple Shaaray Tefila Early Childhood Center
89 Baldwin Rd.
Bedford Corners, NY 10549
 (914) 666-3133
www.shaaraytefila.org/ecc.html
Director: Jerri Rosenfeld

The Country Children's Center (Bedford Hills)
410 Bedford Rd. (Rte. 117)
Bedford Hills, NY 10507
(914) 242-0520
www.countrychildrenscenter.org
Director: Benan Ozkaynak
Infants to 5 years old

Village Green Nursery School
Main St.
Bedford, NY 10549
(914) 234-7967
Director: Kim Bickley

Brewster
Brewster Co-op Nursery School
110 Main St.
Brewster, NY 10509
(845) 278-2661
www.brewstercoop.org
Director: Robin Tedeschi

Briarcliff Manor
Christian Nursery School
25 South State Rd.
Briarcliff Manor, NY 10510
(914) 941-2923
Director: Joanne Borchers

Congregation Sons of Israel
1666 Pleasantville Rd.
Briarcliff Manor, NY 10510
(914) 762-6396
Director: Linda Cindrich

Creative Play Care
All Saints Episcopal Church
201 Scarborough Rd.
Briarcliff, NY 10510
(914) 941-0379
Director: Mary DiDomenico
18 months to 3 years old

The Little School
Faith Lutheran Brethren Church
480 Pleasantville Rd.
Briarcliff Manor, NY 10510
(914) 769-4255
Director: Heidi Roth

Sleepy Hollow Nursery School
201 Scarborough Rd.
Briarcliff Manor, NY 10510
(914) 941-2107
Director: Karen Morris

Young Wonders Preschool/Day Care
446 North State Rd.
Briarcliff Manor, NY 10510
(914) 944-9434
Director: Roy Ammirati
16 weeks to 5 years old

Bronxville

Bronxville Montessori School
101 Pondfield Rd. West
Bronxville, NY 10708
(914) 793-2083
Director: Jean Nelson
18 months and up

Eliza Corwin Frost Child Center
17 Sagamore Rd.
Bronxville, NY 10708
(914) 779-4852
Director: Juli Marvel Arlt
14 months to 5 years old

Sarah Lawrence Early Childhood Center
Sarah Lawrence College
1 Mead Way
Bronxville, NY 10708
(914) 395-2353
Director: Sara Wilford

The Chapel School
Village Lutheran Church
172 White Plains Rd.
Bronxville, NY 10708
(914) 337-3202
www.vlc-ny.org
Director: Camille Strawbridge

The Reformed Church Nursery School
6 Kraft Ave.
Bronxville, NY 10708
(914) 337-6332
Director: Margaret Murtagh

Buchanan

The International Pre-School Center
275 Church St.
Buchanan, NY 10511
(914) 739-0809
Director: Jasmine Aurora Somerste

Chappaqua

Beginning Years Early Childhood Center of Beth El
220 S. Bedford. Rd.
Chappaqua, NY 10514
(914) 238-5735
Director: Janet Goldstein

Chappaqua Children's Workshop
St. Mary the Virgin Church
73 S. Bedford Rd.
Chappaqua, NY 10514
(914) 238-3295
Director: Barbara Klein
Afterschool programs available for older children

Chappaqua Friends Nursery School
420 Quaker Rd.
Chappaqua, NY 10514
(914) 238-6831
Director: Janet Hough

Just 3, Just 4
Horace Greeley High School
Roaring Brook Rd.
Chappaqua, NY 10514
(914) 861-9439
Director: Susan Williams

Oak Lane Child Care Center
49 Memorial Dr.
Chappaqua, NY 10514
(914) 238-3756
Director: Ronnie Weinberger
18 months to 5 years old

Play Care
Congregational Church
210 Orchard Ridge Rd.
Chappaqua, NY 10514
(914) 238-6206
Director: Carol Cleary
2 months to 5 years old

Village Nursery School
120-300 King St.
Chappaqua, NY 10514
(914) 238-4800
Director: Ruth Swetonic

World Cup Nursery School
170 Hunts Ln.
Chappaqua, NY 10514
(914) 238-9267
www.worldcupnurseryschool.com
Director: Pat Vogelsperger

Cortlandt Manor

The Flying Goose, A Child Nurturing Space
100 Oregon Rd.
Cortlandt Manor, NY 10567
(914) 739-5100
Director: Lisa Rodriguez
18 months to 8 years old

Northern Westchester YM-YWHA
3565 Crompond Rd.
Cortlandt Manor, NY 10567
(914) 736-3076
Director: Rhonda Heumann

Croton-on-Hudson

Asbury Play and Learn Nursery School
17 Old Post Rd. S.
Croton-on-Hudson, NY 10520
(914) 271-3628
Director: Jodi Hamlon

Center PreSchool of Croton
52 Scenic Dr.
Croton-on-Hudson, NY 10520
(914) 271-4733
www.centerpreschool.com
Director: Kathy Lawton

Childrenspace
119 Maple St.
Croton-on-Hudson, NY 10520
(914) 271-5056
Director: Sherry Horowitz
2 3/4 years old to 5th grade

Circle School
56 Cleveland Dr.
Croton-on-Hudson, NY 10520
(914) 271-8950
Director: Ellie Hall

Croton Community Nursery School
25 Van Wyck St.
Croton-on-Hudson, NY 10520
(914) 271-4451
Director: Barbara Swanson

Croton Montessori School
Unitarian Meeting House
2021 Old Albany Post Rd.
Croton-on-Hudson, NY 10520
(914) 271-4503
www.crotonmontessori.com
Director: Elizabeth terPoorten

Happy Tots Day Care Center
114 Grand St.
Croton-on-Hudson, NY 10520
(914) 271-6992
www.happytots.org
Director: Maureen Gioio
6 weeks to 5 years old

Temple Israel Early Childhood Program
Glengary Rd.
Croton-on-Hudson, NY 10520
(914) 271-4705
Director: Lori Cohen

Dobbs Ferry

Days of Wonder
343 Broadway
Dobbs Ferry, NY 10522
(914) 693-2980
www.daysofwonder.org
Director: Jennifer Dawber
18 months to 5 years old

Greenburgh Hebrew Center
515 Broadway
Dobbs Ferry, NY 10522
(914) 693-5121
Director: Suzanne Boydstun

The Christian Preschool
Dobbs Ferry Lutheran Church
43 Ashford Ave.
Dobbs Ferry, NY 10522
(914) 693-0026
Director: Sharon Brennen

Eastchester

Woodlot Christian School
Eastchester Community Church
11 Woodlot Rd.
Eastchester, NY 10709
(914) 779-0368
Director: Alice McCullouth

Elmsford

Ann & Andy Preschool
2170 Saw Mill River Rd.
Elmsford, NY 10523
(914) 347-2524
Director: Cheryl Anstett
8 weeks to 5 years old

Bright Horizons Children's Center
77 Executive Blvd.
Elmsford, NY 10523
(914) 592-2890
www.brighthorizons.com
Director: Katherine Grayson
6 weeks to 6 years old

Treetops at Bright Horizons
11 Clearbrook Rd.
Elmsford, NY 10523
(914) 592-6006
Director: Michelle McNally

Granite Springs

Bright Beginnings Preschool Learning Center
Church of the Good Shepherd
Granite Springs Center
Granite Springs, NY 10527
(914) 248-5333
Director: Mara Ziedens

Harrison

Harrison Children's Center
300 Harrison Ave.
Harrison, NY 10528
(914) 835-4271
Director: Virginia Carpenter

JCC of Harrison Nursery School
130 Union Ave.
Harrison, NY 10528
(914) 835-2850, x109
Director: Nancy Isaacs

Harrison Presbyterian Nursery School
231 Park Ave.
Harrison, NY 10528
(914) 835-0055
Director: JoAnn Sarlo

Webster Avenue Nursery School
300 Harrison Ave.
Harrison, NY 10528
(914) 835-4504
Director: Joan Coulter

Hartsdale

Creative Beginnings Children's Center
112 W. Hartsdale Ave.
Hartsdale, NY 10530
(914) 428-1200
www.cbcc.org
Director: Susan Stevenson
18 months to 5 years old

Greenburgh Early Childhood Program
475 W. Hartsdale Ave.
Hartsdale, NY 10530
(914) 949-2745
Director: Dawn Mair-McMillan

Rainbow Nursery School
130 N. Central Ave.
Hartsdale, NY 10530
(914) 949-3736
Director: Gale Kelleher

Sacred Heart PreK Program
59 Wilson St.
Hartsdale, NY 10530
(914) 946-7242
Director: Virginia Salamone

Hastings-on-Hudson

Happy Harbor Child Care Center
95 Broadway
Hastings-on-Hudson, NY 10706
(914) 478-4175
Director: Cindy Veavey
3 months to 4 years old

Hastings Co-op Nursery School
25 Old Jackson Ave.
Hastings-on-Hudson, NY 10706
(914) 478-3777
Director: Robin Tedeschi

Temple Beth Shalom Nursery
740 North Broadway
Hastings-on-Hudson, NY 10706
(914) 478-3833
Director: Judith Michael

Hawthorne

Little Years
1 Skyline Dr.
Hawthorne, NY 10532
(914) 347-7682
Director: Denise Spadaccini

Holy Rosary School
180 Bradhurst Ave.
Hawthorne, NY 10532
(914) 769-0030, ext. 25
www.holyrosaryny.com
Director: Victor J. Presto
Also has kindergarten through 8th grade

Trinity Lutheran Preschool
292 Elwood Ave.
Hawthorne, NY 10532
(914) 773-1108
Director: Carol Rodriguez

Irvington

Good Shepherd Early Childhood Center
25 North Broadway
Irvington, NY 10533
(914) 591-4104
www.gsecc.org
Director: Nancy Brand

Katonah

Hi-Ho Nursery School
Cantitoe Rd.
Katonah, NY 10536
(914) 234-3360
Director: Jill Ann Holland

Katonah Playcare
44 Edgemont Rd.
Katonah, NY 10536
(914) 232-7825
Directors: Gail Porter and Louise Cameron
18 months to 5 years old

Katonah Play School Nursery
31 Bedford Rd.
Katonah, NY 10536
(914) 232-5903
Director: Anne Harris

Little Farm Montessori Nursery
2658 Rte. 35
Katonah, NY 10536
(914) 232-5992
www.onalittlefarm.com
Director: Bonnie Wilder

The Country Children's Center ("The Farm")
466 Cross River Rd. (Rte. 35)
Katonah, NY 10536
(914) 232-9344
www.countrychildrenscenter.org
Director: Noreen Cotter
Infants to 5 years old

The Country Children's Center ("The White House")
412 Cross River Rd. (Rte. 35)
Katonah, NY 10536
(914) 232-9401
www.countrychildrenscenter.org
Director: Shanna Krizan
Infants to 5 years old; they also run an afterschool program for
kindergarteners

Larchmont

Larchmont Avenue Church Preschool
60 Forest Park Ave.
Larchmont, NY 10538
(914) 834-3984
Director: Joyce M. Guimaraes

Larchmont Temple Nursery School
75 Larchmont Ave.
Larchmont, NY 10538
(914) 834-9244
www.larchmonttemple.org
10 months to 5 years old

St. John's Nursery School
4 Fountain Square
Larchmont, NY 10538
(914) 833-2870
Director: Marilyn Pardo

Mamaroneck

Liberty Montessori School
631 Boston Post Rd.
Mamaroneck, NY 10543
(914) 636-3461
www.libertymontessorischools.com
Director: Pushpa R. Jagoda
17 months to 6 years old

Mamaroneck Child Development Center
134 Center Ave.
Mamaroneck, NY 10543
(914) 698-3131
Director: Denise Gilman

Mamaroneck Community Nursery School
501 Tompkins Ave.
Mamaroneck, NY 10543
(914) 381-2655
www.mcnschool.org
Director: Lynda Merchant
18 months to 5 years old

Saxon Woods Country School
2 Fairway Dr.
Mamaroneck, NY 10543
(914) 698-0500
Director: JoAnn Lynch Towle

Westchester Day School
856 Orienta Ave.
Mamaroneck, NY 10543
(914) 698-8900, x104
www.westchesterday.org
Director: Susan Chasen
2 3/4 years to 8th grade

Westchester Jewish Center
Rockland and Palmer Aves.
Mamaroneck, NY 10543
(914) 698-2767
Director: Hanne Holsten
14 months to 4 years old

Mohegan Lake
Tom Thumb Pre-School Center
1949 East Main St.
Mohegan Lake, NY 10547
(914) 528-5600
Director: Nancy Brophy

Montrose
Montrose Child Care Center
FDR VA Hospital Bldg. #29
Rte. 9A
Montrose, NY 10548
(914) 734-2745
www.montrosechildcarecenter.com
Director: Karen Erickson
6 weeks to 5 years old

Mount Airy Nursery School
2124 Albany Post Rd.
Montrose, NY 10548
(914) 736-1447
Director: Jan Seagren

Sunset Nursery School
80 Sunset Rd.
Montrose, NY 10548
(914) 737-1818
Director: Cheryl Martin

Mount Kisco

All Aboard Childcare
100 S. Bedford Rd.
Mount Kisco, NY 10549
(914) 244-1100
Director: Madeline Freed
6 weeks to 5 years old

Bet Torah Nursery School
60 Smith Ave.
Mount Kisco, NY 10549
(914) 241-6339
Director: Mindy Citera

Boys & Girls Club/Cooperative Nursery
351 Main St.
Mount Kisco, NY 10549
(914) 666-8069
www.boysandgirlsclubnw.org/programs.htm
Director: Elizabeth Ostrye

Jennie's School for Little Children
Presbyterian Church
Rte. 133
Mount Kisco, NY 10549
(914) 666-4001
Director: Barbara Esau

The Little Garden Preschool
236 Rte. 172
Mount Kisco, NY 10549
(914) 241-0445
Director: Beatrice Santore

Little Blessing Children's Center
15 South Bedford Rd.
Mount Kisco, NY 10549
(914) 666-0644
Director: Joann Spolzino

Mount Kisco Day Care Center
95 Radio Circle
Mount Kisco, NY 10549
(914) 241-2135
Director: Dottie Jordan
Infants to 4 years old

Rippowam Cisqua School
325 W. Patent Rd.
Mount Kisco, NY 10549
(914) 244-1200
www.rcsny.org
Director: Risa Zayde

The Little Preschool of Mount Kisco
300 Main St.
Mount Kisco, NY 10549
(914) 666-6505
Director: Betty Spano

Mount Vernon

Collin Allen Child Development Day Care Center
103 West Second St.
Mount Vernon, NY 10550
(914) 664-7005
Director: Andrea Brown
6 weeks to 4 years old

Excelsior Learning Center
675 E. Lincoln Ave.
Mount Vernon, NY 10552
(914) 665-2231
Director: Nicole Gaskin-Daniels

Longfellow Pre-K
625 Fourth Ave.
Mount Vernon, NY 10550
(914) 665-5077
Director: Jacqueline Liburd

Mount Vernon Day Care Center
151 S. Second Ave.
Mount Vernon, NY 10550
(914) 664-6557
Director: Linda Iglehart
6 weeks to 5 years old; afterschool program for school-age children
up to 4th grade

New Beginnings Educational Institute
125 Sharpe Blvd.
Mount Vernon, NY 10550
(914) 699-0031
Director: Jessica Vega
6 weeks to 4 3/4 years old; before- and afterschool programs for
6- to 12-year-olds

WestCOP Toddler's Park Head Start Day Care Center
260 South 4th Ave.
Mount Vernon, NY 10550
(914) 699-5039
Director: Michele Holzman

New Rochelle

A Child's Dream
10 Mill Rd.
New Rochelle, NY 10804
(914) 633-4332
Directors: Tiffany Amaya and Ana Caldararo

Barnard Early Childhood Center
129 Barnard Rd.
New Rochelle, NY 10801
(914) 576-4386
Director: Patricia Lambert
Pre-K to 2nd grade

Beth El Synagogue Nursery
North Ave. & Northfield Rd.
New Rochelle, NY 10804
(914) 235-2700, x250
Director: Ronnie Becher
18 months to 5 years old

Children's Corner Nursery School
40 Willow Dr. & 60 Willow Dr.
New Rochelle, NY 10805
(914) 632-6320
Director: Renette Ramaglia
6 weeks to 5 years old

Hudson Country Montessori School
340 Quaker Ridge Rd.
New Rochelle, NY 10804
(914) 636-6202
www.hudsonmont.org
Director: Musya Meyer
18 months to 6th grade

Liberty Montessori School
155 Beechmont Dr.
New Rochelle, NY 10801
(914) 777-1382
Director: Pushpa R. Jagoda

Mother and Child Center
11 Wilmot Rd.
New Rochelle, NY 10804
(914) 235-7917
Director: Mimi Fortunato

Mount Tom Day School
48 Mount Tom Rd.
New Rochelle, NY 10805
(914) 636-8130
Director: Jill Newhouse

New Rochelle Day Nursery
115 Clinton Ave.
New Rochelle, NY 10801
(914) 632-2093
Director: Jean DeVeaux
18 months to 5 years

Pre-School Learning Center
95 Eastchester Rd.
New Rochelle, NY 10801
(914) 654-0339
Director: Joan Godfrey

Temple Israel Early Childhood Program of New Rochelle
1000 Pinebrook Blvd.
New Rochelle, NY 10804
(914) 235-1800 x227
www.tinr.org
Director: Wendy Shemer
4 months to 5 years old

The Caring Place
53 Sixth St.
New Rochelle, NY 10801
(914) 632-7221
Director: Frances Vitale

TLC Transitional Learning Center
555 Davenport Ave.
New Rochelle, NY 10805
Director: Jeannette Mirabile
(914) 738-6760

Trinity Cooperative Nursery School
311 Huguenot St.
New Rochelle, NY 10801
(914) 636-1727
Director: Rani Rangraj

United Child Care Center
60 Willow Dr.
New Rochelle, NY 10805
(914) 632-6320
Director: Sheridan Povemba
6 weeks to 5 years old

Weekday Nursery School
United Methodist Church
1200 North Ave.
New Rochelle, NY 10804
(914) 632-6758
Director: Sara Arnon

Westchester Area School
456 Webster Ave.
New Rochelle, NY 10801
(914) 235-5799
www.westchesterareaschool.org
Director: James M. Bennett
2 3/4 years to 8th grade

Ossining

All Aboard Childcare
255 N. Highland Ave.
Ossining, NY 10562
(914) 923-1700
www.allaboardchildcare.com
Director: Madeline Freed
6 weeks to 5 years old

Briarcliff Nursery School
40 Morningside Dr.
Ossining, NY 10562
(914) 941-4373
Director: Eva Levine
15 months to 4 years old

Noah's Ark Christian Academy & Nursery School
199 Croton Ave.
Ossining, NY 10562
(914) 941-5498
Director: Ruth Hanby

Roosevelt Pre-Kindergarten
190 Croton Ave.
Ossining, NY 10562
(914) 762-2682
Director: Mirla Puella

Small Miracles PreSchool Center
15 Campwoods Rd.
Ossining, NY 10562
(914) 762-0531
Director: Janet Perritano
6 weeks to 5 years old; before- and afterschool programs for 6- to 12-year-olds

St. Ann School Peas and Karrots Program
16 Elizabeth St.
Ossining, NY 10562
(914) 941-0312
Director: Lori Polidoro
www.stannoss.org

St. Matthew's Head Start Day Care Center
50 N. Malcolm St.
Ossining, NY 10562
(914) 941-1715
Director: Judith Byrne
Infants to 5 years old; afterschool program for 6- to 12-year-olds

Torbank Nursery School
108 Pinesbridge Rd.
Ossining, NY 10562
(914) 941-1563
www.torbanknurseryschool.com
Director: Gayle April

Peekskill
Aunt Bessie's Open Door Day Care Center
137 Union Ave.
Peekskill, NY 10566
(914) 737-9166
Director: Doris Boddie
8 weeks to 5 years old

First Hebrew Nursery School
1821 East Main St.
Peekskill, NY 10566
(914) 739-0504
Director: Barbara Kaufman

WestCOP St. Peter's Head Start Day Care Center
1001 Howard Street
Peekskill, NY 10566
(914) 737-9121
Director: Valerie Loscalzo
18 months to 5 years; afterschool program for children K-3rd grade

The Flying Goose
100 Oregon Rd.
Peekskill, NY 10566
(914) 739-5100
Director: Lisa Rodrigues
18 months to 5 years old; afterschool program for 5- to 8-year-olds

The International Preschool Center
1050 Oregon Rd.
Peekskill, NY 10566
(914) 739-7250
Director: Rory Somerstein
6 weeks to 6 years old

Pelham

Huguenot Nursery School
901 Pelhamdale Ave.
Pelham, NY 10803
(914) 738-6346
www.huguenotschool.com
Director: Barbara Klein

Montessori School of New Rochelle in Pelham Manor
1415 Pelhamdale Ave.
Pelham Manor, NY 10803
(914) 738-1127
Director: Elizabeth G. Capuano

The Pelham Children's Center
20 Fifth Ave.
Pelham, NY 10803
(914) 738-3900
Director: Janet Sherman
18 months to 5 years old; two afterschool programs for K through
5th grade at The Colonial and Hutchinson Elementary schools

Pleasantville

Crossroad Kids
70 Bedford Rd.
Pleasantville, NY 10570
(914) 747-0646
Director: Vicki Luongo

Great Beginnings
Presbyterian Church
400 Bedford Rd.
Pleasantville, NY 10570
(914) 773-0414
Director: Ruth Fischer

Pleasant Hill Nursery School
Lutheran Church
197 Manville Rd.
Pleasantville, NY 10570
(914) 769-3418
Director: Roslyn Campanaro

Pleasantville Children's Center
(Behind Presbyterian Church)
400 Bedford Rd.
Pleasantville, NY 10570
(914) 769-8613
Director: Marcie Krauss

Port Chester

Congregation KTI Early Childhood Program
575 King St.
Port Chester, NY 10573
(914) 939-1010
Directors: Eileen Stein and Karen Schek

North Baptist Nursery School
284 King St.
Port Chester, NY 10573
(914) 937-8401
Director: Jean Dinsmore

Port Chester Children's Place Head Start Day Care Center
400 Westchester Ave.
Port Chester, NY 10573
(914) 690-0860
Director: Paula Belli

Port Chester Head Start Therapeutic Nursery
Tamarack Rd.
Port Chester, NY 10573
(914) 937-5863
Director: Terry McCauley
6 weeks to 5 years old

Weber Drive Child Center Head Start Program
11 Weber Dr.
Port Chester, NY 10573
(914) 690-0860
Director: Paula Belli

Westmore Day Care Center
80 S. Regent St.
Port Chester, NY 10573
(914) 937-5250
Director: Lucille D'Arco
8 weeks to 5 years old

Pound Ridge
Montessori School of Pound Ridge
5 Highview Rd.
Pound Ridge, NY 10576
(914) 763-3125
Director: Teresa Whelan

Pound Ridge Community Church Play School
3 Pound Ridge Rd.
Pound Ridge, NY 10576
(914) 764-4360
Director: Doris Forsberg

Purchase
Purchase Children's Center Inc.
3095 Purchase St.
Purchase, NY 10577
(914) 948-2414
Directors: Judy Betz and Donna Tortorici

The Children's Center at SUNY Purchase
735 Anderson Hill Rd.
Purchase, NY 10577
(914) 251-6895
www.ns.purchase.edu/children
Director: Dr. Patricia Amanna
18 months to 5 years old

Rye
Christ's Church Nursery School
Rectory St.
Rye, NY 10580
(914) 967-5758
Director: Mary Jane Burns
18 months to 5 years old

Community Synagogue Early Childhood Center
200 Forest St.
Rye, NY 10580
(914) 967-7698
Director: Marilyn Zelman

Little Angels Child Care Center
Avon Plaza
Rye, NY 10580
(914) 935-1849
Director: Carolyn Martucci
6 weeks to 5 years old

Rye Presbyterian Nursery School
882 Boston Post Rd.
Rye, NY 10580
(914) 967-2073
www.rpnskids.org
Director: Cheryl Flood

Rye United Methodist Nursery School
964 Boston Post Rd.
Rye, NY 10580
(914) 921-1939
Director: Lucia Vassallo

Rye Brook

Ridge Street Country School
N. Ridge St.
Rye Brook, NY 10573
(914) 939-5460
Director: Barbara Schori

The Pre-Day School of St. Paul's Lutheran Church
Comly Ave. & King St.
Rye Brook, NY 10573
(914) 939-8170
Director: Suzanne Newcomb

Scarsdale

Alcott Montessori School
27 Crane Rd.
Scarsdale, NY 10583
(914) 472-4404
Director: Arlene Donegan

Children's Corner Nursery School
10 Alkamont Ave.
Scarsdale, NY 10583

(914) 725-1719
Director: Lisa Mondelli
18 months to 4 years old

Greenville Church Nursery School
270 Ardsley Rd.
Scarsdale, NY 10583
(914) 723-1262
Directors: D'ann Cecere and Marcia Heese

Hitchcock Church Playcare & Weekday School
6 Greenacres Ave.
Scarsdale, NY 10583
(914) 723-0922
Directors: Susan M. Grant and Suzanne Boydstun

JCC of Mid-Westchester
999 Wilmot Rd.
Scarsdale, NY 10583
(914) 472-3300
Director: Jane Seides

Kids BASE and The Little School
307 Mamaroneck Rd.
Scarsdale, NY 10583
(914) 472-5409
www.kbls.org
Director: Deborah Fine
Before- and afterschool programs available for K through 6th grade

Mazel Tots
Scarsdale Synogogue Tremont Temple
2 Ogden Rd.
Scarsdale, NY 10583
(914) 723-3001
Director: Jody Glassman

Our Lady of Fatima
963 Scarsdale Rd.
Scarsdale, NY 10583
(914) 725-3899
Director: Janice Arcaro

Scarsdale Community Baptist Nursery School
Popham & Autenrieth Rds.
Scarsdale, NY 10583
(914) 722-0278
Director: Elaine Ferraro

Scarsdale Congregational Church Nursery School
1 Heathcote Rd.
Scarsdale, NY 10583
(914) 723-2440
Director: Ginny Clark

Scarsdale Friends Nursery School
133 Popham Rd.
Scarsdale, NY 10583
(914) 472-6550
Director: Olivia Hewitt

St. James Nursery School
Crane Rd. at Church Ln.
Scarsdale, NY 10583
(914) 723-1018
www.stjames-scarsdale.org
Director: Sue Fleishaker

Westchester Reform Temple Early Childhood Center
255 Mamaroneck Rd.
Scarsdale, NY 10583
(914) 723-6493 x103
Director: Susan Tolchin

Somers

Tusker Peanuts Playschool
St. Luke's School
Rte. 100
Somers, NY 10589
(914) 277-4963
Directors: Monica Colarco and Debbie Depaoli

South Salem

Center Nursery School
At Jewish Family Congregation
111 Smith Rich Rd. (Rte. 123)
South Salem, NY 10590
(914) 763-3028, x15
Director: Debra Friedman

St. John's Early Learning Center
82 Spring St.
South Salem, NY 10590
(914) 763-3671
Director: Jeanette Rudolph

South Salem Nursery School
111 Main St.
South Salem, NY 10590
(914) 763-3560
Director: Karen Potz

Tarrytown

Children's Garden Center
At Temple Beth Abraham
25 Leroy Ave.
Tarrytown, NY 10591
(914) 631-1607
Director: Susan Grunthal

Elizabeth Mascia Child Care Center
171 Sheldon Ave.
Tarrytown, NY 10591
(914) 631-2126
Director: Shannon Farrell
2 months to 4 years old; afterschool program up to 3rd grade

JCC on the Hudson Early Childhood Division
371 South Broadway
Tarrytown, NY 10591
(914) 366-7898
www.jcconthehudson.org
Director: Barbara Davis

Phelps Child Care Center (Robin's Nest)
3 Phelps Ln.
Sleepy Hollow, NY 10591
(914) 366-3232
Director: Diane Matrafailo
2 months to 5 years old

Tarrytown Nursery School
15 W. Elizabeth St.
Tarrytown, NY 10591
(914) 631-8227
Director: Rosemarie O'Keefe

Tuckahoe

Asbury Nursery School
167 Scarsdale Rd.
Tuckahoe, NY 10707
(914) 779-3762
Director: Linda Smith

Eastchester Child Development Center
35 Bronx St.
Tuckahoe, NY 10707
(914) 337-4492
Director: Ruth Shepard
18 months to 5 years old

Valhalla
All Aboard Childcare
400 Columbus Ave.
Valhalla, NY 10595
(914) 741-1500
www.allaboardchildcare.com
Director: Madeline Freed
6 weeks to 5 years old; afterschool program up to 10 years old

Nursery School at St. Bartholomew's
82 Prospect Ave.
Valhalla, NY 10595
(914) 946-0628
Director: Margaret Ita

Valhalla United Methodist Church Nursery School
200 Columbus Ave.
Valhalla, NY 10595
(914) 289-0489
Director: Lois Whartenby

Virginia Marx Children's Center at Westchester Community College
75 Grasslands Rd.
Valhalla, NY 10595
(914) 606-6644
Director: Susan Zucker
6 weeks to 5 years old

White Plains
BJE Westchester Services
701 Westchester Ave., 2nd Fl.
White Plains, NY 10604
(914) 328-8090
Director: Irene Lustgarten

Congregation Kol Ami
252 Soundview Ave.
White Plains, NY 10606
(914) 949-4717 x107
www.nykolami.org
Director: Nan Blank

Elmwood Nursery School
900 Dobbs Ferry Rd.
White Plains, NY 10607
(914) 592-8577
Director: Jane Arcaya

Grace Church Day Care Center
(for low income families)
33 Church St.
White Plains, NY 10601
(914) 949-3472
http://gracechurchwhiteplains.org/gccc.htm
Director: Joanne Narvaez

Harrison Children's Center
251 Underhill Ave.
West Harrison, NY 10604
(914) 761-8177
Director: Stephanie Donworth

Memorial Methodist Early Childhood Center
250 Bryant Ave.
White Plains, NY 10604
(914) 949-4187
Director: Ann Pardes
21 months to Pre-K

Montessori Children's Center at Burke
785 Mamaroneck Ave.
White Plains, NY 10605
(914) 597-2253
www.cmteny.com
Directors: Pamela Serra and Carole Wolfe Korngold
3 months to 6 years old

Ridgeway Nursery School & Kindergarten
465 Ridgeway Rd.
White Plains, NY 10605
(914) 949-3134
Director: Janice Barnes

Temple Israel Center Nursery
280 Old Mamaroneck Rd.
White Plains, NY 10605
(914) 948-2800, x126
www.templeisraelcenter.org/education/nursery_school.php
Director: Sharon Hirshik
1 to 4 years old

Mohawk Country Home School
200 Old Tarrytown Rd.
White Plains, NY 10605
(914) 948-2800
www.mohawkhomeschool.com
Directors: Mr. and Mrs. Stephen M. Schainman

The Nursery School Westchester
Ethical Culture Society
7 Saxon Woods Rd.
White Plains, NY 10605
(914) 948-1132
Director: Marcia Sindell

United Preschool Center
456 North St.
White Plains, NY 10605
(914) 946-4781
Director: Annabelle Strozza

Union Child Day Care Center
30 Manhattan Ave.
White Plains, NY 10607
(914) 761-6134
Director: Rita Hulkower
6 weeks to 12 years old

White Plains PreKindergarten
Eastview School
350 Main St.
White Plains, NY 10601
(914) 422-2378
Director: Lucia De Rosa
4-year-olds only

White Plains Presbyterian Church Nursery School
39 N. Broadway
White Plains, NY 10601
(914) 761-5528
Director: Gina Cerillo

YWCA Nursery School
515 North St.
White Plains, NY 10605
(914) 949-6227, ext. 142
Director: Bridget Delaney-Messana

Yonkers

Bright Horizons Children's Center
7 Odell Plaza
Yonkers, NY 10703
(914) 376-3241
www.brighthorizons.com
Director: Margaret Rowan
6 weeks to Pre-K

Bryn Mawr Children's Learning Center
20 Buckingham Rd.
Yonkers, NY 10701
(914) 423-5566
Director: Melissa Csanko

Butler Nursery School
St. John's Episcopal Church
100 Underhill St.
Yonkers, NY 10701
(914) 779-7449
www.netministries.org/see/churches.exe/ch04818
Director: Dee Hyde

Children's Playhouse of Yonkers
(3 locations)
286 Mile Square Rd., Yonkers, NY 10701
378 Park Hill Ave., Yonkers, NY 10705
63 Ashton Rd., Yonkers, NY 10701
(914) 476-5852
www.thechildrensplayhouse.net
Director: Dr. Diana Rothenberg

Church of Our Saviour Day Care Center
Park Hill Ave. & S. Waverly
Yonkers, NY 10701
(914) 969-1726
Director: Ernestine Christmas

Lincoln Park Jewish Center Nursery School
Red Brick Building
311 Central Park Ave.
Yonkers, NY 10701
(914) 476-7879
Director: Maxine Handel

Marion & George Ames Early Childhood Learning Center
463 Hawthorne Ave.
Yonkers, NY 10701

(914) 375-8820
Director: Dimitra Dreyer

Queen's Daughters Day Care Center
73 Buena Vista Ave.
Yonkers, NY 10701
(914) 969-4491
Director: Barbara Berrios
18 months to kindergarten

Small World North
600 N. Broadway
Yonkers, NY 10701
(914) 423-2694
Director: Patricia Fusaro

St. Mark's Lutheran School
Kimball Ave. & St. Mark's Pl.
Yonkers, NY 10704
(914) 237-4944
Director: Ann Losee
3 years to 8th grade

St. Peter's Child Care Center
204 Hawthorne Ave.
Yonkers, NY 10705
(914) 476-2152
Director: Laura Strong

Temple Emanu-El
306 Rumsey Rd.
Yonkers, NY 10705
(914) 963-0575
Director: Marilyn Shebshaievitz

The Laurel & Rose Butler Nursery School
St. John's Episcopal Church
100 Underhill St.
Yonkers, NY 10701
(914) 779-7449
Director: Dee Hyde

Whitney Young Head Start
356 Nepperhan Ave.
Yonkers, NY 10701
(914) 965-7386
Director: Danielle Kilcullen

Yorktown Heights

Bright Beginnings Preschool Learning Center
1974 Commerce St.,
Yorktown Heights, NY 10598
(914) 962-2929
Director: Mara S. Ziedins
18 months to kindergarten

Bright Beginnings Preschool Learning Center
2467 Quaker Church Rd.
Yorktown Heights, NY 10598
(914) 245-2020
Director: Mara S. Ziedins
18 months to kindergarten

Montessori Pre-Nursery School
(3 locations)

St. Andrew's Lutheran Church
2405 Crompond Rd., Yorktown Heights, NY 10598

Yorktown United Methodist Church
2300 Crompond Rd., Yorktown Heights, NY 10598

Yorktown Jewish Center
2966 Crompond Rd., Yorktown Heights, NY 10598

(914) 962-9466
www.ourmontessorischool.com
Director: Betty Hengst
6 weeks to 6th grade

Pied Piper Preschool
2090 Crompond Rd.
Yorktown Heights, NY 10598
(914) 962-5196
Director: Kathleen Dineen

SEED Day Care Center
2084 Baldwin Rd.
Yorktown Heights, NY 10598
(914) 962-9622
Director: Diane Turcin

Yorktown Community Nursery School
247 Veterans Rd.
Yorktown Heights, NY 10598
(914) 962-7868
Director: Ann Jaffe

Chapter 13

Those Lazy, Hazy, Crazy Days

Which Is the Right Camp?

Tools to Help You Choose

Right in Your Own Backyard

Camp Supplies

Where can you find a circus camp? Are there camps with peanut-free kitchens? What about a camp that focuses on foreign languages? Believe it or not, if there's a specific thing that your child is inter-ested in, no matter how unusual, there is most likely a camp that caters to it.

But choosing a camp isn't always easy. The American Camping Asso-ciation estimates that there are over 12,000 camps in the United States—8,000 of them "residential," or sleep-away—attended by more than 10 million children each year. So how do you find the right one for your child?

WHICH IS THE RIGHT CAMP?

Word of mouth is certainly an easy way to go about it, especially for day camps. If your child follows his friend to camp, you're not only placing him in an institution that's been already been endorsed by another parent but also ensuring that he'll know someone when he gets there. However, you might want to do more research when looking for a sleep-away camp; there are so many available it's worth a bit of time to explore the various types to find the best fit for your child.

Beyond the primary choice between day or sleep-away camp, there is a broad array of options in terms of focus. There are traditional camps, which include the activities that we usually think of when we think of summer camp, such as sports, arts & crafts, team activities, swimming, etc. They provide the opportunity for your child to try new activities and gain exposure to campers and staff with different interests. There are also specialized camps, which concentrate on one or two areas, such as academics, weight loss, computers, religion or art, and which enable your child to increase her knowledge or proficiency in that area. The focus of specialized camps ranges from the most popular interests, such as sports camps for tennis or soccer, to the most particular, such as computers or science.

❓ Some of the First Questions to Consider When Choosing a Camp ❓

* Does your child prefer a wide variety of activities, such as arts & crafts, nature studies, water sports and outdoor adventures, or would she be happier with a more limited number of activities?
* Are you looking for a camp that provides specific training or skills in things like sports, computers, musical instruments, or drama?
* Would your child benefit from a special needs camp where he can feel comfortable and meet other kids with similar needs?
* Do you have preferences or limitations in terms of location and cost? A private sleep-away camp generally costs about $1,000 a week (YMCA or scout camps cost less), and most children attend for three to eight weeks.
* Do you prefer a coed or a single-sex camp?

Once you have a sense of what you're looking for, there are three main tools you can use to help narrow your search: camp fairs, the Internet and consultants. We've outlined below the pros and cons of each, along with some avenues to try. We've also provided resources for camp supplies and care packages. Finally, please note that you should start looking for a camp the summer before you plan to have your child attend and that you really should try and visit the camp before making a final decision. Some camps have a "rookie day" or introductory weekend when kids and parents can come and check it out.

TOOLS TO HELP YOU CHOOSE

Camp Fairs

These are a great way to collect information and brochures and to meet camp directors or representatives. They can be overwhelmingly large, but if you are just beginning the process and want to speak to a variety of people representing a broad array of camps, the fairs are a good way to start your search.

Westchester County Center Camp Fair

This camp fair includes representatives from sleep-away, day, special interest (e.g., sports, computers), teen travel and special needs (handicapped, disabled) programs. It has taken place in January each year for over twenty years and is sponsored by the Elana Chapter of Hadassah, a non-profit organization. Admission is free and open to the public. For more information, visit www.westchestergov.com/parks/countycenter.htm.

American Camping Association (ACA)— New York Section

The ACA-NY's camp fairs in Westchester include more than 300 accredited sleep-away and day camps New York, New Jersey, Connecticut, Pennsylvania, Massachusetts, New Hampshire, Vermont and Maine. (The ACA has accredited 2,400 camps that go above and beyond state requirements for health and safety and meet 300+ standards on safety, transportation, staffing and management.) Information on their camp fairs—which generally take place in the fall or winter—can be found at www.aca-ny.org.

In addition, you can check out www.acamp4u.org for information on the organization's free referral service to help match your child's interests and needs with an accredited day or sleep-away camp. If you're looking for other areas of the country, go to the main ACA website at www.acacamps.org.

The Internet

Many camp websites provide great descriptions and photos of their campers, facilities and activities. There are also a number of referral sites that allow you to search for a camp based on type (residential vs. day), location, focus (general vs. specialty), gender, cost, special needs, affiliation and more. While the listings are brief and the sites don't claim to be comprehensive, they do include thousands of camps, and can give you some good ideas on how to narrow your search. You will also find links to the individual camps' websites and their contact information.

The referral sites can also be useful in giving first-time campers (and the parents of campers!) some much-needed support and advice. They can provide information and articles on how to choose a camp, how to pack and prepare, and what to do about homesickness. In some cases a camp advisor even will phone you with recommendations. Although Sam's not ready for sleep-away camp yet, Laura "road-tested" a large number of sites. Judging from the breadth and quality of their results, we found the best ones to be the following.

www.campsearch.com
This site allows you to search by state (but not by region), gender, age, price, specialty and length of session.

www.kidscamps.com
This site provides a search engine based on state and region, religion, gender and length of session.

www.summercamp.org
After you fill out an extremely comprehensive questionnaire from the National Camp Association, they will e-mail you a list of recommended camps and send you brochures, DVDs or videos.

Camp Consultants

These professionals will help you read between the lines of the glossy brochures and websites and will assist in matching your child with the right camp or program. They provide you with personalized guidance, educate you about the different types of programs that are available and help you think through what you and your child are looking for. In addition to sleep-away camps, they can also refer to teen tours, academic programs, language immersion programs and community service programs (big with the pre-college application set). Some also refer to day camps, and some to corporate or business internships. Most have been in business for years, and they conduct extensive on-site visits and interviews with directors, making them very knowledgeable about a wide range of programs. Perhaps more importantly, they know the camps' personalities—for instance, which are very outdoorsy and which are less so? Which require uniforms? Which have more competitive environments and which are more nurturing? In effect, the consultants have done the research for you and are objective advisors who can tell you the pluses and minuses of programs and help you compare them. Finally, they will put in the time and effort to get to know you and your child in order to help you find the right program based on your child's personality and interests, your family's financial needs and any other considerations.

Camp consultants generally conduct telephone interviews with parents (and possibly the children, depending on their age) and provide information on several camps. The services are free to you since they earn commissions of 10-15% from the camp (the fact that they don't work for any one camp is supposed to keep them unbiased). The consultants we spoke with all said the vast majority of their clients come to them through word of mouth.

Camp Connection
(914) 944-3030
www.thecampconnection.com
susan@thecampconnection.com

Camp Connection has been in business for over twenty years, and advises thousands of families each year. Susan is their Westchester representative, and they also have offices in New Jersey, Long Island and Manhattan. The Camp Connection advisors visit about seventy programs each summer and meet with program directors in the off season.

The Camp Experts and Teen Summers
(914) 472-4747
www.campexperts.com
joanne@campexperts.com

Joanne and Jack have been camp consultants for almost twenty years, and they help many thousands of families each year. They have eighteen offices across the country and families work with the consultant based in their area. During the summer, all of the Camp Experts travel to see programs in operation, and in the off season program directors come to visit them.

Student Summers Inc. / The Camp Lady
(201) 847-0505
www.campsandtrips.com
sueellen@studentsummers.com

Student Summers Inc./The Camp Lady is one of the oldest camp advisory services. Sue Ellen serves families in Westchester and New Jersey, but since she has several East Coast offices she can tap into the knowledge and experience of her partners if you're interested in going outside of the region. During the summer she visits about seventy camps up and down the East Coast, and off season she meets with educational program directors.

Summer Camp & Trip Resources
(914) 722-2644
www.summercampsandtrips.com

Ellen Schwartz Wylie and her colleague in the Boston area have twelve years of experience, and an expertise in children with special needs. In addition to being a parent with kids at camp, Ellen prides herself on personalized service. She travels all summer, visiting camps and programs.

The Summer Lady
(866) 566-CAMP (-2267)
info@thesummerlady.com
www.thesummerlady.com

The Summer Lady has been a camp consultant for over twenty years, and helps about 3,000 families each year. She visits over thirty sleep-away camps each summer.

Everything Summer
(914) 472-8600
www.everythingsummer.com
jill@everythingsummer.com

This camp consultant works on a fee basis; fees can range up to several hundred dollars. Since Jill does not earn commissions from the camps and programs, she will refer to a wider range of programs (including day camps and programs that have no marketing budget). She specializes in families based in Westchester and Southern Connecticut and visits many programs in the U.S. and abroad every year. In addition, Everything Summer has proprietary tools and a network of professionals that provide the full range of services to make summers stress-free, including planning ahead, organizing, shopping, packing and travel (with or without children).

Savvy Suggestion

Make sure you find out when registration begins for the programs that you are interested in. For our kids' local day camp, we had to register in February. Some of the private camps are full by October. We know of at least one popular camp program that holds a first-come, first-serve lottery where parents line up in the middle of the night to ensure their kids a spot. *Yikes!*

❓ Questions Every Parent Should Ask ❓
When Making a Final Decision

Now that you've narrowed your search down to a couple of great camps, how do you make the final decision? Obviously, the best way is to visit the camp—usually the summer before—and view it "in action" to get a sense of its personality and see whether you can picture your child (and she can picture herself) there. Some camp directors also do "road shows" where they visit prospective families, discuss their camp and answer parents' questions. The questions you might want to ask include:

* What is the camp's philosophy?
* How many children are in the bunk or group and how many counselors?
* How many campers return each year? (The average return rate is 65-70%.)
* How are counselors screened (e.g., work history, criminal background checks, face-to-face interviews, character references)?
* How are counselors trained? How are they supervised?
* Are the sports activities run by people trained in them?
* Is there a doctor at the camp? Where is the closest hospital?
* How often can campers call home? Do they have access to e-mail? (At some camps, children are limited to one call per week, and most camps don't allow cell phones.)

RIGHT IN YOUR OWN BACKYARD

For preschoolers and young children, you'll usually be looking for a day camp, either one that offers shorter sessions (two to three hours each morning) or an all-day option. There are many private day camps in Westchester with fabulous facilities, expert instruction, and even campers bussed up from Manhattan. Some of the camp consultants listed above will help you find day camps. Otherwise, a neighbor's or friend's referral might suffice. In addition to the private camps in your area, most of the communities in Westchester have a town or village recreation program. These are definitely worth looking into—they're neighborhood or community programs that are close by, and they're usually more affordable than some of the private programs. Some community camps have pools (or take the children to a community pool) for swimming lessons and free play while others rely on sprinklers and hoses to cool off the kiddies. Both Sam and Simon have attended the day camp run by Edgemont Recreation and both loved it. They adored their counselors and played sports, did arts & crafts and music, and took nature hikes. And since many of these programs are restricted to local residents (or, at a minimum, local residents are given first crack at registration) your children will get to be with kids their age who they'll be attending kindergarten and elementary school with.

CAMP SUPPLIES

Your little camper will need lots of supplies—from a sleeping bag to stationery to bug spray (and we won't even go into the pillows with built-in stereo speakers!). For one-stop shopping for clothing (with camp logos or without), labeling kits, bedding, bath supplies, duffel bags and trunks, canteens and mess kits, outdoor gear and more, three great resources are:

www.campsupplies.com

www.bunkline.com

www.gilbin.com

Camp Labels

During Sam's first summer at camp, Laura was amazed when she saw the lost & found bin—how could so few kids lose so much stuff? Needless to say, it's unwise to send your children to camp without fully personalized, labeled clothes and belongings. And if your child has a health concern—a serious allergy, for example—you can add that information to the labels for added peace of mind. To help you make sure that your child doesn't lose her very favorite t-shirt, you can use iron-on labels, sew-on labels, clothing tattoos or laundry stamps, which all come in a variety of colors, with or without icons or designs. In addition to clothing labels, many of the below sources offer labels for plastics, as well as bag tags for diaper bags, book bags, lunch boxes, etc. Make sure you choose labels that are easy to read and won't come off in the dishwasher or washing machine. If you don't want to mess around with labels, at the very, very least, invest in a Sharpie or permanent laundry marker and start writing!

www.babylabels.com

www.joline.lovablelabels.ca

www.stuckonyou.biz

Care Packages

Before you send off a box stuffed with sweets and goodies, check the camp's policy. Some require the food to be kosher, whereas others do not permit junk food, so it's best to find out first. Oh, and let's not forget what our teachers always taught us . . . be sure you send enough to share!

These websites will package and mail your hugs and kisses. Some do age– and gender-specific packages, or ones focused on a category of your choice (e.g., sports, beach, pedicure). Some will include games, tricks, jokes, plush toys and treats, and some will even include a postcard to encourage a polite thank-you note from your child. Some even do counselor gifts. Prices range up to about $50 (plus shipping and handling) per package.

www.bunkbuddies.com
(800) 678-9047

www.carepackages.com
(877) 354-1205

www.carepackagestyle.com
(866) 297-8419

www.eswak.com
(800) 888-7925

Summer camp is a wonderful opportunity for kids to learn new skills, enlarge their circle of friends and, of course, to have fun. And in the case of overnight camp, it's a chance to get away from home and gain independence and build confidence. Both of us attended day and sleep-away camps as children and the experiences that we took away from those summers are still with us today. Betsy can't wait until Simon is old enough to go to the same camp she went to for five years . . . and Laura just can't wait for the opportunity to sleep late again!

Party Animals

Puppets, Ponies & Power Rangers:
Sensational Birthday Celebrations

Party Necessities:
Cakes, Rentals & Supplies

Helpful Websites

When we wrote the first version of KidSavvy, *Simon and Sam had only had a few birthdays between them, so our firsthand knowledge of throwing parties was somewhat limited.* However, now that the boys are several years older–and Laura's had a second child–we've thrown a lot more parties...and attended a ton of them. And, as always, we've depended heavily on other "Savvy Suburbanites" to give us their opinions and ideas on the subject. As a result, this is one of the chapters that expanded the most from the last edition: we hope it helps you plan a fun and memorable birthday bash for your child.

For some young ones, a birthday is treated as an epic celebration that can literally become a three-ring circus. (Seriously, you can arrange for live animals to come to your house for pony rides and petting zoos.) On a slightly smaller scale, you can arrange to have in-home entertainment ranging from clowns to magicians to singers to scientists. You can even get the Power Rangers or the Powerpuff Girls to show up, if you and your child are so inclined. Also keep in mind that practically any place that has classes (gym, dance, music) or activities (arts & crafts, sports, karate) also has some sort of birthday party package. So if your child absolutely adores a particular class, you may want to have her birthday there.

The backyard birthday parties of our youth have taken a back seat to the "facility based" parties of today. Why? One word springs to mind: convenience! In many cases these venues provide everything from invitations to goody bags, and they handle the clean up. That being said, if you're looking for a truly original celebration, designing one yourself is probably the best bet–you're limited only by your imagination. Bear in mind that weather is a significant factor to consider when planning larger parties; many of us simply don't have the room indoors for all the partygoers and their parents. When he was younger, Sam, being a summer baby, had backyard barbecue parties that both kids and adults enjoyed. The mess was kept outside and there was ample room for the kids to run around (and Laura just kept her fingers crossed that it wouldn't rain).

This is probably a good time to mention there are a few guidelines to keep in mind if you want a birthday party to run smoothly, particularly if the children are very young (4 and under) or if you're planning to host a party at your house. First, always have a "welcoming" activity that the kids can do until everyone arrives. For example, tape some butcher paper to the floor so the kids can draw and stick stickers on it. Think of the party as being divided into ten- to fifteen-minute increments. For toddlers, you are going to want to change the activity with each block of time, as their attention spans can't handle much more than that. If a particular activity isn't going well you can drop it and move on; if it is going well, you can stretch it out a bit.

It is a must to have some sort of centralized activity so that the children are occupied. At Sam's second birthday a singer (whose services were won at a silent auction) delighted the kids with music, interactive songs and small instruments for them to play. When Laura had asked the songstress to play for an hour, she just laughed: she knew that even the best performer can only captivate a very young crowd for about half an hour. So don't plan on a one-hour mini-concert only to be disappointed that most children have abandoned the singer for something they deem more interesting, like stepping on ant hills.

If you book an entertainer, they should not perform for much longer than thirty to forty minutes. We know what you're thinking: "I'm spending *how* much for half an hour?" But trust us, there is a point of diminishing returns, and in the end you'd rather everyone remember the clown who left them begging for more, not the clown who had them running for the door. Lastly, kids' parties are pretty short: for younger children, about an hour could be enough; older kids can handle two to three hours or more.

Until their children are 4 or 5, most parents assume they will be staying for a party, so it's a good idea to have something for the adults to nibble on. Betsy always has a bagel platter, fruit and coffee on hand; any leftovers can always be brought home.

When you consider the millions of details we all juggle on a daily basis, it's odd how throwing a kids' birthday party can totally stress us out. We can't eliminate the stress for you, but we can provide some advice on party spots, entertainers and activities. We asked a bunch of local moms about their favorites and have listed some of the most popular recommendations below. One thing we've definitely discovered is that there is absolutely no correlation between how much money you spend and how much fun the kids have at the party. The other thing we've learned is that pizza plus cake equals fun; if they served it at the doctor's office, your kids would probably even enjoy going there.

Savvy Suggestion

Party Game Classics
(With a Few New Twists)

* Musical Towels for a pool party (Kids can keep the towels as a party favor.)
* Simon Says (Substitute your child's name for Simon.)
* Freeze Dance
* Pin the Tail on the Donkey
* Treasure Hunt (The treasure is the goody bags.)
* Egg Relays (Hard boiled eggs please!)
* Sand Art (This is much better done outdoors.)
* Face Painting
* Temporary Tattoos
* The Hokey-Pokey

PUPPETS, PONIES & POWER RANGERS: SENSATIONAL BIRTHDAY CELEBRATIONS

Animals

Stew Leonard's
1 Stew Leonard Dr., Yonkers
(914) 375-4700
www.stewleonards.com

It's an hour and a half of non-stop action. From face painting upon arrival to visiting with the farm animals at the small zoo (during the warmer months), the kids are kept entertained. Several of Stew's assistants help kids do an arts & crafts project, make their own sundaes, have pizza and cake, sing songs and do dances. Weather permitting, the party can be held on the outside deck by the zoo. In the colder months, there is a private indoor party

Savvy Suggestion

Never get caught scrambling for a gift again. Buy multiples of children's gifts when you find them on sale and stash them in a closet for future birthday parties.

room. "Wow the Cow" will also make a special appearance—but don't worry, they won't be offended if your child prefers to take a pass on their mooing mascot.

Ages: 3-6

Cost: $219.95 for 10 children, $12.95 for each additional child. The staff does not accept tips.

The Nature of Things
7 Sugar Hill Rd., North Salem
(914) 276-3454
www.thenatureofthings.com

Your child can choose from over 160 animals for this one-hour educational, yet highly entertaining, activity. The staff will bring in ten to twelve animals—ranging from amphibians, reptiles and insects to mammals and birds—for a hands-on visit either in the comfort of your own home or at a rented facility. Parties can include songs and games, and the birthday child gets a free nature book.

Ages: 3 and up

Cost: $235-$410, depending on the number of children and location

Arts & Crafts

Fun Craft
590 Central Ave., Scarsdale
(914) 472-1748
www.funcraftparties.com

You can choose from a wide variety of age-appropriate activities, including "create a mat" (great for the young ones), sand art, puppet making, plastercraft, soap making, and more. Basic parties include a deejay, video games, karaoke, cupcakes, soda, paper goods, balloons, invitations and thank-you cards, as well as goody bags. They will also arrange for food to be brought in if you'd like.

There is an eight-child minimum during the week and a twelve-child minimum on the weekends. Check their website for special printable discount coupons.

Ages: 3-14

Cost: The basic package starts at $8.99 per child, plus the cost of the project. Most projects are $7.99-11.99 per child.

Little Rembrandt
116 S. Ridge St. (Rye Ridge Shopping Center), Rye Brook
(914) 939-1400
www.littlerembrandt.info

They offer two different types of crafts parties: a painting party and a pet party. For the first, each child does a paint-your-own pottery project to take home with him. For the second, each child gets a paintable pet sculpture, paintable t-shirt, pet cradle and pet "birth certificate." All parties include invitations, cake, beverages, face painting and dancing. You can order a piñata, pizza, or platters of food for an additional cost.

Ages: 2 and up

Cost: $225 for 10 kids, $21 for each additional child

Clowns & Characters

Marcia the Musical Moose
(212) 567-0682
www.marciathemusicalmoose.com

Marcia charms youngsters with guitar music, magic and puppets. The show is forty-five minutes for children age 3 and under, and sixty minutes for children age 4 and up.

Ages: 1-7, but best for the younger ones

Cost: $220-$250

Dave's Cast of Characters
(914) 235-7100
www.davescast.com

It seems like there is nothing Dave and his "cast" can't do. From costumed characters to clowns to carnival games—they do it all. Want a ball pit? An inflatable bouncy castle? Laser tag, pony rides or pop diva look-a-likes? No problem. Dave's staff will customize any party to meet your needs and your guest list.

Ages: 1 and up

Cost: $295 and up for 1 hour

Pinkie the Clown
(800) 246-PINK (-7465)
www.pinkietheclown.com

The antidote for those of us with "clown issues," Pinkie is sweet and upbeat without being the slightest bit scary. She wears minimal face make-up and performs magic tricks, tells age-appropriate jokes and makes balloon animals or hats for all the kids.

Ages: 3-7

Cost: $375 for 1 hour

Savvy Suggestion

If you or your spouse is willing to be a clown for a day, you can save money by renting the costume of your choice and making a cameo appearance at the end of the party to help with the cake or hand out party favors.

Beyond Costumes
530 Nepperhan Ave., Yonkers
(914) 963-1333

Hours: Monday-Friday 10 am-5 pm, Saturday 10 am-3 pm

Cooking

Bellizzi
1272 Boston Post Rd., Larchmont
(914) 833-5800
153 Main St., Mount Kisco
(914) 241-1200
www.bellizzi.ws

In addition to a circus room and an "underwater" room, they also have a game room with non-violent video games. Depending on the birthday party package you choose, the cost can include chef hats, make-your-own pizzas, beverages, cake, game-room tokens and invitations. Packages and prices are described on their website.

Ages: 2-10

Cost: $18-24 per child, with a minimum of 15 children

The Cookie Jar

172 Boston Post Rd., Mamaroneck
(914) 835-3738
www.cookiejarparties.com

At these parties children decorate cookies in shapes according to the party theme, which include "Princess," "Rock & Roll," "Creepy Crawly Critters" and "Tea Party." Party activities include age-appropriate games and decorating a chef hat or apron and two cookies. The price includes invitations, bottled water and paper goods. You can "deluxe" any party to include pizza, juice or soda, balloons and cake for an additional cost. You can even do an evening party (after 5:30 pm) where guests can wear their pj's.

Ages: 4 and up

Cost: $18.95 and up per child

Little Cooks

(888) 695-COOK or (201) 493-9412 (ask for Joyce)
www.littlecooks.com

This is a party idea that really cooks! A "chef" will come to your house and help kids whip up a main course and a dessert. Perennial favorites include "tic-tac-toe" pizza and cookie lollipops. The cost includes chef's hats, aprons and ingredients.

Ages: 4-14

Cost: $260 for 10 children; $24 for each additional child

Little Scoops

60-62 Washington Ave., Pleasantville
(914) 741-0011
www.littlescoops.com

An old-fashioned ice cream parlor designed for children. At birthday parties children make their own sundaes and play age-appropriate games. The cost includes invitations and thank-you notes (which you can choose on their website), as well as pizza and drinks. The birthday child gets a t-shirt—to be autographed by the partygoers—and they can put their handprint on the birthday wall. Two more locations of Little Scoops are slated to open in Scarsdale and White Plains; check the website for updated information.

Ages: 3-13

Cost: $375 for 15 children; $21 for each additional child

Main Street Sweets
35 Main St., Tarrytown
(914) 332-5757

Parties include pizza, make-your-own sundaes, traditional games, paper goods and balloons, and end with a craft project.

Ages: 3-13

Cost: $245 for 15 children; $14.50 for each additional child

Scoops Ice Cream and Party Café
23 Taylor Square, West Harrison
(914) 287-7555

Parties include pizza, a craft project, (if you choose photo craft you must pay for the film), hand painting, bingo, brownies and make-your-own sundaes. The birthday child gets to decorate his own little ice cream cake.

Ages: 3 and up

Cost: $20 per child

Dolls

Madame Alexander Doll Company
615 West 131st St., New York
(212) 283-5900
www.madamealexander.com

At parties at this doll-making company—which has been in business for eighty years—touching is allowed. Go on a private factory tour and visit the doll hospital, where Grandma Greta tends to those needing repair. Mini-workshops give children the chance to exercise their own creative expression and decorate their own doll shoes and hats. Parties are available Monday-Saturday.

Ages: 3 and up

Cost: $30-95 per child

Glamour

Sharkey's Cuts for Kids
2100 Boston Post Rd., Larchmont
(914) 834-5300
220 E. Putnam Ave., Cos Cob, CT
(203) 629-KIDS
1866 Post Rd. E., Westport, CT
(203) 254-2200
www.sharkeyscutsforkids.com

Hair, nails and makeup: what more can a girl ask for? Well, how about karaoke, body glitter, a disco ball, sequin dresses and a fashion show? Packages include pizza or tea sandwiches, juice or soda, paper goods and balloons, and a party favor.

Ages: 5-13

Cost: $425 for 12 kids, $20 for each additional child

Magicians

Magically Yours
(516) 677-0883
www.magic-al.com

"Magic Al" (along with his bird, "Poopsie") performs eye-popping illusions and sidesplitting comedy for kids of all ages. A veteran entertainer, he's a popular choice among many local celebrities and will certainly make your child feel like a star. He has also just released a new DVD, *It's a Magic-Al World*, which makes a great party favor.

Ages: 3 and up

Cost: $750 for 1 hour

Simply Magic
(718) 824-7705

John Turbo provides great family entertainment that all the kids participate in. He uses rabbits, doves, guinea pigs and gerbils in his magic show.

Ages: 4 and up

Cost: $150 for 1 hour

Movie Theaters

Reel Kool Party
www.national-amusements.com

The party package includes theater admission, a "Kool Refresh-ment Combo" (popcorn, drink and candy) for each child, a party area for up to one hour before or after the movie (depending on showtime), unlimited popcorn and soda in the party area, all paper goods and invitations, and a complimentary group photo. Additional food (Nathan's or Sbarro's, for example) is optional and at additional cost. Parties are available at the City Center 15 Cinema De Lux (White Plains) and All Westchester Saw Mill Multiplex (Hawthorne) locations.

Ages: 5 and up

Cost: $16.50 per child, with a minimum of 10 children and a maxi-mum of 20

Clearview Cinemas
(877) KID-FUN6
www.clearviewcinemas.com

This package includes a private screening, popcorn, soda, cake, all paper goods, and staff to help. Best of all, your child's name appears on the marquee. If there is not an appropriate movie playing at the time of your child's party, you can bring in a favorite DVD to be viewed on "the big screen." You can also bring in your own cake and additional food. Clearview has locations in Bedford, Bronxville, Larchmont, Mamaroneck, Mount Kisco, Rye, White Plains and Yonkers. Parties are available Monday-Thursday 4-6 pm, Friday 3:30-5:30 pm, and Saturday-Sunday 10 am-12 pm.

Ages: 5 and up

Cost: Monday-Thursday, $395 for 25 kids; Friday-Sunday, $495 for 25 kids

Musical Entertainers

Graham Clarke
(914) 669-5843
www.grahamclarke.com

Silly, zany and all the rage, Graham is beloved by the preschool set. He sings songs that have kids rolling in the aisles and works the crowd into a frenzy. He's recorded several of his own CDs, which can be given away as party favors.

Ages: 3-7

Cost: $350 for 30 minutes, $400 for 45 minutes, $450 for 1 hour

JiJi's
(914) 949-7217

Delores JiJi has a unique music program. She comes to your location with her guitar, puppets, scarves and instruments. Kids participate fully in the program and even put on a parade. Delores performs for 1 1/2 hours.

Ages: 2-6

Cost: $245

A Joyful Noise
(914) 576-3854
www.themusicofbusiness.com/joyfulnoise

Saragail Benjamin is a trained teacher and composer who will engage your children with a highly participatory performance that includes original songs, sing-alongs, puppets, magic, dancing and percussion.

Ages: 1-7

Cost: $250 for 45 minutes

Sing Me a Story
(212) 501-4635
www.susanmirwis.com

Susan Mirwis is a singer and actress who will delight your child with musical storytelling, creative movement and instruments to play along.

Ages: 3-8

Cost: $250 for 45 minutes

Stevie B and Andy
(917) 647-3611
andrewbaum@verizon.net

Manhattan-based singers and guitar players who have teamed up to play and sing songs for children. Their performances are for children of all ages and include a lot of participation. Their two-voice, two-guitar approach brings new life to familiar songs and will introduce your child to new favorites.

Ages: All

Cost: $300; they will play for 30-40 minutes for the kids and then another 30 minutes for the adults.

Savvy Suggestion

Brilliant Birthday Bashes
(That Won't Break the Bank)

* Fill a piñata with pre-wrapped and labeled gifts so every guest gets the perfect prize (an especially good idea if your guests vary widely in age).
* Spread bubble wrap on the floor. Play music and have the kids dance and stomp on the bubbles.
* Have children decorate ceramic flower pots and plant a flower in each to take home.
* For a first birthday, ask everyone to bring something for a time capsule that the child will open on her 21st birthday.
* Pre-bake sugar cookies using fun cookie cutters for children to decorate using colored frosting, mini-M&Ms, sprinkles and other toppings. (For older kids making the cookies can be part of the festivities.)
* Hire some neighborhood teens to help out at your party.

Puppets

Rick Stevens
(917) 301-6778

A primo puppeteer. Rick sets up a mini-theater in your home or party space and delights kids with his famous Sesame send-up, including a certain lovable, furry, blue monster.

Ages: 2-6

Cost: $250 for 35 minutes

Science

Mad Science
(914) 948-8319
www.madscience.org

Kids take part in hands-on experiments like making tornado tubes or unlocking the mysteries of electricity, air pressure and chemical reactions. They supply all the equipment and will come to you. Parties end with children making silly putty or slime. For an additional charge, parties can include a rocket launch or a dry ice option.

Ages: 5-12

Cost: $250 and up for 1 hour

Sports

Coach Jimmy's Sports

10 Mill Rd. (Holy Trinity Greek Orthodox Church), New Rochelle
(845) 629-9169

Coach Jimmy has access to a full-size gym and will lead games of floor hockey, dodge ball, kickball, running bases, soccer, basketball, T-ball, baseball or football. (He also does classes and clinics during the week.) You can invite up to thirty kids to the party.

Ages: 3-12

Cost: $210 for two hours

Court Sports

150 Clearbrook Rd., Elmsford
(914) 592-3005
www.court-sports.com

If your kid loves sports then this is a great idea for a party venue. Older kids can choose basketball, soccer, volleyball or dodge ball; younger kids can have a "gym kids" party. There is also a bouncy castle (for an additional $100 fee) to keep the party hopping.

Ages: 3-14

Cost: $300 for two hours, with a maximum of 15 children

Elmsford Raceway

17 Raceway Ln. (No. Payne St.), Elmsford
(914) 592-5375
www.flatoutfun.com

Parties at this slot-car raceway involve an hour of racing and half an hour of refreshments. Kids have races, and prizes are given out to the winners. You supply food and cake.

Ages: 5 and up

Cost: $250; maximum of 16 children

Frozen Ropes

55 S. Broadway, White Plains
(914) 993-6355
www.frozenropes.com

The first ninety minutes of the party are spent in the batting cages with an instructor who pitches balls and plays games with the kids. For the younger set (3- to 5-year-olds) they have a "Born to Play" party, where the kids play baseball-related age-appropriate games. The last half hour is for refreshments (you supply the food, cake and beverages). The birthday child gets a baseball-related favor.

Ages: 3 and up

Cost: $250 for 10 kids; $12.50 for each additional child

Last Licks

1074 Wilmot Rd. (Golden Horseshoe Shopping Center), Scarsdale
(914) 725-5932
www.lastlicks.net

A great place for sports buffs, this ice cream store is full of memorabilia and is known for its autograph signings by famous pro football and baseball players. Party packages include a craft project, baseball card bingo, pizza, soda, make-your-own sundaes, and gift bags. They also provide a special gift for the birthday child.

Ages: 1 and up

Cost: $25-35 per child

The Little Gym

777 White Plains Rd., Scarsdale
(914) 722-0072
www.thelittlegym.com

Children can literally bounce off the walls at this gym facility. There are trampolines, swings, mats and a trained gym staff to help kids safely enjoy all the fun equipment. This may be a good place to have your party if you have a wide age-range of kids to invite: older ones can enjoy the more advanced options while babies can roll around on the cushiony floor mats (you can rest assured they're clean—no shoes or socks are allowed in the gym!). The party package includes invitations, paper goods and pizza, but you can bring in your own food as well.

Ages: 1 and up

Cost: $400 for up to 12 children; $12 for each additional child

New York Knicks Orange and Blue Birthday Bash
Madison Square Garden (34th St. and 7th Ave.), New York
(212) 465-6080
www.nba.com/knicks/tickets/groups-05.html

Buy fifteen or more tickets to a Knicks game and receive free goody bags and a special birthday gift bag, including an autographed mini-ball. They will even display a free birthday message from the Knicks on the Gardenvision scoreboard.

Ages: 5-12

Cost: Varies based on the cost of the tickets, which start at $25

Renaissance Westchester Hotel
80 W. Red Oak Ln., West Harrison
(914) 694-5400
http://marriott.com/property/propertypage/hpnsh

Throw a pool party any time of year at the Renaissance Westchester's indoor pool! They provide two lifeguards, pizza, ice cream cake, soda and juice for the kids, and coffee for the grown-ups, as well as balloons and paper goods. Parties are available Monday-Thursday 4-6 pm and Sunday 3-5 pm. For the tween set, you can even get a hotel room, order room service and have a sleepover (room rates vary by season; call for prices).

Ages: 5 and up

Cost: $550 for 20 kids and 5 adults; $10 for each additional child

SportTime USA
380 Saw Mill River Rd. (Rte. 9A), Elmsford
(914) 592-2111
www.sportimeusa.com

Bumper cars, batting cages, over 200 arcade games and more. There is also a "soft adventure" area for children age 5 and under. Birthday parties last ninety minutes and include invitations and paper goods, pizza, soda or juice, ride tickets and game tokens, and a gift for the birthday child. There's also a party package featuring Laser Tag.

Ages: 5 and up

Cost: $13.95 and up per child, with a minimum of 10 children

White Plains Lanes
47 Tarrytown Rd., White Plains
(914) 948-2677
www.amf.com

Party packages include bowling, shoe rental, invitations and paper goods, a choice of food, beverages and cake, and an authentic bowling pin that all the guests can sign for the birthday boy or girl. They will put up "bumpers" to avoid gutter balls, so each child will be able to knock down at least a few pins. They also have an "X-treme" bowling package for kids age 8 and up that includes lights, loud music and wild challenges.

Ages: 5 and up
Cost: $19.99 per child

Savvy Superlatives

Our Favorite Party Favors

* Have the kids decorate simple wooden frames (from a craft shop) with paint pens, glitter glue, stickers and pom-poms. Take Polaroid or digital photos of the kids at the party, put them in the frames, and send the guests home with a personalized keepsake.
* *Invisible Ink* or *Mad Libs* books, which you can often find to fit the party theme (Laura found baseball ones for Sam's 7th birthday).
* Buy plastic, kid-sized seats and use a permanent marker to personalize them for each guest.
* Give each guest a mini-photo album. Send one or two photos of the party in each thank-you note.
* Instead of gifts, try a book exchange. Every kid brings a wrapped book, and every kid takes a wrapped book home.
* Burn a compilation CD of your child's favorite tunes or your party theme and give it out at the end of the party.

Pick a Theme, Any Theme

It's My Party

114 Boston Post Rd., Mamaroneck
(914) 381-BDAY (-2329)
www.itsmypartyLLC.com

This all-inclusive party provider will do any theme you choose, from a "Dream Theme" to a "Cooking Celebration," and their interchangeable sliding wall murals will provide the fitting back-drop. At the cooking parties, kids won't just be decorating treats—they'll be creating, from scratch, cakes, pretzels, pancakes, pasta and candy. Parties include custom-made invitations and thank-you notes, cake, food, goody bags and recipes. Nibbles, drinks and coffee for the adults are also included.

Ages: All ages

Cost: $750 and up for 15 children

Kiddie Parties

174 Harris Rd., Bedford Hills
(914) 242-0102
www.kiddieparties.com

This all-inclusive party site offers a wide variety of themes—including bear or doll stuffing, pirate adventures, tea parties, "Razzle Dazzle" glamour parties and more. Parties include an arts & crafts project; with the bear or doll stuffing, each child decorates a t-shirt for their new friend, chooses from a large selection of outfits and receives a "birth certificate." Parents can watch from a "bistro area" while the kids are entertained. Packages include invitations, thank-you notes, paper goods, music, games and food. Optional add-ons include antique popcorn and cotton candy carts, a bubble machine and personalized goody bags.

Ages: 1-12

Cost: Theme parties are $399 for 12 children ($18 for each additional child). Bear and doll stuffing parties are $275 for 12 children, plus the cost of the toy (which start at $10).

The Scholastic Store
450 Central Ave., Scarsdale
(914) 725-7201

Birthday parties are ninety minutes long. Each party includes games, activities and a craft project based on the theme you choose. For example, if you select a princess party, kids can dress up as princes and princesses and decorate a crown or tiara. Other popular themes include the "Klutz Build-a-Book Party" and the "Royal Birthday Bash." Cupcakes, juice boxes and decorations are included. You can order pizza and veggie platters for an additional cost. You supply the cake.

Ages: 3-6

Cost: $375 and up for 15 children, $20 per additional child

PARTY NECESSITIES:
CAKES, RENTALS & SUPPLIES

Cakes

If you're feeling particularly ambitious, take a stab at making your own cake. Many of the party stores listed below have fun cake molds and toppings. If you'd prefer to go the store-bought route you'll be able to get a perfectly delicious cake at your local bakery or supermarket. However, if you're looking for something just a little bit more special (the icing on the cake, so to speak) check out these places.

Lexington Square Cafe
510 Lexington Ave., Mount Kisco
(914) 244-3663
www.lexingtonsquarecafe.com

This restaurant is known for more than its food. They have an eye-popping array of original creations to fit any theme and every budget. A week's notice for cakes is recommended—if you check out the cakes on their website you'll know why.

Riviera Pastry Shop
660 Saw Mill River Rd., Ardsley
(914) 693-9758
www.rivierabakehouse.com

Widely regarded as the most amazing bakery in Southern Westchester, Riviera's selection of whimsical creations is staggering. For specialty cakes you must order at least a week in advance. They can get pricey, but if you want to make your child's special day a little bit more so, these incredible cakes are sure to do just that. Ben's second birthday featured a cake with blue icing, and he looked awfully cute with it all over his face!

Stew Leonard's
1 Stew Leonard Dr., Yonkers
(914) 375-4700
www.stewleonards.com

A slightly less expensive option that doesn't skimp on the splendor. They offer a wide variety of popular character, theme and even photo cakes.

Rentals & Supplies

In addition to the many independent party supply stores in the county, there are two major chains in Westchester that stock lots of goodies: **Party City** (www.partycity.com), with five locations (Mount Kisco, Port Chester, Yonkers, Yorktown Heights and Stamford, CT) and **Rojay Party Super Store** with three locations (Mount Vernon, White Plains and Yonkers). Or, check out the following locations for your party needs.

Accommodating Party Rentals
3663 Lee Rd., Jefferson Valley
(914) 528-1800
www.aprentals.com

They'll rent you everything from tents, linens, tables and chairs to hog dog wagons, carnival equipment and BBQs.

Alperson Party Rentals
107 Fairview Park Dr., Elmsford
(914) 592-8300
www.alpersonpartyrentals.com

If you don't happen to have seating for forty, if you're looking for an industrial-size coffee maker, or if you want those cute little party tables and chairs for kids, you may want to try Alperson. They will deliver and pick up items with a minimum order of $75 (it may be more, depending on where you live). Otherwise, you can load up the back of your SUV with anything and everything you need to complete the perfect party.

Bobby's Balloon Works
129 Main St., Dobbs Ferry
(914) 693-2795
www.balloonworksusa.com

This store has every sort of balloon (including hard-to-find varieties like die-cut mylars), and if they don't, they will order it so that you'll have it in two days. And they deliver too!

Strauss Warehouse Outlet
140 Horton Ave., Port Chester
(914) 939-3544

This discount mega-store carries everything you could need for a birthday party, and at cheaper prices than you'll find anywhere else. It's also *the* place for all your Halloween needs.

HELPFUL WEBSITES

Going online is one of the easiest and most convenient ways of taking care of all your party needs, and, best of all, you can do it from the comfort of your home. These sites let you search by theme, age, favorite characters and more. Plus, you can get everything from invitations to the goodies in your goody bag shipped directly to your front door. Now that's a reason to celebrate!

www.foryourparty.com
This is a great site for your personalized party needs. Choose from a wide selection of napkins, gift cards, party favors and more.

www.oriental.com
Wondering where to find a six-foot inflatable palm tree or pick up a dozen candy necklaces? This is the ultimate resource for fun things that won't cost a fortune. They also have a fabulous selection of stuff for goody bags and party favors.

www.pinatas.com
More piñatas than you can shake a stick at! Also, for those of you who believe blindfolds, bats and small children don't mix, they sell a pull-string conversion kit.

www.plumparty.com
This upscale site has a unique collection of party supplies and gifts, including invitations and serving items, such as the "Andy Warhol Fantastic in Plastic" tabletop collection. You can choose from about a hundred different themes for a party.

www.shindigz.com
Bearing the slogan "The World's Largest Party Superstore," this site offers collections of themes for "First Birthdayz," "Kid Birthdayz" and "Teen Birthdayz," including decorating basics, personalized products, games and crafts, invitations, piñatas, cakes and costumes. They will also personalize balloons, streamers, tableware and more.

www.spitfiregirl.com
Offbeat and unusual party invitations, baby gifts and baby shower favors, including "box" invitations full of kitschy trinkets and toys to fit the party's theme; for example, fiesta invitations contain a mini-blender and a margarita glass.

Following are some additional party sites, where you can get invitations, paper goods, balloons, streamers and more.

* ✱ www.iparty.com
* ✱ www.birthdayexpress.com
* ✱ www.birthdayinabox.com

Savvy Suggestion

One of the coolest gifts we've ever seen is a customized CD where every song contains your child's name. Nothing made our kids feel more special than feeling like the music was literally being sung for them. They have an enormous selection of products, many in several languages and even carry customized books now. Average cost is $14.95 plus shipping. www.cds4kids.com.

At Your Service

Hair Today, Gone Tomorrow: Haircutters

Playing It Safe: Professional Childproofing

Stress-Free Suppers: Fake It, Make It or Take It

Midnight Meds: 24-Hour Pharmacies

A Job Well Done: Handymen (and Women)

Picture Perfect: Photo Studios

Neat-o: Organization Experts

There are tons of books out there that answer the simple questions like "How do I wean my baby?" So we thought we'd attack the truly complicated issues of parenthood, such as where to take your child for his first haircut or where to find take-out food that's as good as homemade. Seriously, we know what it's like to need some good suggestions about miscellaneous daily needs. Hopefully these listings of helpful services will make your life a little easier.

HAIR TODAY, GONE TOMORROW: HAIRCUTTERS

Some kids sprout a full head of hair very early on, while some resemble Caillou longer than we might like. Either way, when the time finally comes for that first (and second and third) haircut, there seem to be more and more places popping up in Westchester where you can go to get it done. The novelty vehicle seats, TV monitors and full range of popular videos that seem to work so well for the other kids didn't distract Sam a bit from the task at hand when he was younger; hopefully, you'll have better luck with your child. (Time heals all wounds, though, and he now happily goes to the barbershop.)

If it's your child's first haircut, most places offer to preserve a lock of his or her hair and give you a certificate commemorating the momentous event. Generally all of these places will take you on a walk-in basis, but we recommend making an appointment to keep waiting time to a minimum. In addition to the spots listed below, four locations of Snip-Its—a national kids' haircut chain with proprietary characters and a unique approach—are slated to open in Westchester; check the website at **www.snipits.com** for updated info.

Bedford Hills

Kidstyles
701 N. Bedford Rd.
(914) 666-7707

Hours: Monday, Tuesday, Thursday, Friday 10 am-6 pm, Wednesday 10 am-7 pm, Saturday 9 am-4 pm

Hartsdale

Central Barber Shop
197 East Hartsdale Ave.
(914) 723-1945

The guys who own this shop are young and know how to give all the "cool" haircuts for boys, especially for tweens and teens.

Hours: Monday-Wednesday 9 am-6 pm, Thursday and Friday 9 am-7 pm, Saturday 8:30 am-5 pm, Sunday 10 am-4 pm

Larchmont

Sharkey's Cuts for Kids
2100 Boston Post Rd.
(914) 834-5300
www.sharkeyscutsforkids.com

Hours: Monday-Friday 10 am-6 pm, Saturday 9 am-5 pm, Sunday 10 am-3 pm

Scarsdale

Cool Cuts for Kids
450 Central Ave.
(914) 472-6400

Hours: Tuesday-Saturday 10 am-5 pm

Happy Kids Haircuts
832 Scarsdale Ave.
(914) 725-2044

Hours: Tuesday-Saturday 9 am-5 pm

The Bronx

Someplace Special for Kids
492 W. 238th St., Riverdale
(718) 432-6622
www.someplacespecialforkids.com

Hours: Wednesday-Saturday 10 am-6 pm, Sunday 11 am-5 pm

Connecticut

Sharkey's Cuts for Kids
(Two locations)
E. Putnam Avenue, Cos Cob
(203) 629-KIDS
1866 Post Road East, Westport
(203) 254-2200
www.sharkeyscutsforkids.com

Hours: Monday-Friday 10 am-6 pm, Saturday 9 am-5 pm, Sunday 10 am-4 pm (Westport location closed on Sundays)

Subway Barber Shop
315 Greenwich Ave., Greenwich
(203) 869-3263

Hours: Daily, 8 am-5 pm, closed Wednesdays and Sundays

Putnam County

Short Cuts
441 Rte. 6, Mahopac
(845) 621-2969

Hours: Tuesday-Friday 9:30 am-5:30 pm, Thursdays 9:30 am-7 pm, Saturday 9 am-5 pm

PLAYING IT SAFE:
PROFESSIONAL CHILDPROOFING

The first step in childproofing your house is to know your child. Some kids will open every cabinet and be inexplicably drawn to the most dangerous items therein, while some will happily ignore them. Both Simon and Sam, for example, were never very interested in opening cabinets, and to the extent that they tried they were deterred with a simple rubber band wrapped around the knobs. (By the way, we're told this is a bad idea, since rubber bands can break and become a choking hazard.) But Ben made a beeline for the Glass Plus as soon as he was mobile and still isn't satisfied until he opens every cabinet, puts his hand in every toilet and touches every electric outlet. The truth of the matter is, you can buy every childproofing product on the market and it still won't guarantee that your child will never get hurt. Most children we know can unlock a childproof lock quicker than their parents can. (Sam is routinely called upon to open toilet locks for adult guests.) But better safe than sorry, right?

As your child becomes more mobile, for the minimum in safety you'll probably want to plug up outlets, cushion sharp corners and move the Drano to a high shelf. Then, once you've determined your specific needs, visit one of the larger baby stores listed in Chapter 1. They carry a wide range of do-it-yourself equipment— from baby gates to toilet seat locks—and the staff can generally answer your questions and point you in the right direction. If you would feel more comfortable having professional input, we've listed below a few services. Many of these are members of the **International Association for Child Safety (www.iafcs.org)**. In-home evaluation costs vary, but are usually credited towards your purchase.

Child Proofers Inc.
(914) 381-5106

For over fifteen years, Child Proofers has been doing in-home evaluations and installations and designing customized childproofing solutions. They carry some products that are exclusive to the professional childproofing industry.

Cost: An in-home evaluation is $75.

Kids Safe Childproofing
(877) 842-KIDS (-5437) or (203) 925-8622
www.ekidssafe.com

Trained by a certified teaching facility, these childproofers will help you identify your needs as well as install the products you purchase, including safety gates, cabinet and drawer latches, plastic for railings, appliance latches, fire safety products and more.

Cost: An in-home evaluation is $25.

Manhattan Childproofers Inc.
(212) 367-3733
www.manhattanchildproofers.com

They conduct comprehensive in-home safety evaluations, sell and install a large variety of child safety products as well as custom fabrications, and provide guidance for the do-it-yourselfer. They also conduct lead inspections and background checks, and install nanny cams and pool fences. They are certified by the American Automobile Association to conduct child car seat inspections and by the American Red Cross to instruct in First Aid and CPR.

Cost: An in-home safety consultation is $75.

Peek-a-Boo Babyproofing
(866) 322-8488
(203) 762-8480
www.peekaboobabyproofing.com

This company will conduct a room-by-room inspection of your house for potential hazards, give you product recommendations and installation, and carry out environmental testing for radon, gas, water quality and lead paint. Safety consultations include education and strategizing about the creation of "safe zones" in your house. They use off-the-shelf as well as custom-designed solutions and also do pool fence installation.

Cost: An in-home safety consultation is $95.

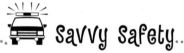
Savvy Safety

Need help making sure your car seat is correctly and safely installed? Many local police and fire departments hold car seat inspection weeks, but they'll usually check yours anytime. Call your local station for details.

STRESS-FREE SUPPERS: FAKE IT, MAKE IT OR TAKE IT

Dinnertime snuck up on you again...yikes! Sound familiar?

When you're dealing with afterschool activities, carpooling and homework, it's no surprise that dinnertime can roll around before you've even had a second to think about what to serve. Betsy is a huge fan of fast food. No, not McDonald's (although she has enough Happy Meal toys to prove otherwise) but great food that can be made fast. There are a number of websites that help you put together easy, healthy meals in a snap; one even gives you a grocery list divided up in convenient categories to make shopping easier. There are also a lot of ways to have a healthy, wholesome meal at home without cooking; supermarkets and gourmet stores offer a wide variety of prepared foods to choose from, such as rotisserie chicken, pastas, fish, side dishes and more. And quite a few services will either help you prepare meals or prepare them for you.

Savvy Suggestion

Leave one kid-level drawer or cabinet un-child-proofed, and fill it with unbreakables that are safe for your child to play with (e.g., Tupperware, wooden spoons). If your child gets frustrated by the other locked doors, you can point him to "his drawer" and let the games begin.

Fake It

There are several services from which you can buy entrées, sides or complete dinners pre-prepared, frozen and delivered to your door. Perfect for busy moms and dads, these services provide everything from hearty, home-style fare to elegant, gourmet dishes. Laura has ordered from all of these services—the food truly is as easy to prepare as they promise, and she and her family have found them to be delicious. Most items are pre-cooked, requiring only reheating, microwaving or a quick simmer, while others (like steak) need to be cooked through, but either way they'll enable you to go from helping with homework to heaping helpings in minutes!

à la Zing
(888) 959-9464
www.alazing.com

This offshoot of Omaha Steaks offers classic "Family Style" meals, "Lighter Side" meals, which contain fifteen grams of fat or less per serving, and "Special Occasion" meals. Recent best sellers include such dishes as stuffed fillet of sole, beef kabobs and boneless pork chops. The Family Style meals serve four and cost from $16 to $40; shipping charges start at $12.99

Artiko
1212 Boston Post Rd., Mamaroneck
(800) 278-4567
www.artikochef.com
The brainchild of Arian Kempera, a Westchester mom who was struggling to get a healthy, family-friendly meal on the table every night, Artiko offers a wide variety of appetizers, main dishes and baked goods, as well as options for special dietary needs. In the "Kids Korner" you can choose from crispy-mashed potatoes in the shape of animals or the alphabet, fish sticks shaped like goldfish, and much more. Most meals are $8-20 per serving ($5-10 for the kids' meals); shipping charges start at $5.95.

Dinewise
(800) 749-1170
www.dinewise.com

Choose from "Family Style", "Express Meals," "Minute Pasta" or "Mix and Match" options, as well as diabetic-friendly dishes. Recent "Chef Selections" included herbed salmon, butternut squash and broccoli and red peppers; seared turkey breast with white and wild rice and baby carrots; and beef top blade with roasted potatoes and asparagus. Complete meals cost approximately $10 to $25 per serving; shipping charges start at $14.99.

Homebistro
(800) 628-5588
www.homebistro.com

Home Bistro carries everything from complete dinners to individual appetizers and desserts, as well as an extensive selection of low carb and "lighter side" meals. They list carb counts, ingredients and nutritional information for each recipe. Recent chef selections included blackened chicken breast in champagne sauce, salmon fillet and shrimp in lobster sauce, and beef stir-fry. Dinners cost $10-20 per serving; shipping charges start at $14.95.

Make It

If you want to say you made it yourself, visit one of these businesses. Select your dishes ahead of time, then, at the kitchen, follow recipes that hang above your work station. Helpful elves have already sliced, diced and prepped the ingredients and, as you follow the simple steps, they will take away the dirty measuring spoons and bowls. You can customize meals if you're watching sodium, fat or any other vice, or even if you just don't like broccoli. You walk out with ready-to-freeze (or refrigerate) meals that need only the final steps of preparation. Each meal is $15-30 and serves 4 to 6 people.

Briarcliff Manor

One...Two...Three...DINNER
North State Rd.
(914) 923-6200
www.onetwothreedinner.com

Scarsdale

Let's Dish!
450 Central Park Ave. (Scarsdale Park Mall)
(914) 722-MEAL (-6325)
www.letsdish.com
Two more Let's Dish! locations are slated to open in Westchester.

Savvy Suggestion

Hit the salad bar at your local supermarket for fresh, pre-chopped ingredients that take less than a minute to assemble. Pour your favorite dressing into the plastic container at home and shake it to create a perfectly tossed, garden-fresh salad. You can use the same trick for a sensational stir-fry shortcut. Get some baby corn, carrots, mushrooms, onions and multicolored peppers, throw them in a pan with some seasonings and voila! Now you're cookin', baby!

Helpful Websites

www.thescramble.com

A weekly e-mail newsletter that gives you five days' worth of recipes and grocery lists. Almost every recipe takes thirty minutes or less to prepare from start to finish, and the meals are kid-friendly without being adult-alienating. The majority of recipes can work for kosher families, vegetarians and those watching their weight. A subscriptions is $5 per month and the newsletter arrives every Wednesday.

www.foodnetwork.com

This is the website for the TV Food Network. The whole site is terrific, but we're huge fans of "30 Minute Meals with Rachel Ray" in particular. If you've ever watched her buzz around a kitchen and pop out a fantastic three-course meal in half an hour you already know she's a parent's best friend. Her recipes—simple to follow and using easy-to-find ingredients—will have you whipping up dinners that are sure to bring your family to the table.

Take It

Waiter on the Run
(800) 460-0090
www.waiterontherun.com

Help is just a phone call away. This service will place and deliver your food order from one of over a dozen local restaurants, including California Pizza Kitchen (pizza and pasta), Casa Maya and Taqueria Mariachi Loco (Mexican), Epstein's Kosher (deli), Sakura

(Japanese), Spiga (Italian) and more, for a $4.99 delivery fee plus 15% tip. You can place your order in advance and request a specific delivery time so that dinner is ready when you are. Currently they serve only central and lower Westchester. They accept orders up to an hour before the restaurant's closing.

Boston Market

Boston Market sells an entire meal that includes your choice of a whole chicken, a pound of turkey or ham, or an entire meatloaf, plus three large side dishes, cornbread, and a whole apple pie for under $20.

Westchester Locations:
* 667 W. Boston Post Rd., Mamaroneck
  (914) 777-1017
* 130 N. Bedford Rd., Mount Kisco
  (914) 241-8800
* 77 Quaker Ridge Rd., New Rochelle
  (914) 235-0550
* 650 Central Park Ave., Scarsdale
  (914) 472-5038
* 32 Xavier Dr., Yonkers
  (914) 963-1305
Connecticut Locations:
* 1345 E. Putnam Ave., Old Greenwich
  (203) 637-4088
* 1018 High Ridge Rd., Stamford
  (203) 321-1410

MIDNIGHT MEDS: 24-HOUR PHARMACIES

Things like croup and vomiting seem to only occur in the wee hours of the night, making them extra challenging to deal with. However, there are several pharmacies in Westchester that are open twenty-four hours a day. So while you're sitting in the steam-filled bathroom singing to your baby, your spouse can head to one of the following stores.

CVS Larchmont
1310 Boston Post Rd. (Ferndale Shopping Center)
(914) 833-3001

CVS Mount Kisco
360 North Bedford Rd.
(914) 241-1260

CVS New Rochelle
309 Main St.
(914) 654-8603

CVS White Plains
325 Mamaroneck Ave.
(914) 287-7650

Savvy Suggestion

Tired of their son always having to pass on birthday cake and other treats due to severe food allergies, Lori Sandler and her husband Mark took matters into their own hands. Divvies is an allergen-conscious bakery in South Salem. They don't use peanuts, tree nuts, eggs or milk in any of their delicious products—like cookies, cupcakes and gourmet popcorn. Everything is made to order in their bakery and can be shipped directly to your home. You can also buy their products in their store, online or at Bloomingdale's in White Plains.

Divvies Bakery
240 Oak Ridge Common (Rte. 123)
South Salem, NY
(914) 533-0333
www.divvies.com

A JOB WELL DONE:
HANDYMEN (AND WOMEN)

The toilet is leaking. A slate is loose on the front walk. The paint on the dining room wall is chipping. You may not have the "handyman skills" to fix these hazards of home ownership, and you probably don't have the time or inclination either. Laura married a very handy guy, but he certainly doesn't want to spend his week-ends plumbing, painting and fixing. Below are several services to help fix what's broken, from a minor leak to a comprehensive remodeling.

These companies will do small repairs and home improvements, including carpentry, minor electrical and plumbing work, painting, wallpaper, tile, masonry, electronic wiring and installations, and odd jobs. Some will even take out, clean and/or store your out-door furniture, perform a "tune up" on your swingset, or conduct a monthly visit to do whatever's on your "honey do" list. Note that Best Kept Home is run by two women with extensive experi-ence in home maintenance. Hey, sometimes the best man for the job is a woman!

Andy On Call
(914) 345-5656
www.andyoncall.com

Best Kept Home
(914) 666-4BKH (-4254)
www.bestkepthome.com

Home & Handy
(914) 698-0164

Home Services Shop
(914) 769-1100
www.homeservicesshop.com

Mr. Handyman of South Central Westchester County
(914) 461-3400
www.mrhandyman.com/MainFranchisee.aspx?loc=9603

Your Home Wish List
(914) 761-6143
www.homewishlist.com

Savvy Suggestion

67% of women describe themselves as a "Do-It-Yourselfer." If you want to take on a home project, you can find thousands of DIY articles, tutorials and tips, specifically aimed at women, at www.be-jane.com.

PICTURE PERFECT: PHOTO STUDIOS

In addition to the many professional photographers in the area, a less expensive alternative is to go to one of the major photo cen-ters around Westchester. All the studios listed below offer cost-saving packages. They have a variety of cute backdrops and props, and you can just walk in to most of them without setting up an appointment. Check their websites for coupons and special offers.

Kiddie Kandids Portrait
2700 Central Park Ave. (Located in Babies "R" Us), Yonkers
(914) 713-1266

Kiddie Kandids is operated independently from Babies "R" Us. Call to schedule appointments. They can also put your photos on a number of items, such as mugs, aprons, totes, etc.

JC Penney Portrait Studio
www.jcpenneyportraits.com
1000 Palisades Center Dr. (The Palisades Center Mall), West Nyack
(845) 348-9313

Sears Portrait Studio
www.searsportrait.com
100 Main St. (The Galleria), White Plains
(914) 686-5098
87N Cross County Parkway (Cross County Center), Yonkers
(914) 968-0312

The Picture People
www.picturepeople.com
100 Main St. (The Galleria), White Plains
(914) 428-2811
1000 Palisades Center Dr. (The Palisades Center Mall), West Nyack
(845) 353-6989

Savvy Suggestion

LifeWorx will help you find a nanny, pet care, cleaning help, organizational help, chef services—whatever you're looking for. They charge a fee for full-time placements, by the hour for part-time (generally $22-28 per hour), and perform pre-screening and background checks.

LifeWorx
(914) 238-7100
www.lifeworx.net

NEAT-O: ORGANIZATION EXPERTS

Sure, you can obsessively watch home improvement shows that make creating a manageable nursery, playroom or family room look oh-so-easy. But we've found that no matter how many methods we've tried or how many bins and plastic drawers we've bought, every room still seems to end up looking like a toy store exploded in it. Fortunately, help is only a phone call away. This service will help you create uncluttered, functional spaces in any room in your house (including your garage). They offer free in-home consultations and customize their solutions to fit your life and lifestyle.

Chaos Commandos
294 West Post Rd., Ste. #1D, White Plains
(914) 949-9742
www.chaoscommandos.com

Cost: $75-$90 per hour

For those whose clutter is more paper-based (you know who you are!), there are also services to help cure you of your addiction to all those mega-piles of mail, bills and magazine articles. They assess where your difficulties may lie and help you figure out a strategy to stay on track and organized.

IN Place Incorporated
(914) 263-4487
inplaceinc@optonline.net

Cost: $75 per hour; four-hour minimum

Oh So Organized!
(914) 271-5673
www.ohsoorganized.com

Cost: Flat rate of $400 for a four-hour visit. Additional time billed at $110 per hour.

Savvy Savings

With gas prices going through the roof, find the cheapest prices on gas by logging onto www.westchestergov.com. There is an area price comparison to locate the station with the lowest prices near you.

Chapter 16

Attention All Shoppers!

Malls

Outlet Centers & Discount Stores

Toy Stores

Bookstores

"Big Kids'" Furniture

Shoes

Bicycles

Baby Gifts

Online Grocery Stores

Fine, our urban counterparts have Fifth Avenue, but for our money we're quite happy with what our fair suburbs have to offer. Frankly, we think Westchester is a shopper's paradise, and best of all, after an especially good haul you can toss the stuff in your trunk instead of having to schlep it home on the subway. And there are even more shopping opportunities now than there were when our first edition came out. White Plains in particular has become a destination spot for shopping, dining and entertainment. In addition to several fantastic malls, there are loads of specialty shops and even some discount stores and an outlet center nearby for the bargain hunter in all of us. The choices out there may seem limitless; below we share a few of our favorites.

MALLS

City Center White Plains
3 City Place, White Plains
(914) 821-0012

With great places to shop for books, bargains and electronics, as well as a New York Sports Club, a multiplex theater and a performing arts venue, City Center has truly become the "centerpiece" of White Plains shopping. (We're huge fans.) There are also a number of restaurants where you can grab a good meal. And although it might not be Vegas, your kids are sure to get a kick out of our very own "dancing fountains" across the street (on Main Street) during the warmer months.

Stores Include: Barnes & Noble (914) 397-2420, Circuit City (914) 272-1060, Filene's Basement (914) 285-1290, Target (914) 821-0012. There is also a seventeen-screen movie theater, an IMAX theater, and the White Plains Performing Arts Center.

Restaurants Include: Applebee's, Atlanta Bread Company, Cold Stone Creamery, Legal Sea Foods and Zanaro's.

What to Know Before You Go: There is a multilevel indoor parking garage with pay meters at the entrance to the mall. The movie theater and restaurants stay open later than the stores. If you are going to the movies, park on the forth level instead of the fifth and take the escalator or elevator up one floor; it makes getting in and out much easier. Also, there are automated vending machines in the lobby outside the theater, avoid long lines by purchasing movie tickets here or online before you go.

Hours: Target daily 8 am-10 pm, other retail stores daily 10 am-10 pm

Fortunoff-The Source @ White Plains
1 Maple Ave. (& Bloomingdale Rd.), White Plains
(914) 287-8700
www.fortunoff.com

This relatively new shopping center next to The Westchester gives us one more reason to love living here. You can shop for maternity clothes, buy a baby gift, do your grocery shopping, grab a bite to eat and check out some serious bling all in one place. Whole Foods encompasses 50,000 square feet. of produce, flowers, seafood, cheeses, baked goods, organic and all natural grocery items, nutritional supplements, vitamins, body care and baby care. There is a hot food bar, salad bar and sushi bar in addition to dozens of daily prepared items. They also have a catering department that Betsy has used as a shortcut for two Thanksgiving feasts.

Stores Include: Fortunoff (914) 287-8700, Destination Maternity (914) 948-1279, The Right Start (914) 686-5880, Whole Foods (914) 288-1300

Restaurants Include: The Cheesecake Factory

What to Know Before You Go: The ground level is where Whole Foods is located; during busy hours parking lot spots are few and far between and competition is fierce. Your best bet is to go up a level or two and park near the elevator bank. During the holiday season, Fortunoff's indoor displays rival those on Fifth Avenue. Stop by and check out the twinkling lights and grab a snack afterwards at one of the local eateries. Be sure to get your parking stub validated from Whole Foods if your purchases are over $15.

Hours: Monday-Saturday 10 am-9 pm, Sunday 11 am-6 pm; Whole Foods daily 8 am-9:30 pm

Galleria Mall at White Plains

100 Main St., White Plains
(914) 682-0111
www.galleriaatwhiteplains.com

This mall has been around for years but has had a recent resurgence with many new, popular stores.

Stores Include: Aeropostale (914) 681-7110, As Seen on TV (914) 686-6687, Champs Sports (914) 328-3715, The Children's Place (914) 997-8133, Claires (914) 686-1821, H & M (914) 422-3777, K*B Toys (914) 948-6686, Kids Foot Locker (914) 421-1857, Macy's (914) 946-5015, Old Navy (914) 682-0482, PacSun (914) 428-3270, The Picture People (914) 428-2811, Sears (914) 644-1400

Restaurants Include: McDonald's, Sbarro, Todai, and an extensive food court

What to Know Before You Go: You can rent strollers shaped like cars and trucks at the customer service booth on the food court level ($5 for a single stroller, $6 for a double); only one of the strollers has an infant seat. Muggsy's Meadow (www.muggsysmeadow.com), a free kids club for ages 0-12, offers kids' activities and weekly discounts for members (registration is free).

Hours: Monday-Saturday 10 am-9:30 pm, Sunday 11 am-7 pm

Jefferson Valley Mall

650 Lee Blvd., Yorktown Heights
(914) 245-4200
www.shopsimon.com

This old standby has Macy's, Sears, over ninety specialty shops, a large food court and an eight-screen United Artists Theater.

Stores Include: BabyGap (914) 245-9013, The Children's Place (914) 245-8818, EB Games (914) 962-8519, Game Stop (914) 245-1503, GapKids (914) 245-9013, Gymboree (914) 243-0625, H & M (914) 962-6660, K*B Toys (914) 245-8274, Kids Foot Locker (914) 248-7337, Limited Too (914) 962-5119, Macy's (914) 962-9100, PacSun (914) 245-2321, The Picture People (914) 245-3151, Sears (914) 248-2500, Stride Rite (914) 245-8553

Restaurants Include: There are no sit-down restaurants, but there is a large food court.

What to Know Before You Go: This is a "Simon Mall"—a national chain of malls and outlet centers. All Simon Malls feature the

Simon Kidgits Club; for a $5 annual membership fee, you get a newsletter, family-friendly coupons for mall retailers, and special offers. They also have a birthday club and gift redemption for kids, and the website features kids' games and puzzles.

Hours: Monday-Saturday 10 am-9:30 pm, Sunday 11 am-6 pm

The Palisades Center Mall

1000 Palisades Center Dr., West Nyack
(845) 348-1000
www.palisadescenter.com

Exit 12 off the New York State Thruway (87 S./287 E.) will deposit you at the second largest indoor mall in America. This huge combination of shopping, entertainment and recreation facilities boasts over 270 specialty shops, fourteen restaurants, an EATery area, an NHL-size ice-skating rink, a sixty-eight-foot Ferris wheel, a restored antique carousel, a twenty-one-screen Loews Theatre, a state-of-the-art IMAX Theatre, and a Dave & Buster's arcade.

Stores Include: abercrombie (845) 348-7044, BabyGap (845) 358-8381, Barnes & Noble (845) 348-4701, Build A Bear Workshop (845) 353-1895, EB Games (845) 348-3698, Filene's (845) 358-7990, Games Workshop (845) 348-1739, Gymboree (845) 358-5336, H&M (845) 727-1958, Hollister (845) 348-9573, JC Penney (845) 348-0382, Lord & Taylor (845) 358-4672, K*B Toys (845) 353-2232, Kids Foot Locker (845) 353-6853, Lego (845) 358-2222, Limited Too (845) 353-4628, Modell's (845) 548-9800, Old Navy (845) 348-0993, Payless Shoe Source (845) 348-4761, Picture People (845) 353-6989, Steve & Barry's University Sportswear (845) 358-1576, Stride Rite (845) 727-5062, Sports Authority (845) 348-8853, Target (845) 348-6440, The Disney Store (845) 348-9262

Restaurants Include: Cheeburger Cheeburger, Cheesecake Factory, Chili's, FOX Sports Grill, Johnny Rockets, Legal's Sea Food and TGIF

What to Know Before You Go: Novelty vehicles on each floor will give your child a short ride for a couple of quarters. Although the mall is vast, it still can get pretty packed on the weekends during prime shopping hours. Go early to avoid lines at the kids' attractions. And once you think you've done it all, don't forget to take your kids on a ride in the glass elevators. Lastly, when we say this place is huge, we mean it's massive—so don't even think of going without a stroller. They are available to rent if you forget yours.

Hours: Monday-Saturday 10 am-9:30 pm, Sunday 11 am-7 pm. The movie theater and restaurants remain open later than the retail stores.

Vernon Hills Shopping Center

(a.k.a. Lord & Taylor Shopping Center)
700-725 White Plains Post Rd., Scarsdale
(914) 472-2000

OK, go ahead and joke about strip malls, but you can do some serious shopping at this one; there's a wide variety of stores on both sides of the street for kids (and for grown-ups!). Plus, Lord & Taylor has a terrific baby and children's clothing section on the bottom floor and they often have coupons available for L & T charge card holders.

Stores Include: American Eagle Outfitters (914) 723-0295, Borders (914) 725-4637, Lord & Taylor (914) 723-7700, Old Navy (914) 722-6576, Park Hill Shoes (914) 725-4664, The Children's Place (914) 722-6249, The Gap and Kids/BabyGap (914) 472-4630, Gymboree (914) 472-5899

What to Know Before You Go: After dragging your kids in and out of stores, reward their good behavior with a snack from Starbucks or the Borders Café (they have a nice patio with umbrella-covered tables, which is lovely in warm weather). Borders is also a great place to while away the time reading books you don't have at home. The stores are on both sides of Post Road: plan your excursion strategically so you don't have to constantly be moving your car. If you're hungry, there's a Bagel Café, which has something to please everyone.

Hours: Varies by store

Savvy Suggestion

Get your shopping done and delight your child at the same time. Some area supermarkets, like Food Emporium and Stop & Shop, have shopping carts with toy cars attached to the front. They safely keep your child strapped in, and he'll love steering his way up and down the aisles.

The Westchester

125 Westchester Ave., White Plains
(914) 683-8600
www.shopsimon.com

Anchored by Nordstrom and Neiman Marcus, this mall contains more than 150 upscale stores. You know you're someplace special when you see the skylights above and the marble and carpeted floors below. The mall is laid out as three different "avenues," with a fountain and sculpture at the end of each.

Stores Include: abercrombie (914) 397-2268, BabyGap (914) 626-2319, babystyle (914) 948-9511, The Children's Place (914) 997-1264, Crewcuts (914) 997-6171, The Disney Store (914) 397-0528, The Gamekeeper (914) 644-8622, GapKids (914) 644-8629, Gymboree (914) 644-8410, Hanna Andersson (914) 684-2410, Janie and Jack (914) 683-1924, K*B Toys (914) 761-0316, Lilly Pulitzer (914) 428-4160, Limited Too (914) 644-8762, Oilily (914) 328-8900, Pottery Barn Kids (914) 949-4947, Starbucks Coffee (914) 949-2470, Stride Rite (914) 686-3584, Talbots Kids (914) 644-8280

Restaurants Include: City Limits Diner, P.F. Chang's China Bistro, Nordstroms Café, and a food court with lots of "quick meal" options.

What to Know Before You Go: Ample indoor parking is available, but for added convenience there is valet parking for an additional $2 charge. Strollers are available at both valet stands on Retail Level 2. Bring a stack of pennies for your kids to throw in the fountains; Sam and Ben both look forward to this as a treat after shopping. A widely known "secret" is that the ladies lounges in Nordstrom and Neiman Marcus are the most pleasant places you'll find to breastfeed your baby. All mall bathrooms offer changing tables, and those labeled "family bathrooms" offer a tot-sized potty for children learning to use them. The Simon Kidgits program is available at this mall (see description in the Jefferson Valley Mall listing).

Hours: Monday-Saturday 10 am-9 pm, Sunday 11 am-6 pm

Westchester Pavilion

60 S. Broadway, White Plains
(914) 993-6320

This shopping center has come a long way and contains some great kid-friendly destinations. As for food, all ages and tastes will be satisfied here with options ranging from "the Golden Arches" to sandwiches or sushi.

Stores Include: Borders (914) 421-1110, BM Kim's Martial Arts Studio (914) 428-0085, Daffy's (914) 761-4477, Educational Warehouse (914) 682-2223, Sports Authority (914) 993-0212, Toys 'R' Us (914) 683-5437

Restaurants Include: McDonald's, Outback Steakhouse, Subway and Sushi Corner.

What to Know Before You Go: The restaurants and martial arts studio are open later than 9 pm. There is parking available starting at $3 for the first hour, but McDonald's and Daffy's will validate your parking stub for the first hour. Parking is free for thirty minutes or less.

Hours: Daily 10 am-9 pm

 Savvy Shopping

Many parents would rather defuse a live bomb than shop for clothes with their teen or tween. For you brave sorts, here are some of the coolest places around. In fact, you might even say they're "da bomb."

All Dressed Up: 17 Rye Ridge Plaza, Rye Brook
(914) 690-1593
Boo Girls: 151 Katonah Ave., Katonah
(914) 232-8082
Buttermilk Blue: 49 Main St., Irvington
(914) 591-6277
Chelsea's Closet: 541 Warburton Ave., Hastings
(914) 478-3553
Gingerbread Kids: 1 Chase Rd., Scarsdale
(914) 472-1930
Havana Jeans: 365 Central Park Ave., Scarsdale
(914) 722-9221
Knoyzz (three locations):
13 Rye Ridge Plaza, Rye Brook
(914) 690-1607
41 S. Moger Ave., Mount Kisco
(914) 242-0030
147 Post Rd. E., Westport, CT
(203) 341-9144
Neil's: 1132 Wilmot Rd., Scarsdale
(914) 472-8120

OUTLET CENTERS & DISCOUNT STORES

If you're like Betsy, you approach shopping as you would a competitive sport. Outlet centers represent the ultimate score, with name-brand clothing, shoes and toys at prices 20-70% under retail. Sure, the clothes they have in stock when you're there may not fit your child today, but just buy one size larger and wait. The best part is, with the money you save buying your kids' shoes at half price, you can justify picking up those designer shoes for yourself!! And, what could make you happier than finding exactly what you need when you're shopping? How about getting it for a fraction of the original cost? The discount stores listed below have a little bit of everything, from crafts supplies and toys to suitcases and electronics. When it comes to finding party favors or presents they're the first place we hit since the selection is great and the prices are awesome. (For Sam's 6th birthday party, Laura found lava lamps at Amazing Savings to give as party favors.) The one thing to remember is, if you see something you like, buy it: it may not be there the next time you visit (and you can always return it if you need to.)

Woodbury Commons Premium Outlets
498 Red Apple Court, Central Valley
(845) 928-4000
www.premiumoutlets.com

This massive outlet center is located less than an hour north of central Westchester. It's worth the trip for the extensive selection of premium stores offering merchandise that is often still in season. We recommend stocking up on clothing mainstays in several different sizes so that you're all set as your child grows.

Stores Include: Carter's (845) 928-9498, The Children's Place Outlet (845) 928-5365, Gap Outlet (845) 928-3122, JM Originals (845) 928-5125, K*B Toy Outlet (845) 928-9424, Little Me (845) 928-7343, NauticaKids (845) 928-8386, Oilily (845) 928-4384, OshKosh B'Gosh (845) 928-4449, Petit Bateau (845) 928-8850, Stride Rite Keds Sperry (845) 928-5104, World of Fun (845) 928-6012

What to Know Before You Go: This has been called the third biggest tourist site in New York, so you can imagine the crowds as the day goes on. Aim to get there early and try to park in the parking lot closest to the stores you want to check out (the website will show you all the store locations). There are close to twenty different places to choose from for a meal, snack or coffee. But here's the real insider's secret: if you're a member of AAA, go to a customer service desk and pick up a free coupon book filled with additional savings—it can save you literally hundreds of dollars.

Hours: Monday-Friday 9 am-9 pm, Saturday 9 am-10 pm, Sunday 9 am-8 pm

Amazing Savings
The name says it all: they have a wide variety of books, puzzles, games, toys, school supplies and baby items (towels, onesies, etc.), greatly discounted. We recommend visiting often as the merchandise is constantly changing.

925 Central Park Ave. (Midway Shopping Center), Scarsdale
(914) 472-1320

88 Rte. 59, Monsey
(845) 426-2020

Hours: Monday-Thursday 9:30 am-9 pm, Friday 9 am-1:45 pm, Sunday 10 am-6 pm, closed Saturday

Family Discount Center

This Westchester chain has two locations where you're certain to find everything you need—and some things you didn't even know you needed—all at a discount. From clothes and toys to stationery and party goods, these stores have it all.

Harrison
270 Halstead Ave., Harrison
(914) 835-0123

Hours: Monday-Friday 9 am-9 pm, Saturday 9 am-6 pm, Sunday 9 am-5 pm

Rye Brook
Rye Ridge Shopping Center, Rye Brook
(914) 939-4321

Hours: Monday-Friday 9 am-9 pm, Saturday 9 am-8 pm, Sunday 9 am-7 pm

Savvy Style

Your kid can look like a million bucks without you spending a fortune on clothes. Be sure to check out chains like Marshall's and TJ Maxx for brand-name clothes at a big discount, as well as stores like Target, Old Navy and H & M.

TOY STORES

Besides the traditional chains, there are a few stand-out independent toy stores in the area. These specialty shops focus on customer service and have staffs with an impressive knowledge of all their merchandise.

Educational Warehouse

60 S. Broadway (Westchester Pavilion), White Plains
(914) 682-ABCD (-2223)
www.educationalwarehouse.com

Educational Warehouse "brings fun and education together." They stock teaching supplies, educational tools and games, as well as a great selection of arts & crafts supplies, infant and baby toys, and seasonal and holiday items like books, videos and decorations. They also have two other locations in Danbury and Norwalk, Connecticut.

Hours: Monday-Saturday 10 am-9 pm, Sunday 11 am-6 pm

Lakeshore Learning Center

969A Central Park Ave. (Midway Shopping Center), Scarsdale
(914) 472-1820
www.lakeshorelearning.com

Lakeshore Learning Center is where teachers shop, so you know you're going to find lots of innovative learning materials and top-quality educational products for children of all ages. Check out the free craft activities every Saturday from 11 am to 3 pm for kids ages 3 and up. Sponsored by vendors, these activities include opportunities for kids to create various fun—and sometimes seasonal—items, such personalized key chains, jeweled "Treasure Chests" and Thanksgiving centerpieces.

Hours: Monday-Saturday 10 am -9 pm; Sunday 10 am-6 pm

Learning Express

21 Spencer Pl., Scarsdale
(914) 723-3700
www.learningexpress.com

With a great selection of toys, games, arts & crafts supplies, science kits, dolls and many other play items, this store is geared towards carrying products you might not find in other places. They also have a serious commitment to customer service: they offer free gift-wrapping and free personalization services. In addition, they have "express lane service:" if you call ahead, they will select, wrap and personalize your gift and deliver it to you curbside so you never have to leave your car. (A great thing if you've ever tried to find parking in Scarsdale Village!) They're also a great source for birthday party goody bags and will help you fill them with theme- age- and price-appropriate items.

Hours: Monday-Saturday 9:30 am-6 pm, Sunday 11 am-4 pm

Miller's

335 Mamaroneck Ave., Mamaroneck
(914) 698-5070
www.millerstoys.com

Miller's has been around over for over fifty years (it originally opened in Harlem) and houses a remarkable selection of train hobby paraphernalia, bikes, outdoor swing sets, books, furniture and, of course, toys. They carry all the usual brands as well as a few harder-to-find ones. Many of the staff have worked there for years and are incredibly helpful. If they don't have something that you want, they'll get it for you. They even offer free gift-wrapping and assembly services. And if you need a present in a pinch, they offer a "Shop & Stop" program where you can contact them via phone or internet, let them know what you need (or how much you'd like to spend) and when you'll be coming by. They can have it wrapped and waiting for you at their back door pick-up location within three hours.

Hours: Monday-Saturday 9 am-6 pm. (Later hours offered on Thursdays by appointment.) Extended hours around the winter holidays.

NOKA
25 Katonah Ave., Katonah
(914) 232-7278
www.nokashop.com

Looking for gifts that are a little bit kooky? This store specializes in the unique, the wacky and fun. Located upstairs from a beautiful floral shop, NOKA has a little something for everyone—from band-aids decorated with pictures of sushi to pencil sharpeners that look like a nose (give it a minute... you'll get it... it's funny). Owner Jennifer Cook is a Westchester mom who loves what she does but also wants to give back to the community: her Helping Hands program donates $2 to a local charity (including A-Home, The Community Center and Katonah Elementary School PTO) each time you make a purchase of $20 or more.

Hours: Monday-Friday 9 am-6 pm, Saturday 9 am-5 pm, Sunday 12 pm-4 pm

Penny Auntie 5 & 10
11 King St., Chappaqua
(914) 238-3242
www.pennyauntie.com

A blast from the past with toys from today. This old-fashioned toy store has a wide variety of brands kids love, including Lego, Wild Planet, ALEX, Melissa & Doug, Manhattan Toy, Groovy Girls, International Playthings and Insect Lore, as well as teen jewelry, stuffed animals, cosmetic sets, play figures, sleds, games and spy toys.

Hours: Monday-Saturday, 9:30 am-5:30 pm, closed Sunday

The Scholastic Store
450 Central Park Ave. (Rte. 100), Hartsdale
(914) 725-7201
www.scholastic.com/scarsdalestore

A must-see destination for kids of all ages; in fact, Laura's kids can spend most of a day here. They offer a full selection of Scholastic products, including books, toys, plush, puzzles, CD-ROMs, videos, games and interactive books from Klutz. The store also holds special events and drop-in, hands-on activities—including author signings, arts & crafts, storytelling, character visits (from the likes of Clifford the Big Red Dog) and themed interactive workshops for teachers, parents and children. They also have an activity and party space where children can throw customized birthday parties. Check the website for a calendar of events. So far they only have one other location, in SoHo—so you know it's gotta be cool.

Hours: Monday-Saturday 10 am-7 pm, Sunday 12 pm-5 pm

Wondrous Things
4 Old Post Rd. S., Croton-on-Hudson
(914) 271-3044
www.wondrousthings.com

A great store for all your gift needs, whether it be for a house-warming or a four-year-old's birthday party. They carry high quality brands including Thomas Wooden Railway, Playmobil, Brio, Kettler, Calico Critters, Creativity for Kids, Klutz and many other educational and creative toy collections. Their website allows you to search by occasion, recipient, or age-range of child. And almost everything they sell is available on the selling floor for hands-on "test runs."

Hours: Monday-Saturday 10 am-6 pm and Sunday 11 am-4 pm

Savvy Suggestion

Bed Bath & *Way* Beyond. This location now carries an extensive line of toys and crafts as well as a Harmon Discount Drug store right on the main floor which also accepts the ubiquitous Bed, Bath and Beyond coupons.

Bed Bath & Beyond
251 Tarrytown Rd. (Rte. 119), Elmsford
(914) 345-2701

BOOKSTORES

As people who have a special interest in bookstore customers, we wanted to make sure that all our readers knew where to, well ...buy *KidSavvy Westchester*!

Seriously, reading with or to your children is a great way to instill in them a lifelong love of books. It's fun both to share your own childhood favorites with your kids and to discover some new "classics" (like *Captain Underpants*). Laura and her kids love to spend rainy afternoons in the neighborhood bookstore, perusing books that they don't yet own, and Sam—a master salesman—is usually able to convince her that he "needs" to buy one more.

INDEPENDENT BOOKSTORES

The people who own and run independent bookstores throughout Westchester do it out of a passion for and belief in what they do. They may not always be the biggest or best-known, but there's something special about shopping in a store where the sales help knows you and your children by name. For being such an important part of our communities, they've certainly got our support—and we hope yours too.

Bedford Hills

Bhoomi
41 Main St.
(914) 241-2661

Bronxville

Womrath Bookshop
76 Pondfield Rd.
(914) 337-0199

Chappaqua

Second Story Book Shop
75 North Greeley Ave.
(914) 238-4463
www.secondstorybookshop.com

Hastings-on-Hudson

Galapagos Books
22 Main St., #A
(914) 478-2501

Good Yarns
8 Main St.
(914) 478-0014

Larchmont

Anderson's Book Shop
96-98 Chatsworth Ave.
(914) 834-6900

Pleasantville

The Village Bookstore
2 Washington Ave.
(914) 769-8322

Rye

Arcade Book Sellers
15 Purchase St.
(914) 967-0966

Parkers
43 Purchase St.
(914) 921-6400

Scarsdale

Reading Writing & Wrapping
30 E. Parkway
(914) 723-1278

Tarrytown

Bilingual Books for Kids
451 Martling Ave.
(914) 524-7325
www.bilingualbooks.com

ROCKLAND COUNTY

Hopscotch
24 Marion St., Nyack
(845) 642-0807

J. Dunnigan Books
6 S. Broadway, Nyack
(845) 358-9126

DUTCHESS COUNTY

Merritt Bookstore
57 Front St., Millbrook
(845) 677-5857
www.merrittbooks.com

PUTNAM COUNTY
Merritt Bookstore Vol. III
66 Main St., Cold Spring
(845) 265-9100
www.merrittbooks.com

NATIONAL CHAINS
The large chains are located conveniently throughout Westchester and set the standard for selection, prices and a variety of activities and amenities. With cafés, coffee bars and snacks available at almost all of them, you really can make an event of your visit. Many of these stores also offer storytimes, which we discuss in Chapter 6.

Hartsdale
Barnes & Noble
111 S. Central Ave.
(914) 948-1002
www.barnesandnoble.com

Mohegan Lake
Barnes & Noble
3089 E. Main St. (Rte. 6)
(914) 528-6275
www.barnesandnoble.com

Mount Kisco
Borders
162 E. Main St.
(914) 241-8387
www.bordersstores.com

Rye Ridge
Waldenbooks
106 S. Ridge St.
(914) 937-3370
www.bordersstores.com

Scarsdale
Borders Books
680 White Plains Rd.
(914) 725-4637
www.bordersstores.com

White Plains

Barnes & Noble
230 Main St. (City Center)
(914) 397-2420
www.barnesandnoble.com

Barnes & Noble
431 Tarrytown Rd. (Crossroads Shopping Center)
(914) 946-3337
www.barnesandnoble.com

Borders Books
West Chester Pavilion
(914) 421-1110
www.bordersstores.com

Yonkers

Barnes & Noble
2614 Central Park Ave.
(914) 771-6400
www.barnesandnoble.com

Waldenbooks
8 Mall Walk
914) 476-6900
www.bordersstores.com

Yorktown Heights

B. Dalton Booksellers
650 Lee Blvd. (Jefferson Valley Mall)
(914) 962-2570
www.barnesandnoble.com

ROCKLAND COUNTY

Barnes & Noble
1000 Palisades Center Dr. (The Palisades Center), West Nyack
(845) 348-4701
www.barnesandnoble.com

Barnes & Noble
140 Rockland Plaza, Nanuet
(845) 624-2920
www.barnesandnoble.com

Waldenbooks
197 Nanuet Mall, Nanuet
(845) 623-4146
www.bordersstores.com

CONNECTICUT

Borders Express
173 Greenwich Ave., Greenwich
(203) 869-6342
www.bordersstores.com

"BIG KIDS'" FURNITURE

When your toddler outgrows her crib you'll be on the hunt for "big kids'" furniture. You may just be looking for transitional stuff until you're ready to redo her room for real, or this might be the bed she'll sleep in until she goes to college. In an attempt to make Simon's transition from crib to bed an easy one, Betsy ended up with something in her house that she could have never foreseen—a giant, plastic, racecar bed. Tacky? Maybe. Successful? Absolutely. On the down side, it meant buying new furniture a few years later, but she was able to move the bed along through Craigslist.com (see Chapter 17). Below are some of the county's best.

Bellini Baby and Teen Designer Furniture
495 Central Park Ave., Scarsdale
(914) 472-7336
1305 Second Ave., New York
(212) 517-9233
175 W. Rte. 4, Paramus, NJ
(201) 845-7336
www.bellini.com

This is a company that believes in quality over quantity. The store features many hand-painted, personalized options for accenting your child's room, and they also carry a few lines of bedding, including their exclusive styles. They have an in-home delivery and assembly service that starts at $95.

Hours: (For Scarsdale) Monday-Saturday 10 am-6 pm (Thursday until 7 pm), Sunday 11 pm-5 pm

Bombay Kids
2564 Central Park Ave. (Central Plaza), Yonkers
(914) 771-6793
1000 Palisades Ctr. Dr. (The Palisades Center Mall), West Nyack
(845) 353-4060
www.bombaykids.com

A great place to find different, unusual items. They carry a large selection of furniture, beds and lighting, as well as inventive and whimsical bedding and accessories.

Hours: Monday-Saturday 10 am-9 pm, Sunday 11 am-6 pm

Crib & Teen City Expo
183 S. Central Park Ave., Hartsdale
(914) 686-3331
159 Rte. 4 West, Paramus, NJ
(201) 843-1505
www.cribteencity.com

This store strikes a comfortable balance between the high-end boutiques and the baby megastores. Their slogan is "We take your baby from cradle to college," so it's no surprise that you'll find a wide range of furniture to select from. And for the "big kids" they have a superb assortment of twin beds, bunk beds, loft/desk combinations and more.

Hours: Monday and Wednesday 10 am-9 pm, Tuesday and Thursday-Saturday 10 am-6 pm, Sunday 11 am-5 pm

Pottery Barn Kids
125 Westchester Ave. (The Westchester Mall), White Plains
(914) 949-4947
www.potterybarnkids.com

A version of Pottery Barn just for kids. They don't have everything in the store that they carry in the catalogue, but you'll save on shipping charges if they do. Many of the toys sold in the store are out on display and you can feel free to allow your child to play with them. The sales help is just that: helpful.

Hours: Monday-Saturday 10 am-9 pm, Sunday 11 am-6 pm

Wendy Gee Home Accessories
1949 Palmer Ave., Larchmont
(914) 834-8507
42 Greenwich Ave., Greenwich, CT
(203) 422-2811
www.wendygee.com

If you're looking for something unique and whimsical, this is the place to go. Although they carry tons of adorable gifts and accessories, they also are one of the largest retailers of Maine Cottage furniture, offered in a kaleidoscope of colors, which they sell at a 15% discount. Maine Cottage is known for their high-quality pieces, which may still be around (and in style) even after the kids are off to college. The bigger of the two stores is in Larchmont, but both stores have a good selection of samples on the floor. You can also check out all the furniture choices at www.mainecottage.com.

Hours: Monday-Saturday 9:30 am-6 pm

One-of-a-Kind-Finds

Below are two stores that specialize in custom-made furniture. They will build a bed, desk, bookshelf or bunk bed to suit your style and needs exactly. When ordering custom furniture you have to expect about a ten- to twelve-week turnaround time, so it's not the way to go if you need something quickly. However, if you have the time and patience, the results can be well worth the wait.

Kid's Supply Co.
14 Railroad Ave., Greenwich, CT
(203) 422-2100
1343 Madison Ave., New York
(212) 426-1200
www.kidssupply.com

If you're looking for both style and substance, this is a store you won't want to miss. They do have quite a few items in stock but the real specialty of this store is custom-made furniture for children; their products have been featured in many children's and design magazines. They create custom bedding as well.

Hours: Monday-Friday 9:30 am-5:30 pm, Saturday 10 am-5 pm

NYC Hours: Monday-Friday 10 am-6 pm, Saturday 10 am-5 pm, Sunday 12 pm-4 pm

Go To Your Room
27 S. Greeley Ave., Chappaqua
(914) 238-7105
234 Mill St., Greenwich, CT
(203) 532-9701
www.go2uroom.com

Fernando Martinez and his wife have been running this store for years. Fernando is a master craftsman and designer, and they also have an artist on staff who can custom-paint anything—from headboards to drawer pulls—to complete the look of your child's room.

Hours: Monday-Saturday 10:30 am-5 pm

SHOE STORES

Besides the moment of their child's birth, one of the most significant memories for many parents is buying their child's first pair of shoes. Although neither of us has gone so far as to have them bronzed, Betsy still has Simon's tucked away in a special place (Laura saved Sam's for Ben). It seems like kids can outgrow shoes faster than you can buy them; below is a list of both specialty and chain stores to help you with the task of putting your child's best foot forward.

INDEPENDENT STORES

Chappaqua

Squires Family Clothing & Footwear
41 S. Greeley Ave.
(914) 238-4511

Irvington

The Perfect Pair
51 Main St.
(914) 479-1602

Specializes in women's and girls' footwear and accessories.

Mount Vernon

Heide Shoes
71 Fourth Ave.
(914) 668-7287

Rye

Shoes 'N More
67 Purchase St.
914) 921-1526

Rye Brook

Foot Steps
120 S. Ridge St.
(914) 934-7676

 **Savvy Shopping**

Check out www.zappos.com for a staggering selection of shoes for everyone in your family. They offer free shipping, no tax and an easy return policy. If you're not sure which size will fit, buy more than one; you can always return the one that didn't work out, at no charge.

Sportstech
124 S. Ridge St.
(914) 934-0001

Specializes in athletic footwear and apparel.

Scarsdale

Fun Steps
590 Central Park Ave.
(914) 722-6645

Heathcote Bootery
1086 Wilmot Rd. (Golden Horseshoe Shopping Center)
(914) 472-3939

Park Hill Shoes
686 White Plains Rd. (Vernon Hills Shopping Center)
(914) 725-4664

Tuckahoe

Epstein's
21 Columbus Ave.
(914) 961-2833

White Plains

Nordstrom
135 Westchester Ave. (The Westchester Mall)
(914) 946-1122

CONNECTICUT

Little Eric of Greenwich
12 E. Elm, Greenwich
(203) 622-1600

Grossman's Shoe Store
88 Greenwich Ave.
(203) 869-2123

Shoes 'N More
251 Greenwich Ave.
(203) 629-2323

CHAIN STORES

Payless Shoe Source
www.payless.com

Mamaroneck
407 Mamaroneck Ave.
(914) 698-2204

Mohegan Lake
3137 E. Main (Cortlandt Town Center)
(914) 528-0650

Mount Vernon
54 S. 4th Ave.
(914) 664-0971

White Plains
387 Tarrytown Rd. (Crossroads Shopping Center)
(914) 684-8137

14 Mamaroneck Ave.
(914) 328-1553

Yonkers
750 Central Park Ave. (Cross County Square Mall)
(914) 709-9495

2500 Central Park Ave.
(914) 395-0935

424 S. Broadway
(914) 963-8494

Yorktown Heights
341 Downing Dr.
(914) 962-7428

650 Lee Blvd. (Jefferson Valley Mall)
(914) 245-6189

Stride Rite
www.striderite.com

Mount Kisco
55 S. Moger Ave.
(914) 241-7663

White Plains
125 Westchester Ave. (The Westchester Mall)
(914) 686-3584

Yorktown Heights
650 Lee Blvd. (Jefferson Valley Mall)
(914) 245-8553

Central Valley
439 Evergreen Ct. (Woodbury Commons Premium Outlet)
(845) 928-5104

West Nyack
1000 Palisades Center Dr. (The Palisades Center Mall)
(845) 727-5062

Target
www.target.com

Mount Vernon
500 E. Sandford Blvd.
(914) 530-3000

White Plains
9 City Place (City Center)
(914) 821-0012

West Nyack
1000 Palisades Center Dr. (The Palisades Center Mall)
(845) 348-6440

BICYCLES

What's nicer on a warm day than rallying the troops for a family bike trip? (Check out Chapter 5 to find a park with a bike path near you.) You can equip your bike with a trailer or bike seat so that even the youngest child can tag along and, as he gets older, you can buy him some wheels of his own. Here are some great places to get set up when you're ready to hit the road.

Danny's Cycles
644 Central Park Ave., Scarsdale
(914) 723-3408
www.dannyscycles.com

Danny, a second-generation bike dealer, knows his stuff, and he and his staff provide friendly, personalized attention. Whether you're buying your child's first tricycle or outfitting the whole family, this is a great place to go. If your child is too young for her own set of wheels, they can set you up with bike seats, trailers and other add-ons you can use to take your little one out for a spin. They also carry a wide range of safety equipment, including children's helmets.

Hours: Monday 10 am-6 pm, Tuesday-Thursday 10 am-9 pm, Friday-Sunday 9 am-7 pm

Millers
335 Mamaroneck Ave., Mamaroneck
(914) 698-5070
www.millerstoys.com

See the listing under Toy Stores for more information.

Piermont Bicycle Connection
215 Ash St., Piermont
(845) 365-0900
www.piermontbike.com

The village of Piermont has always been a haven for cyclists because it's situated directly along 9W—a bike route stretching as far north as Buffalo. This shop, which carries bikes and equipment for all ages, is located in one of the cutest waterfront towns around, filled with art galleries, restaurants, boutiques and more.

Hours: April 1-September 30: Monday, Tuesday, Thursday-Sunday 9 am-8 pm; Wednesday-closed. October 1-March 31: Monday, Tuesday and Thursday 11 am-6 pm; Wednesday-closed; Friday 11 am-8 pm, Saturday and Sunday 9 am-6 pm

BABY GIFTS

From burp cloths and blankets to rocking chairs and step stools, there are many ways to welcome a new baby into the house or to make a new big brother or big sister feel special. Personalized gifts are not only great and thoughtful presents, they're also impossible to re-gift. And there seems to be no end to what you can paint or embroider a child's name on. The big chain emporiums all offer a selection of personalized furniture, frames, and keepsakes, but below are some specialty stores that are definitely worth a look.

Blue Tulip
116 Pondfield Rd., Bronxville
(914) 337-1480
www.bluetulip.com

Blue Tulip is a store built around celebrating family, friends and the occasions that bring people together. You'll find personalized stationery and baby items, as well as unique gifts from around the world. No matter what the occasion, Blue Tulip is a fun place to shop, and you'll probably walk away with a special gift for yourself!

Hours: Monday-Saturday 9 am-8 pm, Sunday 11 am-6 pm

Small Joys
11 Court Rd., Bedford Village
(914) 234-9736

While browsing in this adorable village do not miss Small Joys. The most frequently overheard comment in the store is "I want everything." You'll find gifts for brides, babies, homes and yourself—all carefully selected.

Hours: Monday-Saturday 9:30 am-5 pm

Thigamajigs! by Andrea
(914) 762-8650
thigamajgs@aol.com

Uniquely personalized gifts for all ages and occasions. Andrea hand-paints a wide variety of wood and ceramic items, including picture frames, step stools, rocking chairs and toy chests, and she will work with you to create a theme (trucks, moon and stars, hearts, etc.) and choose the colors for each gift. Prices range from $6 to $300, depending on the item. She's located in Central Westchester, but will ship anywhere.

And for You Internet Junkies

www.chooseydiapers.com
You can order everything from cloth diapers, organic and natural diapers, and diaper covers to mothering needs, baby skincare products, toys, bibs and gifts.

www.mybambino.com
An extensive collection of personalized items, including baby gifts and furniture, toys and sports gifts, piggy banks, school supplies, even Madame Alexander dolls. You can even get your child a personalized book for potty training (as Betsy did for Simon) that mentions where he lives and refers to his best friend by name.

www.personalizedforbaby.com
This site specializes in embroidered gifts but also has some hand-painted items. They will do gift baskets to fit any budget, and if you're not sure about a friend's taste they even have gift certificates.

And Now for Something a Little Different

www.wrybaby.com
While the items here are not "personalized," they are the ultimate anti-frou-frou baby gifts. Basic white onesies, bibs, burp cloths and more are printed with graphic slogans like "I might barf" and "I can't read"–the perfect gift for anyone who has a new baby and a great sense of humor.

ONLINE GROCERY SHOPPING

It's a scene you know all too well. It's raining and you've managed to wrangle your child in and out of the car and into a shopping cart. You're halfway through your grocery list when you reach the dreaded cereal aisle. The battle ensues. You just wanted to pick up some healthy, low-fat flakes for yourself, but now your daughter is screaming for the bright box with her favorite cartoon character on it (only 39 grams of sugar per serving).

Thank goodness for the Internet. Now you can get your grocery shopping done whenever it's convenient for you, and you can even stock up on necessities like jumbo quantities of diapers, wipes, baby formula and more. Some delivery fees apply, and these sites don't necessarily offer the lowest prices around. But they do deliver–and not just right to your door, but into your house! This is a major benefit for anyone who has ever dragged both a twenty-pound toddler and a twenty-pound container of laundry detergent up a flight of stairs.

www.freshdirect.com
Their goal is to provide incredibly fresh food and meal solutions. They carry produce, meat, poultry and fish (both organic and conventional), as well as baked goods, coffee, tea and dairy products. The idea is that the food comes directly from farms, dairies and fisheries (not through middlemen), so it's several days fresher and a lot less expensive when it gets to your table. They can deliver an order as soon as the next day after it's placed, on every weekday from 2 to 11:30 pm, plus all day Saturday and Sunday. You can even order up to a week in advance. The company has only recently expanded into the Westchester market; they currently deliver to parts of Pelham, Rye, New Rochelle, Harrison, Mamaroneck and Larchmont, but they're expanding all the time, so check the website to see if your area is covered.

Cost: $40 minimum order. Delivery fees are $5.95 for orders over $100, $7.95 for orders from $75-$100, and $9.95 for orders under $75.

www.peapod.com

Offered through Stop & Shop Supermarkets, this website is very easy to use. You can use your Stop & Shop card number to take advantage of extra discounts, and when you select a particular item, if a comparable item is on sale they will let you know. You can even redeem coupons when the driver arrives with your groceries. Once you've shopped through the site, you can store a "shopping cart" list of frequently bought items to speed up future visits. If you place your order prior to 11 am you can often get delivery that same day; otherwise next-day delivery is available at a convenient time that you select.

Cost: Minimum order is $50. Delivery fees are $6.95 for orders over $100 and $9.95 for orders less than $100.

www.yourgrocer.com

This warehouse club carries the major brands you'll find at a Costco or Sam's Club, but there is no membership fee. Stock up on heavy items like cases of soda, laundry detergent and cleaning supplies; they also carry fresh produce, meat and baked goods. You can store your shopping list on their site to speed up your future virtual visits, and next-day delivery is almost always available.

Cost: Minimum order is $75 (excluding tax and delivery). Delivery fee is $9.95.

Chapter 17

Give a Little Bit

Sell Your Stuff

Donate Your Stuff

Donate Your Time

There comes a time in all of our lives when our children stop playing with those huge pieces of primary-colored plastic. They've stopped wearing the onesies and the sleep-sacks, and they no longer need the crib and the changing table. Or maybe you've decided you're really never going back to that corporate office job and it's time to get rid of all those Tahari suits you'll never wear again. Or perhaps you know you won't need those baby accoutrements anymore, not to mention the maternity clothes; let's face it, if you haven't burned them or given them to your girlfriends, all they're doing is taking up valuable closet space!

When you have to make room for the big-boy bed and bureau, ice skates, tennis rackets, and other gear—or to free up some much-needed closet space of your own—you have two basic options. You can sell all that stuff you've accumulated—through a yard sale, a newspaper ad, a consignment shop, or a website—and make some extra cash to pay for Junior's skating lessons (or a facial for Mommy, perhaps!). Or you can donate all that stuff to some deserving souls and, in the process, begin to teach your kids the value of giving to those who have less then yourselves. Whichever option you decide to take, we've included many suggestions in this chapter to help get you started.

We've included some information on ways to donate your time as well. Whether it's volunteering in a soup kitchen, building a house or reading to kids, these acts of kindness give us the opportunity to work side-by-side with our children to help out those in need. Volunteer positions are usually not a major time commitment; you can do it just once or twice a year if you like. Moreover, most of our kids have so much, we should begin teaching them at an early age to "give back" and help others who might be less fortunate.

SELL YOUR STUFF

If you want to sell your stuff, the first thing you'll need to decide is whether you'll go it alone or have someone sell for you. Selling your things yourself will help maximize your profits, since there will be no middleman to pay—and sometimes it's so much fun it can even develop into a new hobby! However, the obvious downside is that it takes much more time and effort than having someone else do the work for you.

Yard or Garage Sale

If you have a lot of things to sell, a yard or garage sale can be a good way to go. The best time to hold a sale is in the spring or fall, when the weather is still nice. You might want to coordinate with some neighbors, both to establish critical mass and to take turns "minding the store." Post flyers nearby and especially on busy main streets where passing traffic will see them, but do so at your own risk—the practice is frowned upon, or even illegal, in some communities. You might also put an ad about your sale in the *Pennysaver* or *The Journal News* to draw more customers. Call your town or village clerk's office to find out if you need a permit for your sale—rules and regulations vary across the county. One thing to keep in mind as you weigh your options is that it may run you several hundred dollars to promote your tag sale, which may be all you stand to make in the end. When Betsy had her first (and probably last) tag sale she did make a few hundred dollars, but turn-out was pretty low and many unsold items ended up being donated anyway.

Websites

Craigslist (http://newyork.craigslist.org) and eBay (www.ebay.com) are two of the most popular sites for selling anything from books, toys, and clothing to furniture, electronics, motorcycles, and cars. It's free to post an ad on craigslist, and you can limit your posting specifically to Westchester if you want. Laura's husband Andrew has sold both a living room furniture set and a wheelbarrow on the site for pretty good prices. With eBay you'll need to set up an account first, and you'll have to pay both a nominal listing fee and a small percentage of the item's sale price. On either site, before posting your listing you should look at existing listings for similar items that have already been sold, to determine how to describe your items and how to price them. It's also a good idea to include a photo of what you're selling. And, you should consider setting up a PayPal account for easy payment transactions. Online selling takes some work to get up and running, but the sites are pretty user-friendly and self-explanatory.

Pennysaver or Your Local Newspaper

Laura has sold both a treadmill and a car by posting ads; it took very little time, she got the price she wanted, and the cost of the ad was negligible. Try the *Pennysaver/Shoppers Guide* at (914) 592-5222 or www.tri-statepennysaver.com, *The Journal News* at 800-300-SOLD or www.nyjournalnews.com (click on the "Local Classifieds" link), or your local community paper.

Consignment Shops

A nice alternative to doing all the work yourself is using a consignment shop; they will sell your stuff for you, and all you have to do is drop it off. These shops sell secondhand merchandise at fifty percent or more off the retail price and pay the seller a percentage of the proceeds if and when the item is sold. Most reputable consignment shops are very particular about what they sell, accepting only "gently used" items in good condition for resale. These shops tend to maintain limited inventory; before schlepping your things to your local secondhand store, make sure they are accepting goods. Below are some consignment shops that accept children's items.

Affordables
10 Main St., Dobbs Ferry
(914) 693-3610

Maternity clothes, children's clothes (sizes 0-14), baby equipment, toys, books, games, videos, skates and cleats. The store has regular hours but meetings with sellers are by appointment and are scheduled seasonally. Twice a year the store has a dollar sale for all of their overstock.

Kid Stuff
107 North Broadway, Tarrytown
(914) 366-4657
www.kidstuffclothing.com

Children's clothes (sizes 0-6), baby equipment, toys, books, videos, and maternity clothes.

Milk Money
579 Warburton Ave. (#6 Moviehouse Mews), Hastings-on-Hudson
(914) 478-4378
www.milkmoney.biz

This consignment store sells kids' clothes, maternity clothes, toys furniture, equipment, books and videos. They also have a playroom for kids. At the end of the "season," whatever hasn't sold is donated to local charities (or you can retrieve it).

Twice Upon a Time
33 North Riverside Ave., Croton-on-Hudson
(914) 271-8466

Children's, ladies' and men's clothes, baby equipment, toys, household items and antiques.

Vintage Kidz
2124 Boston Post Rd., Larchmont
(914) 834-0862

Children's clothes and shoes, equipment, room furnishings, toys and accessories.

Savvy Suggestion

The National Association of Resale and Thrift Shops (NARTS) has over 1,000 members, ranging from small chain stores to individuals reselling all kinds of merchandise. Visit their website at www.narts.org and click on the "Shopping Guide" link to find a list of stores in your area. Or you can send $4 to NARTS, P.O. Box 80707, St. Clair Shores, MI, 48080, for a hardcopy list of stores.

DONATE YOUR STUFF

While you're "making room for more" it's nice to think of those less fortunate who could truly benefit from the things you no longer need. There are many organizations throughout the county to which you can donate anything from clothes, toys, baby equipment, and furniture to computers, cell phones, and even cars! And you can help yourself while doing good: donations to charitable organizations are almost always tax deductible (but make sure you get a receipt for your tax returns). Below we list some organizations that accept donations; your synagogue or church or your child's school may take donations or may be able to provide you with references to other programs. Some of these organizations will pick up items at your house—particularly if it's furniture or large items—and some have drop boxes around the county, so you can put that bag of clothes in your trunk and donate it in between errands.

Big Brothers Big Sisters of Westchester

c/o Family Services of Westchester
9 Romaine Ave., Yonkers
(914) 963-4453

Accepts donations of clothes, shoes, linens, accessories, toys, videos and books. They will pick up items (mostly in lower Westchester); call for the pick-up schedule in your area. They no long accept furniture or household items and will only pick up to fifteen items or bags at a time. They also have bins throughout the county where you can drop off clothing. If you use the drop-off bins, just call for a receipt to be mailed to you. Big Brothers Big Sisters volunteers serve as role models to boys and girls ages 7-15 who live in single-parent homes; it's part of Family Services of Westchester, a private, not-for-profit, non-sectarian agency founded in 1954. Donated goods go directly to needy families in Westchester.

Career Closet

Briarcliff Congregational Church
South State Rd. and Elm St., Briarcliff Manor
(914) 747-1344

Accepts men's and women's work-appropriate clothes and accessories. Donations are accepted only on Saturday mornings. Career Closet provides clothing for interviews and office work to public assistance recipients actively moving from welfare to work.

Dress for Success

42 East Third St., Mount Vernon
(914) 664-8680
www.dressforsuccess.org

Accepts clothes and accessories for men and women. They try to provide at least two outfits for job interviews for low income women. Dress for Success is part of the Mt. Vernon Community Action Program.

Goodwill Industries

440 South Riverside Ave., Croton-on-Hudson
(914) 827-9311
www.goodwillny.org

Accepts donations of clothes, shoes, accessories, small appliances, toys, and household goods (no large appliances, computers, or furniture) at their stores in Somers and Croton-on-Hudson, as well as at drop-off bins across the county. To find one near you, call (718) 777-6323 or visit their website. (The website also has instructions for obtaining receipts.) Goodwill Industries is a leading provider of vocational, youth, and community redevelopment services for people with disabilities and other special needs. Revenue generated by reselling donated merchandise supports Goodwill's programs.

Grace Church Community Center
171 East Post Rd., White Plains
(914) 949-3098
www.gracecommunitycenter.org

Accepts donations of children's supplies, including computers; sports equipment, board games, bathing suits, towels, and backpacks; food; linens, towels, nightgowns, toiletry items, and bedroom slippers; and, in winter months, coats, sweaters, hats, socks, and other warm clothes. GCCC runs a day care center, a summer camp for disadvantaged children, a shelter and social service center, a home healthcare program for the elderly and disabled, a homelessness prevention service, and a soup kitchen. For over thirty-five years, it has provided services for people in need, with a guiding vision of turning no one away.

My Sister's Place
2 Lyon Pl., White Plains
(914) 683-1333

While My Sister's Place always needs donations (including kitchen items, linens, clothes, and furniture), they have different needs at different times; please call to find out what they're looking for as you get ready to make donations. My Sister's Place provides confidential shelter, counseling, education, and advocacy for battered women and their children; donations of merchandise are provided to women setting up homes once they leave the shelter.

The Piggy Bank Shop
4 Grayrock Rd., Scarsdale
(914) 723-9440

Accepts children's, women's, and men's clothes, shoes, and accessories. Proceeds go to the White Plains Hospital.

Room to Grow
54 West 21st St., #401, New York
212-620-7800
www.roomtogrow.org

Accepts new or nearly new baby items in excellent condition, including clothes (up to size 4T), toys, books, videos or music tapes, blankets, bedding, towels, strollers, highchairs, bassinets, baby carriers, swings, exersaucers, baby proofing items, and baby room accessories. They do not accept furniture, car seats or stuffed animals. Room to Grow is dedicated to enriching the lives of babies born into poverty throughout their critical first three years of development; parents living in poverty obtain essential items, as well as guidance and support.

Salvation Army
(914) 664-0800
www.salvationarmy-newyork.org

Accepts clothes, furniture, shoes, linens, accessories, toys, and books at their thrift stores and at Salvation Army Centers. They will pick up furniture and large amounts of clothing. Donated merchandise is resold in their thrift stores; proceeds support Salvation Army programs, including emergency disaster services, family counseling, feeding and clothing the homeless, and other community activities.

WestHab
85 Executive Blvd., Elmsford
(914) 345-2800
www.westhab.org

Accepts children's clothes, business clothes for men and women, good-condition children's books, educational software, board games, and arts & crafts supplies, as well as furniture and small kitchen items. The items are used in Westhab's shelters for homeless and low-income families in Westchester County, and are provided to clients moving into transitional and permanent housing.

Westchester Access
(914) 995-6490
www.westchestergov.com/westchesteraccess

Accepts old computers and related equipment for nonprofit organizations.

Westchester/Verizon Wireless HopeLine
(914) 813-5441
www.verizonwireless.com/hopeline

Accepts cell phones and equipment in any condition from any service provider. Phones are accepted at all Verizon Wireless Stores in Westchester County. The phones are refurbished or recy-

Savvy Suggestion

Go to www.westchestergov.com/treasures/ to find local residents who are in need of specific items. They will be responsible for removing it from your house and in return they receive it at no cost. You can set up a posting for something you may be looking for as well.

Savvy Suggestion

Upgraded your cell phone recently? Donate your old phones to charity! Phones 4 Charity is a national program designed to remove discarded wireless phones from the country's environment while directly benefiting charitable organizations. To learn more log onto www.phones4charity.org.

cled; proceeds fund donations to local domestic violence shelters and help purchase phones and airtime for victims.

Got Books?

As you children grow you're left with lots of board-, picture- and other books that they no longer need but other children would love. Try the major charities listed in this chapter, your local hospital or your local library (some libraries accept books into their collections, while some hold used book sales to raise money for operations). Or, try one of these organizations:

www.betterworldbooks.com—Book donations are sold to raise money for non-profit literacy partners, sent directly to those in need, or, at the very least, recycled.

www.booksforfreedom.org—Books are used in libraries, for academic study and for professional reference as well as children's schools in developing nations and, in particular, Afghanistan. They need children's books, secondary education textbooks (K-12), and native language books (Arabic, Farsi, Pashto).

www.booksforsoldiers.com—A non-profit corporation part of a non-denominational church in North Carolina, which runs a self-service site that helps you send books directly to the troops.

DONATE YOUR TIME

Once the little ones are off to school, you might find yourself with some extra time on your hands. This might be the perfect opportunity to become involved in a charity. There are a lot of people who could use your help: over 70,000 people in Westchester live in poverty, and over 4 million pounds of food were distributed last year.

Chances are you'll get the most gratification from volunteering with an organization you have a personal connection to. You might also try religious-affiliated organizations such as Hadassah, UJA, St. Vincent De Paul, and Catholic Charities. Hospitals also offer volunteer opportunities, from interacting with patients to working at the front desk, or in an "office" type setting preparing mailings.

If you're not sure what exactly you'd want to do, here are some ideas to get you started. In addition to opportunities for adults, some of these organizations provide opportunities for children, especially those nearing Bar/Bat Mitzvah age or high school students who are often looking for community service opportunities.

Children's Village
(914) 693-0600, ext. 1586
www.childrensvillage.org

Volunteer mentors at this Dobbs Ferry residential treatment center spend ten hours a month with a child; tutors in math, English, social studies or science commit to once-a-week visits during the school year.

Dorot
(800) 499-0840
www.dorotusa.org

Through its Friendly Visitors program, volunteers are paired with an older person for regular conversation and visits.

Family-to-Family
Pjkcallyn@aol.com
www.family-to-family.org

Based in Westchester, F-to-F connects "families with more" with "families with less". Sponsor families "adopt" a receiving family and are provided with information on the receiving family's children (their number, names, ages, etc.). Each month the sponsor family pre-

Savvy Suggestion

Public schools often encourage charity giving, especially around the holidays. Local elementary schools often collect leftover Halloween candy, conduct food drives around Thanksgiving, and have toy drives around the winter holidays to collect items to give to needy children and families.

Savvy Suggestion

Have a car, truck, boat, plane, motorcycle, or RV to donate? Visit www.donationline.com to donate one of these items to the American Red Cross, Habitat for Humanity, or one of eighty other charities. Or visit America Can! Cars for Kids at www.americascarsforkids.org—they sell donated vehicles (running or not) at auction and use the proceeds to provide second-chance educations for 6,000 at-risk youths each year.

pares a box of food for shipment directly to their own "adopted" family based on a shopping list provided by F-to-F. Boxes are delivered to a central drop-off point; FedEx (the national corporate sponsor) donates its services to deliver the boxes. Each month "the community" of sponsors also sends clothing, books, medicines, and other necessities to the adopted community's food pantry for general distribution.

Food-P.A.T.C.H.
Food-People Allied To Combat Hunger, Inc.
(914) 923-1100
www.foodpatch.org

A certified affiliate of Second Harvest, the largest domestic hunger relief charity in the United States, the mission of Food P.A.T.C.H. is to alleviate hunger and minimize food waste in Westchester County. Volunteer opportunities include administration, food preparation, and serving the hungry.

Gilda's Club Westchester
(914) 644-8844
www.gildasclubwestchester.org

Provides a support community for people living with cancer, their families, and friends. Volunteer opportunities include working with children in their supportive play program, working in the clubhouse, helping prepare for workshops, and preparing monthly mailings and fundraising events.

Habitat for Humanity of Westchester
(914) 636-8425
www.habitatwc.org

An affiliate of an international Christian housing ministry, HFH of Westchester seeks to eliminate poverty housing and homelessness throughout Westchester County, and to make decent, affordable shelter available by building houses with families in need. Volunteer opportunities are available in construction as well as other areas; attending a volunteer orientation session is mandatory for all volunteers.

Literacy Volunteers of Westchester County
(914) 592-2656
www.literacywestchester.org

Volunteers work with American-born adults who have limited literacy skills, or help non-English speakers learn the language.

The Lord's Pantry
(914) 682-4306
www.pipeline.com/~emu/tlp

The Lord's Pantry delivers hot, nutritious meals to homebound AIDS patients, their caregivers, and children in the Westchester area. Volunteer opportunities include delivery, food preparation, and administration.

Reach Out and Read
(212) 242-5339
www.reachoutandreadnyc.org

Reach Out and Read is a national program that promotes early literacy; volunteers read aloud to children as they wait for their pediatric clinic appointments. You can volunteer to read at medical offices (there are six locations in Westchester, as well as locations in New York City and Long Island) or donate gently used children's books. Children also receive a new children's book at every well-child visit from six months to five years of age.

Savvy Suggestion

At www.womenforwomen.org, you can "adopt" a woman who has lost everything in a country at war, such as Darfur. Women for Women International helps these women rebuild their lives by providing financial and emotional support, job skills training, rights awareness and leadership education and access to business skills, capital and markets.

S.P.C.A. of Westchester
(914) 941-2894, ext. 19
www.spca914.org

Volunteers supplement the staff by taking care of and playing with the animals. There is also a visitation program where you can take a shelter pet—or your own pet—to cheer residents of local nursing homes and hospitals.

Volunteer Center of the United Way of Westchester and Putnam
(914) 948-4452
www.volcenterwest.org

Offers a variety of community services with which you can get involved. The website provides an interactive feature to search for and select volunteer opportunities in your area.

WestHab
(914) 345-2800
www.westhab.org

Westhab is the largest not-for-profit provider of housing and social services for homeless and low-income families in Westchester County. Volunteer opportunities are available in tutoring, gardening, directing youth programs (e.g., book clubs, crafts, music) in homeless shelters, and more.

Westchester Coalition for the Hungry and Homeless
(914) 682-2737
www.westchesterchh.org

A coalition of over 143 shelters, food pantries, and soup kitchens across the county that connects volunteers with programs that can use their help.

Chapter 18

Special Stuff for Special Needs

New York State Services

Useful Resources

Preschools for Children with Special Needs

In the first edition of KidSavvy Westchester *we included a chapter on the New York State Early Intervention Program.* For parents whose children have been diagnosed with some sort of developmental delay (from the most minor to the more significant) this state-funded program is a godsend. The program offers evaluations, therapies and support while you and your child work on strengthening his or her abilities.

For our second edition we've expanded this chapter to include the services after your child "ages out" of Early Intervention at age 3. For children 3 to 5 years old there is the CPSE (Committee on Preschool Special Education) program, and then for children 5 to 21 years old there is the CSE (Committee on Special Education) program. We explain what these programs are and offer useful resources to assist you in getting your child the services she requires. No one knows better than Betsy that navigating the process can be a bit daunting, but keep in mind that a little bit of knowledge can be a powerful thing.

If at any point in your child's life you suspect a developmental delay, the first step is to speak to your pediatrician. Even if your child's doctor is dismissive of your concerns, don't be dissuaded: no one knows your child better than you. And don't procrastinate. If it turns out that your child does have some developmental delays, the earlier you get your child help, the faster the problems may be resolved.

Below we describe how to get your child evaluated and diagnosed, as well as the various services available (at no cost to you) once your child has been deemed eligible. Armed with the following information and resources, you should have no problem getting your child the services he or she requires.

NEW YORK STATE SERVICES

Early Childhood Direction Center (ECDC)

One of the best ways to get an overview of the programs available is to contact the Early Childhood Direction Center. This isn't mandatory, but it can be a great resource for you to learn more about programs and services and to gain additional support.

ECDCs are administered by the New York State Education Department and are a resource for professionals and parents of children with disabilities from birth through 5 years of age. ECDCs provide information about programs and services available in your community, as well as support and advice during the process and assistance in accessing these services. They also provide information about:

* Infant and toddler services

* Preschool programs

* Special education services

* Evaluation and assessment services

* Transportation

* Medical, educational and social services

* Day care and Head Start programs

* Early intervention services

* Financial assistance, including questions on insurance and Supplemental Security Income (SSI)

* Health services

* Respite and recreation programs

* Parent education programs and support groups

Children's Rehabilitation Center
Westchester Region (Putnam, Rockland and Westchester Counties)
317 North St., White Plains, NY 10605
Director: Maureen Tomkiel
(914) 597-4054
www.crcny.org

The New York State Early Intervention Program (EIP)

Your second step is to contact the appropriate program based on your child's age. For instance, the Early Intervention Program is available for children from birth to 3 years old.

Bureau of Child and Adolescent Health
New York State Dept. of Health
Corning Tower, Rm. 208, Albany, NY 12237-0618
(518) 473-7016
(914) 813-5094
www.health.state.ny.us/nysdoh/eip/index.htm

You will be assigned an EIO (Early Intervention Official) who will get the process rolling and set up the necessary evaluations. Once your child is evaluated, one of two things will happen: either the therapist will reassure you that your child is within the normal range of development and you have nothing to worry about, or she will pick up on some issue that in many cases can be successfully resolved with a little extra help from an appropriate therapist.

If your child qualifies for services, therapies can take place at home, at a day care or nursery facility, in a classroom, in a professional's office or at a center designed specifically for developmental therapies. Services may include speech, physical or occupational therapy; social work and/or psychological counseling; nursing services; and audiology.

There are many different types of interventions. Here is a listing of some of the most common ones.

Family Training: A family trainer provides parental support and often acts as a therapist for parents who may have difficulty at times dealing with their child or with their child's special needs. The trainer meets alone with the parent(s).

Feeding Therapy: This is often conducted by a speech therapist or nutritionist with a specialty in this area. Feeding therapy may be needed if your infant is having difficulty or discomfort feeding (either by breast or bottle), or if your child is having problems chewing and/or swallowing or is perhaps not eating at all.

Occupational Therapy (OT): Often acting as the "catchall" therapy, this is used particularly to improve "fine motor skills," the ability to use hands for manipulation, coordination and smaller, more refined tasks. Occupational therapy is also widely used in treating Sensory Integration Dysfunction (SID).

Physical Therapy (PT): This type of therapy usually addresses issues with "gross motor skills," that is, large muscle functions like crawling, standing, walking, balance and overall coordination.

Special Education: These educators or instructors have a background in special education and/or social work. Through the use of play therapy they work with your child on improving cognitive skills and on social and emotional development. Their goal is to help the child reach her full potential in learning and interacting with the environment.

Speech Therapy: This therapy can be used to treat speech delays and oral motor issues and to improve articulation and interpersonal language skills.

The Committee on Preschool Special Education (CPSE) Program

CPSE services are available for children 3-5 years old and are organized through your school district. Contact your local school district directly, and if you are not already registered with them you will have to do so. They'll assign someone to assist in setting up the necessary evaluations and will provide a list of evaluation sites approved by the New York State Education Department for you to select from.

After the evaluation the CPSE determines your child's eligibility for the program. If eligible for services, your child will be classified as a "preschool student with a disability," with no additional medical or educational diagnosis.

The CPSE will set up an Individualized Educational Plan (IEP) that will list the services your child will receive and how often. These services are provided on a school calendar year for either ten or twelve months, depending on the child's needs.

The goal of the CPSE is to place your child in the least restrictive environment possible. In other words, they will try to put him in classes with his peers. Unlike Early Intervention, the services do not take place in your home; you will take your child to an approved facility or, in the case of a special education preschool, he will receive therapies on site during the school day.

Here are some common CPSE terms and definitions:

Related Services: Provided by a certified or licensed professional, these may include speech, occupational and physical therapies; counseling; one-to-one aid; and vision and/or hearing education services.

SEIT (Special Education Itinerant Teacher): A SEIT assists your child in the classroom and helps her deal with any issues that may cause difficulty in school. SEIT services are provided for a minimum of two hours a week.

Special Class in an Integrated Setting (SCIS): This program is run by the State Education Department-approved preschool special education program and serves children with and without identified special needs. The classroom staff includes at least one special education teacher and an aide in addition to a regular teacher and aide, which significantly increases the teacher-to-child ratio. Children approved for SCIS may also receive related services as part of their program. Services in this program are provided for a minimum of two hours a day, and transportation to the program is provided at no cost.

Special Class: These classes are provided in a State Education Department-approved preschool special education program. Children are classified as "preschoolers with special needs," and classes are staffed by at least one special education teacher and one aide. Children attend the class for at least two hours per day, two days per week, and may also receive related services as part of their program. Transportation is provided at no cost. See our listing on special needs preschools at the end of this chapter.

USEFUL RESOURCES

Some helpful phone numbers and websites:

New York State Education Department
(914) 245-0010
www.nysed.gov

National Dissemination Center for Children with Disabilities (NICHCY)
(800) 695-0285
www.nichcy.org

National Center for Learning Disabilities
212-545-7510
www.LD.org

CHADD of Westchester County
(Children with Attention Deficit Disorders)
(914) 278-3020
www.chaddonline.org/chapters/chadd180.html

Parentlink
Westchester Advocates for Individuals with High Functioning Autism, Asperger Syndrome and other PDDs (pervasive developmental delays)
(914) 666-2099
www.westchesterparentlink.org

"Growing up Healthy" 24-Hour Hotline
(800) 522-5006

New York Parent's Connection
(800) 345-KIDS
www.sensorysmarts.com

This website is aimed towards parents of children with sensory integration issues. It features information, shopping, services and more. The site is run by Lindsey Biel and Nancy Peske, authors of *Raising a Sensory Smart Child.*

PRESCHOOLS FOR CHILDREN WITH SPECIAL NEEDS

Not only does Westchester have some of the top school districts in the country, it also has a terrific selection of specialty preschools. We've listed them below, including the services they provide and the needs that they serve, so you can more easily narrow down your search. Obviously there are additional considerations when looking at a special needs preschool, but take a look at Chapter 12 for some advice and guidelines about choosing the right preschool for you and your child.

Briarcliff

Clear View School Therapeutic Nursery
550 Albany Post Rd., Briarcliff, NY 10510
Director: Karen O'Gara
(914) 941-9513

Ages: 3-5 years old

Needs Served: Emotional and behavioral difficulties, PDD (pervasive developmental delays)

Services Provided: Psychology, Psychiatry, Social Work, Speech and Language Therapies

Cortlandt Manor
The Children's School for Early Development
SCIS at Walter Panas High School
300 Croton Ave., Cortlandt Manor, NY 10567
Director: Fran Porcaro
(914) 347-3227, ext. 106

Ages: 3-5 years old

Needs Served: Children with developmental delays or disabilities, including speech and language delays and learning difficulties

Services Provided: Physical, Occupational and Speech Therapies, Psychology, Social Work, Parent Support Groups (available at the Hawthorne location)

Hartsdale
Greenburgh Central School District #7
Early Childhood Program
475 W. Hartsdale Ave., Hartsdale, NY 10530
Director: Dawn Mair-McMillan
(914) 949-2745

Ages: 3-5 years old

Needs Served: Learning, speech, emotional and hearing impairments

Services Provided: Physical, Occupational and Speech and Language Therapies, Play Therapy, Social Services and Counseling for Families

Hawthorne
Hawthorne Country Day School
5 Bradhurst Ave., Hawthorne, NY 10532
EI Director: Jean Korchma
(914) 592-8526, ext. 147
CPSE Director: Kelly Hobbins
(914) 592-2484

Ages: Birth to 3 years old (EI), 3-5 years old (CPSE)

Needs Served: Autism/PDD, MR, speech/language disorders, behavior disorders

Services Provided: EI, Home-Based Occupational Therapy, CPSE, Occupational and Speech Therapies, Parent Training

The Children's School for Early Development
40 Saw Mill Rd., Hawthorne, NY 10532
Director: Phyllis Rizzi
(914) 347-3227, ext. 105

Ages: 3-5 years old

Needs Served: Autism/PDD

Services Provided: Physical, Occupational and Speech Therapies, Psychology, Social Work, Parent Support Groups

Katonah
The Children's School for Early Development
SCIS at The Country Children's Center
412 Cross River Rd., Katonah, NY 10536
Director: Fran Porcaro
(914) 347-3227, ext. 106

Ages: 3-5 years old

Needs Served: Children with developmental delays or disabilities, including speech and language delays and learning difficulties

Services Provided: Physical, Occupational and Speech Therapies, Psychology, Social Work, Parent Support Groups (available at the Hawthorne location)

Lincolndale
The Children's School for Early Development
SCIS at Little People's Learning Center
Lincoln Ave., Lincolndale, NY 10532
Director: Fran Porcaro
(914) 347-3227, ext. 106

Ages: Birth to 5 years old

Needs Served: Children with developmental delays or disabilities, including speech and language delays and learning difficulties

Services Provided: Physical, Occupational and Speech Therapies, Psychology, Social Work, Parent Support Groups (available at the Hawthorne location)

Mamaroneck
Mamaroneck Pre-K
Mamaroneck Avenue School
850 Mamaroneck Ave., Mamaroneck, NY 10543
Director: Roni Kramer
(914) 220-3060

Ages: 3-4 years old

Needs Served: Autism, language delays, cognitive delays

Services Provided: Physical, Occupational and Speech Therapies, Counseling

Mount Kisco

Bedford Central School District
Special Class in the Integrated Setting Program
632 S. Bedford Rd., Mount Kisco, NY 10549
Coordinator: Danielle Levin
(914) 241-6024

Ages: 3-4 years old

Needs Served: Developmental delays including speech and language, social, cognitive and motor delays

Services Provided: Physical, Occupational and Speech Therapies, Psychology, Social Work, Parent Support Services

The Children's School for Early Development
SCIS at the Boys & Girls Club
351 Main St., Mount Kisco, NY 10549
Director: Fran Porcaro
(914) 347-3227, ext. 106

Ages: 3-5 years old

Needs Served: Children with developmental delays or disabilities, including speech and language delays or learning difficulties

Services Provided: Physical, Occupational and Speech Therapies, Psychology, Social Work, Parent Support Groups (available at the Hawthorne location)

Mount Vernon

Mount Vernon Public Schools/Pre-K Program
625 South 4th Ave., Mount Vernon, NY 10550
Director: Jacqueline Liburd
(914) 665-5077

Ages: 2 3/4-5 years old

Needs Served: Speech, learning and emotional development delays

Services Provided: Speech, Physical and Occupational Therapies, Psychology, Social Work, Parent Education, Counseling, SEIT (Special Education Itinerant Teachers)

New Rochelle

Preschool Speech Language Learning Center
Barnard School
129 Barnard Rd., New Rochelle, NY 10801
Director: Gloria Strauss
(914) 576-4390

Ages: 3-5 years old

Needs Served: Speech and hearing difficulties, autism, learning delays, emotional difficulties.

Services Provided: Psychology, Social Work, Audiology, Occupational and Physical Therapies

The Children's School for Early Development
SCIS at the Children's Corner
60 Willow Dr., New Rochelle, NY 10605
Director: Fran Porcaro
(914) 347-3227, ext. 106

Ages: 3-5 years old

Needs Served: Developmental delays or disabilities, including speech and language delays and learning difficulties

Services Provided: Physical, Occupational and Speech Therapies, Psychology, Social Work, Parent Support Groups (available at the Hawthorne location)

The Therapeutic Nursery at the Guidance Center
70 Grand St., New Rochelle, NY 10801
Director: Karen Farber
(914) 636-4440, ext. 228

Ages: 3-5 years old

Needs Served: Emotional difficulties, speech and language delays, multiple handicaps, PDD

Services Provided: Speech and Occupational Therapies, Counseling, Parent Training

Ossining

The Children's School for Early Development
SCIS at Roosevelt School
(Ossining School District residents only)
190 Croton Ave., Ossining, NY 10562
Director: Phyllis Rizzi
(914) 347-3227, ext. 105

Ages: Birth to 5 years old

Needs Served: Children with developmental delays or disabilities, including speech and language delays and learning difficulties

Services Provided: Physical, Occupational and Speech Therapies, Psychology, Social Work, Parent Support Groups (available at the Hawthorne location)

The Children's School for Early Development
At Small Miracles Preschool Center
15-17 Campwoods Rd., Ossining, NY 10562
Director: Phyllis Rizzi
(914) 347-3227, ext. 105

Ages: 3-5 (SCIS), 18 months-CPSE transition date for EI

Needs Served: Autism/PDD or similar learning profile

Services Provided: Physical, Occupational and Speech Therapies, Psychology, Social Work, Parent Support Groups (available at the Hawthorne location)

Peekskill
Cornerstone Therapeutic Nursery
50 Dayton Ln., Peekskill, NY 10566
Director: Dr. Marcy Atkins
(914) 949-7680

Ages: 2 1/2-5 years old

Needs Served: Emotional, developmental, behavior management, internalizing and externalizing problems

Services Provided: Family Therapy, Behavior Management, Speech Therapy, Parent Support Groups

Port Chester
Port Chester Head Start
Therapeutic Nursery
17 Spring St., Port Chester, NY 10573
Director: Karen Cohen, MSW
(914) 937-5863

Ages: 3-5 years old

Needs Served: Emotional, learning, and speech difficulties, multiple handicaps

Services Provided: Speech, Physical and Occupational Therapies, Psychology, Social Work, Parent as Teacher Program, Parent Guidance

Scarsdale
JCC of Mid-Westchester
Toward Tomorrow Program
999 Wilmot Rd., Scarsdale, NY 10583
Director: Linda Helfman
(914) 472-3300, ext. 347

Ages: 3-5 years old

Needs Served: Speech/language delays, motor delays, PDD spectrum, behavioral issues, ADHD

Services Provided: Speech/Language and Occupational Therapies, Counseling, Parent Training

Tarrytown

The Children's School for Early Development
SCIS at the Elizabeth Mascia Childcare Center
171 Sheldon Ave., Tarrytown, NY 10591
Director: Phyllis Rizzi
(914) 347-3227, ext. 105

Ages: 3-5 years old

Needs Served: Autism/PDD or similar learning profile

Services Provided: Physical, Occupational and Speech Therapies, Psychology, Social Work, Parent Support Groups (available at the Hawthorne location)

Valhalla

Blythedale Children's Hospital
Early Childhood Center
95 Bradhurst Ave., Valhalla, NY 10595
Director: Denise Mulverhill
(914) 592-7555, ext. 475

Ages: Birth to 5 years old

Needs Served: Health and physical needs for rehabilitation services

Services Provided: Medical Management/Intervention, Speech, Physical and Occupational Therapies through EI and CPSE

Project Explore
70 Columbus Ave., Valhalla, NY 10595
Director: Rea Davidson
(914) 328-1578

Ages: 3-5 years old

Needs Served: Developmental delays and disabilities of all kinds

Services Provided: Speech, Physical and Occupational Therapies, Counseling

Westchester Center for Educational & Emotional
Development (WCEED)
503 Grasslands Rd., Ste 101, Valhalla, NY 10595
Director: Sharon Luby
(914) 593-0593

Ages: Birth to 3 years old (EI), 3-5 years old (private program with related services through CPSE)

Needs Served: Children in need of special education, occupational and physical therapies, and speech services

Services Provided: Occupational, Speech and Physical Therapies, ABA on as-needed basis

White Plains

Children's Rehabilitation Center
317 North St., White Plains, NY 10605
Director: Maureen Tomkiel
(914) 597-4054

Ages: 1-7 years old (Center Based)

Needs Served: Orthopedic impairments, multiple disabilities, preschoolers with disability

Services Provided: Physical, Occupational and Speech Therapies, Psychology, Social Work, Teacher of Visually Impaired, Assistive technology

Cornerstone Therapeutic Nursery
19 Greenridge Ave., White Plains, NY 10605
Director: Dr. Marcy Atkins
(914) 949-7680

Ages: 2 1/2-5 years old

Needs Served: Emotional, developmental, behavior management, internalizing and externalizing problems

Services Provided: Family Therapy, Behavior Management, Speech Therapy, Parent Support Groups

Lighthouse International Parent-Infant Training Program
170 Hamilton Ave., White Plains, NY 10601
Director: Linda Shulz, CSW
(914) 683-7543

Ages: Birth to 5 years

Needs Served: Visual impairment

Services Provided: Teachers of the visually impaired, Social Work, Low Vision Optometrist, Parent Support Group

New York School for the Deaf
555 Knollwood Rd., White Plains, NY 10603
Director: Cathy Milliren
(914) 949-7310, ext. 424

Ages: Birth to 5 years old

Needs Served: Hearing difficulties and deafness

Services Provided: Speech, Physical and Occupational Therapies,

Audiology, Psychology, Social Work, Adaptive Physical Education, Parent Support Group

Prime Time
456 North St., White Plains, NY 10605
Director: Barbara Sommer
(914) 872-5295

Ages: 3-5 years old

Needs Served: Speech, learning and emotional problems, PDD

Services Provided: Counseling, Speech and Occupational Therapies

Stepping Stones
30 Manhattan Ave., White Plains, NY 10607
Director: Dr. Janet Massotti
(914) 761-6134, ext. 310

Ages: 3-5 years old

Needs Served: Speech, learning and emotional difficulties, PDD, autism

Services Provided: Speech, Occupational and Physical Therapies, Psychological Counseling, Parent Training, SEIT

The Children's School for Early Development SCIS and Mommy & Me (EI) at the Church in the Highlands
35 Bryant Ave., White Plains, NY
Director: Fran Porcaro
(914) 347-3227, ext. 106

Ages: 3-5 (SCIS), 18 months-CPSE transition date (Mommy & Me)

Needs Served: Children with developmental delays or disabilities, including speech and language delays and learning difficulties

Services Provided: Physical, Occupational and Speech Therapies, Psychology, Social Work, Parent Support Groups (available at the Hawthorne location)

United Preschool Center
456 North St., White Plains, NY 10605
Director: Annabelle Strozza
(914) 946-4781

Ages: 3-5 years old

Needs Served: Developmental, orthopedic, speech, learning and hearing problems, PDD, multiple handicaps

Services Provided: Speech, Occupational and Physical Therapies, Social Work, Technology and Computer Services, Toy Library, Animal Therapy, Music Therapy, Psychology, Nursing

Yonkers

Alcott School Little Class Program
306 Rumsey Rd., Yonkers, NY 10705
Site Director: Suzanne Block
(914) 969-9676

Ages: 3-5 years old

Needs Served: Learning, speech and language difficulties, autism spectrum disorders, developmental delays

Services Provided: Speech and Occupational Therapies, SEIT, Counseling, Parent-Child Groups, Evaluation Site, Special Ed., E.I. and Integrated Classrooms.

Cornerstone Therapeutic Nursery
35 Dock St., Yonkers, NY 10701
Director: Dr. Marcy Atkins
(914) 949-7680

Ages: 2 1/2-5 years old

Needs Served: Emotional, developmental, behavior management, internalizing and externalizing problems

Services Provided: Family Therapy, Behavior Management, Speech Therapy, Parent Support Groups

Fred S. Keller School
One Odell Plaza, South Westchester Executive Park
Yonkers, NY 10701
Director: Robin Nuzzolo, PhD
(914) 965-1152, ext. 202

Ages: 18 months-5 years old

Needs Served: Autism, speech impairment, learning, emotional and behavioral disorders

Services Provided: Speech and Occupational Therapies, Related Service Aides, SEIT, Parent Education, Consulting Behavior Analyst

Marion and George Ames Early Childhood Learning Center
463 Hawthorne Ave., Yonkers, NY 10705
Director: Ivonne Dominguez
(914) 375-8820

Ages: 18 months-5 years old

Needs Served: Developmental delays

Services Provided: Speech, Hearing, Physical and Occupational Therapies, Counseling, Social Work, Nursing

Westchester School for Special Children—Preschool
15 Leroy Ave., Yonkers, NY 10705
Director: Pricilla Scampoli
(914) 963-7990

Ages: 3-5 years old

Needs Served: Developmental and learning difficulties, hearing impairment, orthopedic impairment

Services Provided: Speech, Physical and Occupational Therapies, Adaptive Physical Education, Psychology, Behavior Management Therapy, Social Work, Nursing

Yorktown

The Children's School for Early Development Mommy & Me (EI) at Yorktown
2880 Crompond Rd., Yorktown Heights, NY 10598
Director: Phyllis Rizzi
(914) 347-3227, ext. 105

Ages: 18 months to CPSE transition date

Needs Served: Children with developmental delays or disabilities, including speech and language delays or learning difficulties

Services Provided: Speech, Physical and Occupational Therapies, Psychology, Social Work, Parent Support Groups (available at the Hawthorne location)

The Children's School for Early Development SCIS at Yorktown Head Start
1974 Commerce St., Yorktown, NY 10596
Director: Fran Porcaro
(914) 347-3227, ext. 106

Ages: 3-5 years old

Needs Served: Children with developmental delays or disabilities, including speech and language delays and learning difficulties

Services Provided: Physical, Occupational and Speech Therapies, Psychology, Social Work, Parent Support Groups (available at the Hawthorne location)

Chapter 19

Westchester Suburbs Simplified

Cities, Towns, Villages, Hamlets & Zip Codes

Westchester County Map

If you check out the local real estate listings you'll see that Westchester is a confusing puzzle of cities, towns, villages and hamlets, many of which overlap in one way or another. For example, a Yonkers address might have a Bronxville or a Scarsdale P.O. but still be within the Eastchester school district. Depending on where you live, these strange arrangements can have an impact on which schools your children attend, which authority provides your municipal services (garbage collection, etc.), how high your taxes are and which swimming pool you're allowed to use. While writing the first edition of this book, Betsy and Laura lived less than a half a mile apart in Hartsdale—but Betsy's school district was Edgemont, while Laura's was Greenburgh. To help you figure out this puzzle, here's a list of Westchester's cities, towns (with their hamlets) and villages, as well as contact phone numbers, websites and Zip codes.

Savvy Suggestion

Some cities and towns have more than one Zip code code. Use the postal service website at www.usps.com to look up the correct one using the exact address.

Cities

Mount Vernon
(914) 665-2300
www.cmvny.com
Zip codes: 10552-10553

New Rochelle
(914) 654-2000
www.newrochelleny.com
Zip codes: 10801-10805

Peekskill
(914) 737-3400
www.ci.peekskill.ny.us
Zip code: 10566

Rye
(914) 967-7404
www.ryeny.gov
Zip code: 10580

White Plains
(914) 422-1200
www.cityofwhiteplains.com
Zip codes: 10601-10607, 10610

Yonkers
(914) 377-6000
www.cityofyonkers.com
Zip codes: 10701-10710

Towns

Bedford
(includes the hamlets Bedford Hills and Katonah)
(914) 666-6530
www.bedfordny.info
Zip codes: 10506, 10507, 10536

Cortlandt
(includes the hamlets Crugers, Montrose and Verplanck)
(914) 734-1000
www.townofcortlandt.com
Zip codes: 13045, 10521, 10548, 10596

Eastchester
(914) 771-3300
www.eastchester.org
Zip codes: 10707, 10709

Greenburgh
(includes the hamlets Fairview, Glenville, Greenville and Hartsdale)
(914) 993-1540
www.greenburghny.com
Zip code: 10530

Harrison
(includes Purchase)
(914) 670-3000
www.harrison.americantowns.com
Zip code: 10528, 10577

Lewisboro
(includes the hamlets Cross River, Golden's Bridge, Lewisboro, South Salem, Vista and Waccabuc)
(914) 763-3511
www.lewisborogov.com
Zip codes: 10590, 10518, 10526, 10597

Mamaroneck
(914) 381-7805
www.townofmamaroneck.org
Zip code: 10543

Mount Kisco
(914) 241-0500
www.mountkisco.org
Zip code: 10549

Mount Pleasant
(includes the hamlets Hawthorne, Pocantico Hills, Thornwood and Valhalla)
(914) 742-2300
www.mtpleasantny.com
Zip codes: 10532, 10591, 10594, 10595

New Castle
(includes the hamlets Chappaqua and Millwood)
(914) 238-4771
www.town.new-castle.ny.us
Zip codes: 10514, 10546

North Castle
(includes the hamlet Armonk)
(914) 273-3321
www.northcastleny.com
Zip code: 10504

North Salem
(includes the hamlets Croton Falls, Peach Lake, Purdys and Salem Center)
(914) 669-5110
www.northsalemny.org
Zip codes: 10560, 10519, 10578

Ossining
(914) 762-6000
www.townofossining.com
Zip code: 10562

Pelham
(914) 738-1021
www.townofpelham.com
Zip code: 10803

Pound Ridge
(includes the hamlet Scotts Corners)
(914) 764-5511
www.townofpoundridge.com
Zip code: 10576

Rye
(914) 939-3075
www.townofryeny.com
Zip code: 10580

Scarsdale
(914) 722-1100
www.scarsdale.com
Zip code: 10583

Somers
(includes the hamlets Amawalk, Croton Falls, Golden's Bridge, Granite Springs, Lincolndale, Purdys, Shenorock and Somers)
(914) 277-3323
www.somersny.com
Zip codes: 10589, 10501, 10519, 10526, 10527, 10540, 10578, 10587, 10589

Yorktown
(includes the hamlets Crompond, Croton Heights, Huntersville, Jefferson Valley, Kitchawan, Mohegan Lake, Shrub Oak, Sparkle

Lake, Teatown, Yorktown and Yorktown Heights)
(914) 962-5722
www.yorktownny.org
Zip codes: 10598, 10517, 10535, 10562, 10547, 10588

Villages

Ardsley
(in Greenburgh)
(914) 693-1550
www.ardsleyvillage.com
Zip codes: 10502, 10503

Briarcliff Manor
(in Ossining and Mount Pleasant)
(914) 941-4800
www.briarcliffmanor.org
Zip code: 10510

Bronxville
(in Eastchester)
(914) 337-6500
www.villageofbronxville.com
Zip code: 10708

Buchanan
(in Cortlandt)
(914) 737-1033
www.villageofbuchanan.com
Zip code: 10511

Croton-on-Hudson
(in Cortlandt)
(914) 271-4781
www.village.croton-on-hudson.ny.us
Zip code: 10520

Dobbs Ferry
(in Greenburgh)
(914) 693-2203
www.dobbsferry.com
Zip code: 10522

Elmsford
(in Greenburgh)
(914) 592-6555
www.elmsfordny.org
Zip code: 10523

Hastings-on-Hudson
(in Greenburgh)
(914) 478-3400
www.hastingsgov.org
Zip code: 10706

Irvington
(in Greenburgh)
(914) 591-7070
www.village.irvington.ny.us
Zip code: 10533

Larchmont
(in Mamaroneck)
(914) 834-6230
www.villageoflarchmont.org
Zip code: 10538

Mamaroneck
(in Mamaroneck and Rye)
(914) 777-7700
www.village.mamaroneck.ny.us
Zip code: 10543

Mount Kisco
(in Mount Kisco)
(914) 241-0500
www.mountkisco.org
Zip code: 10549

Ossining
(in Ossining)
(914) 941-3554
www.village.ossining.ny.us
Zip code: 10562

Pelham
(in Pelham)
(914) 738-2015
www.pelhamgov.com
Zip code: 10803

Pelham Manor
(in Pelham)
(914) 738-8820
www.pelhammanor.org
Zip code: 10803

Pleasantville
(in Mount Pleasant)
(914) 769-1900
www.pleasantville-ny.gov
Zip codes: 10570-10572

Port Chester
(in Rye)
(914) 939-2200
www.portchesterny.com
Zip code: 10573

Rye Brook
(in Rye)
(914) 939-1121
www.ryebrook.org
Zip code: 10573

Scarsdale
(in Scarsdale)
(914) 722-1100
www.scarsdale.com
Zip code: 10583

Sleepy Hollow
(in Mount Pleasant)
(914) 366-5100
www.villageofsleepyhollow.org
Zip code: 10591

Tarrytown
(in Greenburgh)
(914) 631-7873
www.tarrytowngov.com
Zip code: 10591

Tuckahoe
(in Eastchester)
(914) 961-3100
www.tuckahoe.com
Zip code: 10707

Westchester County

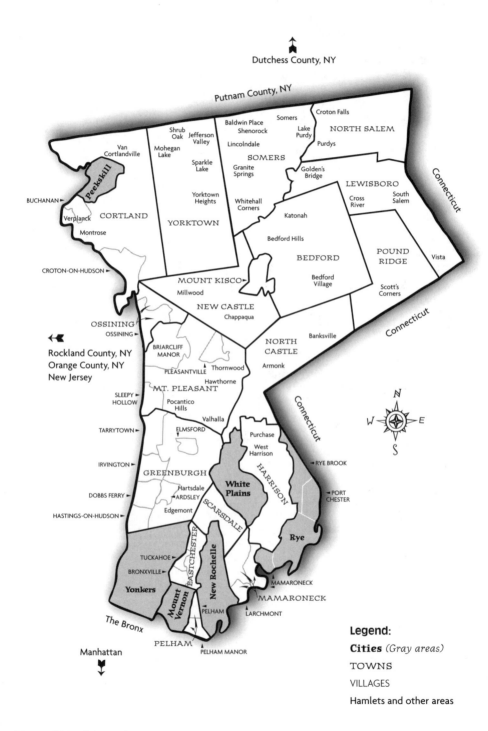

Dutchess County, NY

Putnam County, NY

Somers · Croton Falls

Shrub Oak · Jefferson Valley · Baldwin Place · Shenorock · Lake Purdy · NORTH SALEM

Van Cortlandville · Mohegan Lake · Lincolndale · Purdys

SOMERS

Sparkle Lake · Granite Springs · Golden's Bridge

Peekskill · LEWISBORO

BUCHANAN · Yorktown Heights · Whitehall Corners · Cross River · South Salem

Verplanck · CORTLAND · YORKTOWN · Katonah · Connecticut

Montrose · Bedford Hills

CROTON-ON-HUDSON · BEDFORD · POUND RIDGE · Vista

MOUNT KISCO · Bedford Village

Millwood · Scott's Corners

NEW CASTLE · Chappaqua

OSSINING · Banksville

OSSINING · NORTH CASTLE · Connecticut

Rockland County, NY · BRIARCLIFF MANOR

Orange County, NY · PLEASANTVILLE · Thornwood · Armonk

New Jersey · Hawthorne

SLEEPY HOLLOW · MT. PLEASANT

Pocantico Hills

TARRYTOWN · Valhalla

ELMSFORD · Purchase

West Harrison

IRVINGTON · RYE BROOK

GREENBURGH · HARRISON

DOBBS FERRY · Hartsdale · White Plains · PORT CHESTER

ARDSLEY

HASTINGS-ON-HUDSON · Edgemont · SCARSDALE

Rye

TUCKAHOE · EASTCHESTER · New Rochelle

BRONXVILLE

Yonkers · MAMARONECK

Mount Vernon · MAMARONECK

PELHAM · LARCHMONT

The Bronx

Manhattan · PELHAM · PELHAM MANOR

Legend:
Cities *(Gray areas)*
TOWNS
VILLAGES
Hamlets and other areas

N · W · E · S

Index

Listings By Subject and Location

About the Authors

Ben, Laura, Sam, Betsy and Simon

Laura E. Wilker lives in Edgemont with her husband, Andrew Jeske, and sons, Sam and Ben. She's had a career in corporate communications, investor relations and public relations for almost twenty years, and continues to work full-time in Manhattan. She serves as a member of the Second Shift Advisory Board, is a dedicated Little League cheerleader, loves sitting on the front porch blowing bubbles and still wants to be President when she grows up.

Betsy Cadel, a former advertising copywriter, also lives in Edgemont with her husband, Andy, and son, Simon. She currently does freelance writing and is in the process of developing some children's books. Chances are you'll see her around Westchester doing more research for the next edition's shopping section—hey, anything for KidSavvy readers.

Notes